HOW I WISH I'D
TAUGHT
WRITING

TIM MILLS
CLARE SEALY

Together we unlock every learner's unique potential

At Hachette Learning (formerly Hodder Education), there's one thing we're certain about. No two students learn the same way. That's why our approach to teaching begins by recognising the needs of individuals first.

Our mission is to allow every learner to fulfil their unique potential by empowering those who teach them. From our expert teaching and learning resources to our digital educational tools that make learning easier and more accessible for all, we provide solutions designed to maximise the impact of learning for every teacher, parent and student.

Aligned to our parent company, Hachette Livre, founded in 1826, we pride ourselves on being a learning solutions provider with a global footprint.

www.hachettelearning.com

To order, please visit www.HachetteLearning.com or contact Customer Service at education@hachette.co.uk / +44 (0)1235 827827.

ISBN: 978 1 0360 1410 0

© Tim Mills and Clare Sealy 2026

First published in 2026 by
Hachette Learning (a trading division of Hodder & Stoughton Limited),
An Hachette UK Company
Carmelite House
50 Victoria Embankment
London EC4Y 0DZ
www.HachetteLearning.com

The authorised representative in the EEA is Hachette Ireland, 8 Castlecourt Centre, Dublin 15, D15 XTP3, Ireland (email: info@hbgi.ie)

Impression number   10 9 8 7 6 5 4 3 2 1
Year   2030 2029 2028 2027 2026

Cover phot : Shutterstock/UmerDeArtist
Illustrations by DC Graphic Design Limited, Hextable, Kent.
Typeset in the UK.
Printed in the UK.

A catalogue record for this title is available from the British Library.

MIX
Paper | Supporting responsible forestry
FSC™ C104740

To all the kids we failed...

Acknowledgements

Photo credits

p121 © ChocoPie/Shutterstock.com; p136 © AaronChenPS2/Shutterstock.com

Text credits

p18 Sedita, J. (2019). The Writing Rope. Rowley, MA, Keys to Literacy. Reprinted with permission from Joan Sedita All rights reserved.; p91 © Gary Provost, THE WRITER'S WRITER

About the authors

Dr Tim Mills

Tim led the expert panel and he was lead drafter of the DfE's Writing Framework. Tim is currently a DfE RISE Advisor and lead drafter of the revised National Curriculum for English at KS1 and KS2 for England.. He was previously Executive Director of Primary Education for STEP Academy Trust and helped build the Trust into one of the highest performing in the primary sector. His doctoral study focused on teaching phonics in KS2 with the published research building on the growing understanding of 'decoding threshold' – how much phonics is enough phonics. He is a visiting professor at the University of Coventry and has published a number of academic peer-reviewed papers. Prior to working in education, Tim was a feature writer for the *London Evening Standard*, wrote the award-winning Channel 4 short film *Sunny Spells* and in 1985 was booed off stage at London's Comedy Store.

Clare Sealy

Clare works as Head of Education Improvement for the States of Guernsey, working across primary, secondary and tertiary phases. Prior to this role, she was a primary headteacher for over 22 years in Tower Hamlets, East London. During the latter part of that time, she also worked on a consultancy basis as a school improvement partner for Essex local authority.

Clare writes about curriculum, assessment and pedagogy. She is a member of the Ofsted reference group for curriculum, teaching and assessment, having previously been on the Ofsted reference group for maths. She was part of the sector panel for the recently published DfE Writing Framework and was previously on the DfE panel for the revised Early Learning Goals. She is a member of the Advisory Committee leading the development of a new National Curriculum for Northern Ireland. In 2018 she was named by the TES as one of the ten most influential people in education and in 2022 she received an OBE for services to education.

Clare's publications

- ResearchED Guide to the curriculum: editor.
- ResearchED Guide to primary literacy: contributor.
- ResearchED education myths: contributor.
- Early Career Teaching handbook: contributor.

Clare blogs at www.primarytimery.com

Review quotes

This book starts with the simple but enormously important insight that writing is hard – one of the most cognitively challenging tasks we teach children. From that basic premise flow so many implications, which are explored brilliantly in this book. Progress depends on secure sentence structures, fluent transcription and sustained practice. The authors make a compelling case for building writing capacity gradually, focusing on the fundamentals so that pupils are not overwhelmed, and so that self-expression can emerge from growing competence.

Daisy Christodoulou

Writing is much harder than reading, but teachers rarely get effective training in how to teach it – and far fewer books have focused on writing instruction than on reading instruction. This volume goes a long way toward rectifying that situation, providing a thorough but accessible overview of the scientific research on writing and key takeaways. From the connections between both oral language and reading to writing, to the importance of explicitly teaching students how to construct sentences and plan paragraphs and essays, every page is brimming with valuable information and insights, delivered by two educators who aren't afraid to share their own past missteps. If you're one of the many teachers and school leaders who desperately want to help their students write clearly and coherently but aren't sure how to go about it, *How I Wish I'd Taught Writing* is for you.

Natalie Wexler, co-author of The Writing Revolution.

Somehow, Clare and Tim have written a deep dive into writing research which is also a very practical how-to *and* an exploration of some of the history of writing instruction (and its lack), peppered additionally with entertaining – often rueful – anecdotes. I will be recommending this to every English lead and headteacher – everyone interested in the writing process – that I know, for its engaging, easy-reading deluge of useful information. I'm loathe to use the term 'common sense' but I don't know how else to describe the balanced approach best summed up by the authors themselves thus: 'Teaching the technical without it feeding into the creative is pointless. Teaching the creative without building technical competence is futile.'

Lindsay Pickton, literacy consultant.

Helping children to learn to write is one of the most vital acts in education. It is also something that is incredibly difficult! Sealy and Mills do a brilliant job in communicating the complexity of writing, from its history to its present in the classroom. Most importantly, they offer an array of practical insights and strategies to support every developing writer to succeed, from handwriting and spelling and grammar, to writing for an audience with precision and pleasure. Every teacher and leader looking to build strong foundations for writing should invest in this book!

Alex Quigley, author of Closing the Writing Gap

This is quite simply the most useful book on writing instruction that I have read. Clare and Tim's honesty and humility about the way they used to teach writing invite the reader to examine their own preconceptions and potential blind spots. The volume of research behind their conclusions – and the perfectly pitched advice for teachers – make this an essential read for anyone interested in improving the teaching of writing.

Andrew Percival, Deputy headteacher at Stanley Road Primary School, Oldham

This book is a revelation. It tackles the perennial question of why writing feels so punishingly difficult to teach and answers it with uncommon clarity and compassion. The authors take the reader from first principles to classroom practice without ever simplifying the intellectual terrain. What emerges is a portrait of writing as a human activity of extraordinary cognitive weight that can, with deliberate teaching, be made accessible to every child.

One of the book's great strengths is its refusal to hide from complexity. Where others gesture vaguely at 'creative expression,' Sealy and Mills confront the hard truth: writing is the most demanding cognitive task children will ever routinely encounter. The opening chapters, mapping the sheer effort required to encode thought into text, are striking in their honesty.

The book illuminates writing's social purpose with unusual depth: writing as inclusion, identity, voice and participation. The section on the 'non-present reader' is especially compelling. It captures the strange, counterintuitive discipline required of young writers who must imagine an audience they cannot see and shape ideas accordingly. Few books manage to explain this moment of cognitive rupture so well.

The historical sweep of the early chapters is another delight. The exploration of how the writing systems evolved – from pictograms to morphophonemic English – furnishes teachers with a rationale for why English writing is so arduous to master and why explicit instruction is essential.

Perhaps the book's most valuable contribution is its treatment of working memory. The authors marry cognitive science with classroom wisdom in a way that is rare in educational writing. Their account of how handwriting, spelling, syntax and compositional strategy compete for the same limited mental workspace is both sobering and liberating. It equips teachers with a lens that instantly makes sense of the stumbles, hesitations and apparent carelessness they see in children's writing. The portrait of the 'full-time overloaded' writer is one that will stay with readers long after they close the book.

Handwriting and spelling are not treated as decorative extras but as emancipatory tools without which young writers cannot flourish. The anecdotes about classrooms shaped by romantic assumptions about 'creativity' are both funny and devastating, offering a candid account of the consequences of neglecting the technical foundations of writing. By the time the authors show how systematic phonics and fluent handwriting intersect to support composition, the argument is irresistible: transcription is not the enemy of creativity but its prerequisite.

What sets this book apart is its blend of scholarly breadth, practical insight and moral seriousness. It offers a coherent framework rooted in cognitive science, linguistic history and classroom realism, always returning to the central conviction that writing is teachable, and that children's futures depend on us teaching it well.

How I Wish I'd Taught Writing deserves to become the definitive guide for anyone serious about improving the teaching of writing. It is learned, lucid and often unexpectedly moving. Most importantly, it gives teachers much more than another list of strategies; it offers a way of seeing that reveals writing as both a cultural inheritance and a profoundly human act.

David Didau, educator and author of Making Meaning in English and Bringing the English Curriculum to Life

Contents

Foreword

Professor Steve Graham, Arizona State University

I recently ran across a single panel cartoon created by Dave Blazek where Yoda, the wise Jedi master, is told by a teacher his attempt to diagram a sentence about fear, a topic he advises Anakin Skywalker about in the *Star Wars* saga, is nowhere close to correct. If you are not familiar with sentence diagraming, it is a technique where a learner demonstrates the inherent structure in a sentence by using horizontal and vertical lines to show how the grammatical parts of a sentence are separate and related to each other.

I smiled at the premise and whimsical nature of the cartoon and, as I rose from my chair, a childhood memory slid into my consciousness. I slipped back through time to a rural school house in New Mexico. Inside a sixth-grade classroom at the end of the hall, the school principal stood at the blackboard patiently teaching our class how to diagram sentences, providing his charges with a good dose of: 'Practicing this skill so I know you got it.' We did this for one hour every Thursday afternoon.

To borrow a line from the *Star Wars* saga, this happened 'a long time ago in a galaxy far, far away.' Even so, I am pretty sure I was better at sentence diagraming than our friend Yoda. I am also sure that learning how to diagram sentences did not make me a better writer. I had no idea how to make this skill apply to the stories and other texts we occasionally wrote for class.

I do not mean to disparage my former principal or those I met over the years who claim they learned to write as a result of sentence diagraming – a sum total of one very prolific academic writer named Lynn Fuchs – but the available evidence does not support the use of this method as a means for improving students' writing. I first became aware of this when conducting a meta-analysis with Dolores Perin entitled *Writing Next*. Since its publication in 2007, I often find myself wondering why so few evidence-based practices make their way into classrooms, and so many practices with no or questionable evidence do?

As I wrestled with this question, I realized there is no single answer. A variety of factors and actors contribute to this paradoxical situation.

How I Wish I'd Taught Writing by Timothy Mills and Clare Sealy addresses one of the most critical contributors and solutions to making evidence-based writing practices a common feature in classrooms. Put simply, many teachers are not aware, or only superficially familiar with, evidence-based writing practices. Other teachers know only a few such practices well. Teachers cannot apply the many validated writing practices now available if they are unfamiliar with them or do not know how to use them effectively. This book provides a solution to this issue by offering teachers the knowledge needed to bring evidence-based writing practices into their classroom in a thoughtful and informed manner.

I want to make clear that teachers are not to blame for a lack, or limited knowledge, of evidence-based practices. This is a systems problem. The organisations that prepare teachers commonly place little emphasis on teaching them how to teach writing, much less use evidence-based practices to do so. While schools may provide teachers with some preparation on teaching writing, this occurs infrequently and only occasionally focuses on practices with a proven track record. As a result, much of the burden for learning how to be an effective writing instructor falls on teachers personally. This book provides a valuable resource not only for preparing teachers, but for fostering their own efforts to become a great teacher.

So why is it worth you investing your effort and time to read, reflect on and apply the practices presented in *How I Wish I'd Taught Writing*? I would argue this is because writing is not an optional skill. Rather it is one students must master if they are to realise their full educational, social and occupational potential. We use writing to communicate with friends, share and record information, entertain others, discover who we are, tell who we were, heal physiological and psychological wounds, show what we know and persuade other people. Writing about material read or presented in class makes it more understandable and memorable, whereas teaching writing makes students better readers. Writing is a powerful tool that is ubiquitous and central to life in the 21st century.

Of course, you may think my argument about the importance of writing is in need of revision with the advent of ChatGPT and other large language models (LLM). These tools can produce text that appears to be both natural and intelligent. While LLMs can create stories, essays and arguments, there are things they cannot do. They cannot think for you.

The beauty of writing is that it engages you in thinking. When we write about a topic, for instance, we select which ideas are important, consider these ideas in light of what we already know, organise our understandings into a coherent whole, make decisions about what is to be written and analyse and reflect on our understanding as ideas are transformed into text. When a LLM writes for us, these thinking processes are not engaged, limiting what, if anything, is learned.

So, what should we do? We need to take the bull by the horns, as we say in the United States, and decide how our students will learn to use LLMs in an ethical manner and in ways that maintain thinking and learning when writing. Just as importantly, as students learn to use LLMs as a writing partner, they will still need to learn the skills, processes, strategies and knowledge necessary to write effectively, as well as also needing to acquire new writing skills.

Take, for instance, writing an essay using multiple source materials. This is a challenging task. Students must locate appropriate material that fits their writing goals, analyse each source in terms of their writing intentions and what they know about the topic, integrate these old and new understandings into a coherent mental model and use these understandings to craft a suitable text. When students draw on LLM-generated source materials to carry out such a task, it becomes even more challenging. Source material can change depending on how the prompt to locate it is worded, the validity of the source material is uncertain as its generation is not transparent, and students act as co-constructor of the LLM-generated text as they create the prompts used to access it. In this scenario, students need to know more, not less, in order to use a LLM effectively. This will undoubtably place additional challenges on teachers as this new writing era crystalizes. Teachers who understand how writing works and how to teach writing effectively will be best prepared to ensure their students are successful in this new and evolving writing landscape.

Introduction

Craig Barton's (2018) seminal work *How I Wish I'd Taught Maths* describes how, after 12 years of teaching, and after talking to experts and reading research, he realised that much of what he had thought was good practice was actually mistaken. We (Clare and Tim) have between us over 70 years of experience within primary education and it is only fairly recently that we too now appreciate how far our practice when teaching – or not actually teaching – writing deviated from what experts and the research evidence indicates are likely to be the most effective strategies. We don't think we are alone in this! Oddly, unlike reading, the teaching of writing has hardly featured in education debates.

This book is an attempt to help other teachers understand what the best evidence tells us is most likely to work. Like Craig's book, it also shares along the way some grizzly confessions of things we did with the best of intentions, that with hindsight we now know were counterproductive.

What has been salutary writing this book is how blown by the winds of edu-fashion we were! And how the profession – including us – often takes a good idea and overextends it to the exclusion of all else.

We hope this book goes some way to helping the current generation of teachers base their professional decision-making on evidence rather than fad, trendiness and what seems superficially plausible or to placate an accountability system.

Why is writing so difficult to teach?

Writing is difficult; even writing something relatively simple like an email or letter. The difference between having an idea that you want to communicate and then actually committing it into writing is stark. At times you can feel your brain seizing up with the demand of trying to put ideas into writing. It's why professional writers talk about doing every conceivable chore in the house before finally sitting down to face that blank page. Patricia Cornwell talks about the long walk down the corridor to her writing room every morning. Writing, even for successful, professional writers is really hard. And for the rest of us, who are merely trying to achieve competence in our daily communications, it can be excruciatingly challenging.

And if writing is so difficult, how much more difficult is it to teach? We learn to talk naturally, through our interactions with others, unless we have specific learning difficulties.

Reading, on the other hand, is a taught process. Even the two sides engaged in 'the reading wars' are fighting over *how* reading should be taught and not *that* it should be taught – although the whole language advocates[1] came pretty close to insinuating that it was as natural as speaking.

Writing is also a taught process and although reading and writing interact, children who are able to read are not automatically able to write.

So, although speech, reading and writing are interrelated, they are not inverses and of these three, writing is the most complex...by quite some distance. The US psychologist Ronald Kellogg's (1994) research indicated that the cognitive effort required for planning, composing and rewriting a text was twice that needed for reading a very complex text (try Hegel or Joyce) and not dissimilar to the effort exerted by an expert chess player encountering a formidable opponent.

The researcher Debra Myhill (2010) maintains that learning to write is one of the most challenging undertakings facing young children. Gunther Kress (1994) hypothesised that writing is more difficult than reading because when we read, we make meaning *from* text whereas when we write we make meaning *through* text. Myhill explains that reading is a receptive process, whereas writing is a productive process, and this means that writing development *is extremely susceptible to teaching* or in other words, the explicit teaching of writing is highly effective at making children better at writing. And it is therefore also extremely susceptible, in a negative sense, to the absence of explicit teaching. Recognising a word someone else has written is much easier than recalling a word we want to write. We all recognise a £5 note instantly but might struggle to recall what's on it. We might understand what someone is saying in French (because that involves recognition) yet struggle to formulate a reply (because that involves recalling vocabulary and grammar). Explicit teaching of the various components of the writing process develops the ability to recall – to bring back to consciousness – the meanings, syntax,

---

1   Whole language reading theory posited that as we read to create meaning, it is the words and sentences that hold the meaning and not the graphemes and phonemes. So they eschewed phonics.

structures, strategies, audience awareness and transcriptional enablers that combine together when we write. It is why improvements in writing are seldom rapid and why long periods with no writing instruction (persistent absence, holidays, pandemics) often stall progress.

The research into the teaching of writing is far more modest and less definitive compared with reading instruction. Sample sizes are smaller, the quality of studies is often less robust, and therefore meta-studies lack the research weight associated with reading instruction meta-studies. However, there is a growing body of research from which is emerging greater evidence of where the basis of instruction might be most fruitfully focused, and which practices have the greatest likelihood of supporting children's development.

A brief history of writing

Part of the difficulty of transferring thoughts and speech into text is related to the intricacy of our writing system. The English that we write today has been encoded with one of the most complex alphabetic codes that exists.

Humans have been using symbols to communicate for tens of thousands of years. Cave paintings developed from three-dimensional images to a few marks that represented objects, animals and information. However, all of these symbols suffered from the difficulty that the pictograms often lacked consistency so were open to interpretation. Standardised systems were developed about 5000 years ago in Mesopotamia (modern-day Iraq) by the Sumer civilisation originally as a system to record transactions. This evolved to enable complex language and ideas to be recorded and is how we have records of Enheduanna's poetic verses and the beginnings of literature. We call these standardised and systematised communication symbols that can record speech, writing. Other writing systems also developed later and *completely independently* in China and Mesoamerica (central America). The problem with all early writing systems was that humans can only remember in the region of 2000 symbols and most languages have vocabularies of hundreds of thousands of words.

The breakthrough came with the realisation that if symbols represented sounds rather than ideas, then only a few symbols needed to be remembered. When the Phoenicians added vowels to this rudimentary alphabet, they were able to represent any word using fewer than thirty symbols. The modern-day alphabet was born and, according to Eric Havelock (1976), has never been improved on.

The complexity of the English alphabetic code along with its vast vocabulary is due to its chaotic evolution as a result of invasions and the subsequent integration of other languages into its orthography (spelling). This was further compounded with the introduction of the printing press. With no common agreement about how words should be spelled, printers made spelling decisions at random. By the time Samuel Johnson cemented English spelling with his dictionary in the eighteenth century, English had developed into a morphophonemic language. That means that English spellings indicate pronunciation *and* meaning. So, the 'sign' in '*sign*ature' is indicating meaning but the pronunciation is different to the root word 'sign'. It is why English has so many homophones ('maid' and 'made'), but it is also why English tends to have shorter words, gifting it a certain efficiency once mastered – unlike the long compound words of German (*Geschwindigkeitsbegrenzung*: speed limit).

This means that mastering the English alphabetic code takes longer than languages like Finnish and Italian, which have more consistent letter to sound correspondences. These languages are said to be transparent whereas those with a more complicated system are said to be opaque. English is the opaquest of all alphabetic writing systems. As encoding (writing the letters of a word in the correct order) lags behind decoding (blending the encoded sounds to read the word), this means that not only does learning to read English take longer than other alphabetic languages; learning to write (and spell) English takes even longer. As a result of its evolution from many languages, English also has one of the largest vocabularies (why we have words for animals and their meat – 'pig' and 'pork'), which is an advantage when creating expressive text and communicating with great clarity and specificity, but adds to the cognitive demands of learning to write a vast lexicon.

There are four myths that have emerged around the teaching of writing:

1. Because it is so difficult to do, it is just too difficult to teach in any coherent way.
2. The key to teaching writing is to get children to do lots of reading.
3. The research into teaching writing is so thin that it gives little indication of how to teach it.
4. Writers are born not made and the ability to write is a blessing from on high, so, really, what's the point in teaching it.

We shall attempt to dispel all four of these myths.

4

Key messages

- Writing is one of the most cognitively demanding activities undertaken by humans. As a result, it is difficult to teach writing in any language.

- The English alphabetic code is one of the most complex, so it takes much longer to learn to decode it than other more transparent orthographies. As a result, it also takes longer to learn to encode English.

- English has one of the largest vocabularies. Although this offers greater opportunity for clarity when writing, it places further cognitive demands.

- The morphophonemic nature of the English orthography makes spelling English more demanding. This adds a further cognitive demand to writing.

Chapter 1
Why writing matters

For many centuries most people couldn't read, and it didn't much matter because there was precious little to read. Stories were delivered orally; travelling players and storytellers gave you the occasional narrative dopamine hit. You weren't even expected to read the Bible – that was the job of your priest. Even when Martin Luther insisted that you interpret it for yourself, most people couldn't read because an hour's instruction every week at Sunday School just wasn't enough. But in the modern world, we all know that learning to read is important. It is the sine qua non of primary education. If you can't read, then it is extremely difficult to navigate modern life. But is learning to write so important?

Tim writes: I'm not sure that I ever placed the importance on teaching writing that I placed on teaching reading. If a child in my class couldn't read well, then I had failed; if they couldn't write well, did I really give myself such a hard time? And I'm not even sure that I knew what not writing well was – usually poor handwriting and spelling and missing capitals and full-stops. I assumed that handwriting was the child's business as long as I arranged some handwriting practice on special paper, spelling was somehow down to reading more, and I banged on about capitals and full-stops ad nauseum with some short-term improvement but little effect in the longer term. Some children learned to write well regardless, some got by and some produced indecipherable and/or incoherent offerings under duress. I had no idea how to do better, but I religiously followed the advice to inspire my classes with interesting and enigmatic picture cues. I dressed up as a character to motivate them and created moments of awe and wonder by wandering the countryside fondling leaves and tree bark and listening to Beethoven's Pastoral Symphony. To be fair, this approach did promote some wonderful discussions and 'turns of phrase', particularly among my 'top' writers, but it did little to improve the actual written work and almost nothing for the coherence of their texts. I became quite adept at improving children's writing, but I was markedly ineffective at improving children as writers. I'm not sure that anyone really knew how to do this – and I'm not sure anyone much cared.

Clare writes: *I trained to teach in the heyday of a highly ideological stance on the teaching of both reading and writing that believed that children were only motivated to learn through immersion and creating their own meanings. Approaches that focused on particulars rather than whole language – be that phonics or grammar – were viewed as not just inferior, but actually evil, imperialistic impositions that killed motivation and creativity and imposed an authoritarian fixed meaning onto vulnerable children. In the same way that I was taught to teach reading by immersing children in beautiful books, with the belief that this alone would inspire children to derive meaning from the printed word, I was taught that the key to teaching children to write was to position them as publishers. The creation of physically beautiful objects was promoted as the essential driver of enabling children to write well. Even when work was a couple of paragraphs, ensuring the children added, at the very least, a beautiful border was the indispensable element of acceptable writing. I went on a course teaching me how to do Japanese book binding for example, because if children could make beautiful books, then that would activate their inner author and all would be well. (Note to reader: All was not well.) So, my early experience as a teacher was that writing was seen as important because it was about children's self-expression. However, there was a high degree of magical thinking from the adults about how that self-expression might be cultivated.*

And yet this is not entirely wrong. Writing is at least in part about self-expression and that expression needs an audience. Writing is, as we have already said, extremely hard. Ronald Kellogg (1994) remarks that learning to write is like 'digging trenches.' In the same way that digging a trench is backbreaking, onerous physical labour, writing is cognitively gruelling. So, if writing is such a cognitively demanding activity, then there has to be a very strong reason for us to bother to undertake it and, what's more, undergo the often arduous task of learning to do it. Charles Bazerman (2016) insists that we need to consider this when teaching writing. Developing children's motivation to undertake an activity that will take many years to achieve any sort of competence is a major challenge. With this in mind, it is understandable why approaches to teaching writing that emphasise above all else the provision of motivating contexts and the creation of beautiful products have such allure. If only such approaches were – by themselves – effective!

So why is writing important?

Writing enables social inclusion

As we will discuss later, what is valued in the teaching of writing seems to have done a 180 degree turn from when Clare started teaching. At that point, writing for an audience was the only thing that mattered. Nowadays, the social aspect of writing appears to have all but vanished within many contemporary classrooms. This is equally misplaced.

Charles Bazerman (2016) argues that as a social animal, the payoff of any communicative activity is going to be the anticipation of a shared communal utility. Becoming a competent writer enables us to share communications across space and time. At its most refined, this may be through literature – novels, poetry – but also, more prosaically, through emails, texts, social media and through work- and study-related communications. Adults who are unable to write or who struggle with writing are excluded from this social and cultural environment. We write, according to Ken Hyland (2021), for our words to be read by others; to communicate our ideas, thoughts, opinions and information. This ability to share ideas with others and our future selves infuses writing with social value, according to Anne Dyson (2002). Because writing is perceived as socially valuable, this encourages children to undertake the necessary arduous mental exertion of writing. So, Bazerman (2016) suggests, it is important for teachers and schools to understand the social imperative of writing and to try to create a pedagogy, environment and culture that flicks this social switch.

Ensuring a social purpose to writing in class can motivate and improve writing. Classrooms offer the potential for an immediate and supportive readership, the opportunity of having a rich social knowledge of one's readership and the opportunity of conversing with readers and receiving feedback. Having an explicit understanding that writing is communication and has the purpose of informing, persuading, entertaining and expressing feelings to others – even in its earliest stages – can help develop a young writer's purpose and motivation. Furthermore, developing an awareness of the social purpose of writing helps develop children's understanding of the difficult and abstract concept of the non-present reader – so necessary for the emergence of cohesion and coherence within writing. For some young writers, this communication may initially only occur within the social structure of their classroom.

Writing develops thinking

If writing is a social activity permeated by culture and identity that gives us voice and influence, and develops our identity, then what are the deeper psychological drivers that motivate us to engage in this frustrating and demanding activity? And what are the deeper psychological advantages?

Writing demands thinking and so encourages thinking

Ronald Kellogg (1994) insisted that writing cannot be achieved without thinking, and quality writing cannot be achieved without quality thinking. He suggests that thinking well and having cogent and interesting ideas is a necessary but not sufficient condition of having willing readers. There will be other influences on how drawn the reader is – personal interests, language, structure and cohesion for example – but, Kellogg argued, poor writing reflects a failure to develop interesting ideas, communicate them clearly and sequence them lucidly. It fails to consider the reader's needs sufficiently. And when the reader's needs are not met, they have a tendency to stop reading and do something less frustrating. It is this pervasive consideration of the non-present reader that requires deep contemplation when writing. We need to help novice writers develop an understanding of this concept and we need to help pupils build mental models of how to address it. We will return to this throughout the book: is the writing we are teaching our children to create sufficiently clear and interesting to help their non-present reader stay the distance?

It is worth reflecting on the difference in thinking required when reading as opposed to that required when writing. A good writer has often done much of the cognitive heavy lifting for the reader so that the reader is using their own thinking pathways to read the words fluently, engage with the language used and draw on long-term memory to illuminate the writer's ideas and fill in the blanks that the writer is assuming the reader already knows. Although this can be cognitively taxing when the text and subject matter are complicated, it is far less demanding than constructing the text in the first place.

The writer has not only to consider the thoughts and ideas they are trying to communicate that derive from their own personal construct system, but they must also attempt to consider the construct system of the unknown readership. As we write, we overlay our own perspectives with the consideration of our perceived perspectives of others – writing is not merely a one-dimensional activity where the writer communicates their ideas and never mind the reader. This task of representing our own thoughts and ideas such that they can be shared in a public forum is, according to Kellogg (1994), 'monumental' and 'the crux of the challenge facing each writer' and why writing demands so much penetrating thinking – it will have taken you a few minutes to read this section but it has taken us many hours to write, revise, rewrite and edit it and part of the reason for that, is that we don't know you and we don't know exactly what you know, but we are still writing for you…the individual.

What this all means is that the better we write, the better we think and the better we think, the better we write. And to link back to the importance of writing, voice and power, when someone writes well, Raymond Nickerson (1985) and his colleagues suggest, 'one tends to believe that a person has the ability to think effectively.' That is quite some cultural capital to endow on our pupils.

Writing is a means for thinking and an exemplary process of thinking

By writing about a subject, we learn to think about a subject. Some subjects, suggests Susan Horton (1990), are so complex that merely thinking about them is insufficient; they require writing about for us to really cohere our thoughts. We can add 2 + 3 in our heads but reach for pen and paper to add 15,623 + 7683. We can easily answer the question 'What shall we eat tomorrow?' in our heads but 'What were the causes of World War I?' requires writing if we are to consider and communicate all our thoughts and ideas to address the question in its full complexity. Horton suggests that developing scientific and legal thought and argument may actually be impossible without the tool of writing to facilitate the demands of the thinking required: a written record of complex arguments and thoughts permits, encourages and facilitates examination, elaboration and reaction in a manner that spoken language cannot.

This is why Horton (1990) states that it is important not to wait to start writing until fully formed and fleshed out ideas have solidified. The mere process of writing will help with the thinking which will in turn help with the writing. This is, she argues, a vital concept for beginning writers to start to understand. Their first drafts – whether a draft sentence, paragraph or longer text – will almost certainly be unsatisfying. It is worth remembering Isabelle Allende's (2025) observation that one can always edit a poor piece of writing, but one can never edit a blank page. So, writing improves with more thinking, thinking improves with more writing, which gives us the really big payback: writing improves with more writing. This is seldom communicated to children, yet, according to Perry Klein's team's (2022) research, they can find this highly motivating and particularly so for struggling writers. It's why Stephen King (2020) doesn't always know the ending to his stories before or while writing them. He knows that the writing will promote his thinking which will in turn enable him to 'find' his story's ending. In fact, David Galbraith's (1996) research suggests that writers who solve problems during the planning phase produce less coherent text and discover fewer new ideas than those who discover ideas spontaneously during their writing.

So, writing not only *demands thinking* but is also a *means for thinking*. This is a crucial benefit for those of us in the business of promoting thinking. Any activity that inherently ensures thinking has to happen is going to be high on our list of important pedagogies and writing seems to be at the very top of this hierarchy. This is why AI must not replace learning to write in schools. If writing is outsourced to AI, so too is the thinking. Schools are nothing if they are not places that develop children as thinkers.

Writing develops metacognition

Writing requires the writer to monitor and evaluate their thinking and writing during the process. Thus, when we write we are required to think about our thinking: writing is not a motor skill like riding a bike, it requires mindful and effortful engagement (thinking, in other words) and never becomes fully automatised. As such, it is a far more conscious cognitive process than speaking. When we speak, we communicate spontaneously, whereas self-monitored communication is almost always written, and anything but the most routine writing is tough – digging trenches.

Writing promotes creative thinking and well-being

There appears, according to Charlene Tan's (2021) research, to be a reciprocal relationship between creative acts and well-being. Robert Sternberg (1988) suggested that all writing is a creative act. He argued that although original, innovative and important writing satisfied the definition of *product creativity*, writing that was the result of simply applying relevant knowledge inventively to achieve a goal resulted in *process creativity*. The written outcomes, he argued, would vary, but they were, nonetheless, still creative acts. As long as the written output is novel to the individual mind which had the idea, even if fairly imitative, the person has engaged in creativity.

Writing develops language

Noam Chomsky's (1965) work in the 1960s suggested that we are prewired for spoken language and although there has been some argument as to whether this is an evolutionary trait we certainly develop spoken language before we are able to read or write, and before we attend formal schooling. David Geary (2002) suggests that spoken language is biologically primary, meaning that we learn to speak through exposure to it and don't have to be schooled in it. However, as Debra Myhill (Fisher *et al*, 2010) noted, writing is not merely speech written down. Written language, although built upon spoken language and interrelated to it, is different – not only is written syntax different and much more complex but, as Maria Korochkina's (2024) research team discovered, when children read books, they are likely to be exposed to a vast number of words that they will never have encountered aurally and that includes encounters through radio and television (up to 28% – and these books are ordinary children's books and not for the most part great children's literature). Written vocabulary is far richer than spoken vocabulary – it has to, both for clarity and engagement.

However, written language is also more difficult to produce. Arthur Applebee (1978) found that an eight-year-old's written story was the equivalent to that of a four-year-old child relating the story orally. Deborah McCutchen (1995) proposes that some of this divergence will be as a result of the complexities and demands of automatising the procedural knowledge associated with writing (handwriting, spelling, grammar and sentence structures). However, as Michel Fayol (2016) muses, this is a pretty strange evolution: moving from coherent and cohesive oral narratives to sketchy, allusive and poorly organised written ones. He suggests that much of the difficulty pupils have with communicating in writing has to do with the conditions specific to written language.

When children relate their ideas in speech, they are able to monitor the listener's reactions and responses in the moment and clarify and adapt both the language and their oral register. However, when children translate their ideas into written language, they discover that they must imagine the recipient of their message and self-regulate their language production with the reader in mind. This requires being more specific and introducing language markers to prevent ambiguity – these markers are not necessary in speech. Furthermore, writing requires different patterns in word choices and the use of less frequent words, requiring the acquisition of a larger and more precise vocabulary. Children will also have to learn new syntactic structures that differ from the syntax of spoken communication, eschew the reliance on verbal and contextual cues, and adopt the use of linguistic markers that connect ideas for their readers and help the reader to signal relationships between successive statements and ideas. Not only does writing require the coordination of ideas between sentences but it demands the inclusion of subordinating ideas – and all this while maintaining the continuity of the theme. Fayol (2016) considers this move from the 'here and now' language of speaking to the 'there and away' language of writing to be one of the foremost threshold concepts of learning to translate ideas into written language.

So, Fayol (2016) suggests, learning to write requires a significant development of language, and the effort required to achieve this development delivers important linguistic advantages. Whereas spoken syntax can seldom be applied in writing without the writer appearing unclear and confused, the syntax of writing can enhance speech and, in the hands of a great orator, can sound impressive and important. Basil Bernstein (1964) highlighted the use of this more complex syntax in an 'elaborated' code of speaking and suggested it is often used where the speaker does not know the listener well – similar to the relationship between the writer and the reader. Bernstein suggested that this elaborated code had social implications, and Pierre Bourdieu (1974) associated the use of more complex language structures with linguistic capital – the language version of cultural capital.

As Isabel Beck (2013) and her colleagues indicated in their book *Bringing Words to Life*, the requirement of specific and precise vocabulary in writing means that words must be used in context and not merely recognised or guessed (as in reading) with the result that these words are far more likely to be remembered. Using words and syntax that promote clarity and coherence – a requirement of writing – develops not only written language, but also oral language.

The effects of written language on oral language are often overlooked. Much time is rightly spent on the bridge between talking and writing, and how talking can improve writing, but there appears to be a payback dividend as well as a pay forward investment. Written language can improve oral language as Scott Payne and Paul Whitney (2002) discovered. Their second-language students who used digital written chatrooms developed significantly improved oral language when compared to students in the control group who did not write. The Romans were fully aware of the power of writing to improve speech. They used writing almost exclusively for this purpose. Success for Roman elites was founded on the making of great speeches, so Roman pupils were taught to write in order that they become great orators rather than to become great writers.

The language developments associated with writing also deliver positive effects on reading particularly in developing writers. Yusura Ahmed (2014) and her team found that although reading influenced writing more than writing influenced reading, at the sentence level, expertise in writing offered significant advantages to reading comprehension. Spelling also affects reading more than reading affects spelling, with better spellers reading faster than poorer spellers.

Key messages

- Writing is a social activity that gifts social voice and power. We write to have our words read. A classroom offers a unique opportunity to create a safe, supportive and experimental environment where the social and cultural imperative of writing can be fostered and positive writing identities developed.

- Writing is a powerful tool for thinking. Not only is the writing process an exemplar for the thinking process, but it also supports long-term memory, enhances problem solving and is inherently creative. If we want our pupils to think better, remember more and be more creative we need them to write more.

- Writing is an inherently creative activity.

- Writing builds language. The more complex syntax of written language builds vocabulary and develops language, enabling pupils to not only write more effectively but also to speak with greater accuracy and coherence.

Chapter 2
A cognitive perspective on writing (the overloaded writer)

Tim writes: *My teacher training was rooted in the principles of 'child-centred education' and constructivism and was situated far along the 'progressive' continuum in terms of educational philosophy. 'Traditional' approaches were frowned upon and ignored and the concept of discovery-based approaches to learning were prominent. I was genuinely quite happy with this, never questioned the approaches, even when I couldn't get them to work, and still feel that there is a deal of sense associated with much of the philosophy, particularly for more competent learners who have mastered much of the required procedural knowledge and can apply some agency to their learning. There was, however, precious little talk of memory, and the idea of remembering was redundant because once 'discovered', learning did not require remembering. Because remembering stuff was not important, I had little idea about memory and the research in cognitive science as they related to learning and therefore teaching. This now seems a gaping hole in my development as a teacher, especially as much of the research is over 100 years old – Ebbinghaus was conducting his memory experiments in the 1880s. If there was one aspect that I would have found profoundly useful, it is the concept of working memory. Once I 'discovered' this keystone – it would have been nice if someone had just told me about it on my PGCE – so much about my pupils' struggles with writing started to make sense, and I was able to help them develop as writers much more effectively.*

Clare writes: *This echoes my training too. It wasn't until about 25 years after my training that I stumbled across teachers talking about the importance of memory as the essential matrix within which learning is constituted. It is so obvious yet hit me like a sledgehammer! Even so, among some teachers, I still encounter a violent, almost emetic reaction to 'memorisation' as anathema to real 'learning' which is spoken about in hushed tones as some sort of spiritual enlightening that does not need anything as base as* *memory formation within physical brains. There's a deep-seated fear that if you start talking about memory, then education will be reduced to learning meaningless, disconnected facts. Whereas understanding working memory, cognitive load, long-term memory and schema formation actually makes it much easier to help children learn things that are meaningful and connected and that they can use to think critically and to be creative.*

A conceptual model of writing development

You have probably heard of Philip Gough and William Tunmer's (1986) seminal model for reading, 'The Simple View of Reading'. Their model maintains that reading comprehension (the ability to extract meaning from text) is the result of the ability to decode words (read words almost instantly) multiplied by the ability to understand language. Development in one, but preferably both abilities, will multiply the reader's ability to comprehend what they read. And conversely, since the relationship is a multiplicative one, and anything multiplied by zero is zero, lack of development in one will undermine the reader's ability to comprehend what they read, however advanced the other. The model is supported by significant research. It undermined the 'Whole Language' theory of Ken Goodman (1970) and Marie Clay (1991) by highlighting the importance of code knowledge and systematic phonics teaching and shifted the reading paradigm in England from multi-cueing, language-based approaches (the Searchlights model of the old Literacy Strategy) to alphabetic code approaches to early reading. The Simple View of Reading is essentially why we teach phonics every day in Reception and KS1 in England.

Philip Gough, in the same year as he devised the Simple View of Reading, developed along with Connie Juel and Priscilla Griffiths a simple view of writing (Juel, Griffith and Gough, 1986). They proposed that in the same manner that reading comprehension development was dependent on decoding and language comprehension, writing development was dependent on the ability to spell multiplied by ideation (the generation and organisation of ideas). In other words, if you had an idea and could write it down in a readable form you were writing. They acknowledged that both spelling and ideation were complex processes but posited that in the absence of ideas, spelling is an empty skill and that even the best ideas cannot be written without the ability to spell.

A model is not wrong because it is simple, but there appeared to be something missing. By aligning writing with reading, it failed to acknowledge the added complexity of writing. Reading comprehension requires the reader to interpret the words and ideas of the writers…but the writer has to have those ideas in the first place and organise and write them into a coherent and cohesive text. In other words, the writer has to do much of the cognitive heavy lifting – all the reader has to do is read them and understand them. It's the difference between watching a film, however critically, and making a film. Or playing a piece of music and composing a piece of music. Virginia Berninger and her colleagues (2002) suggested that what was missing was an acknowledgement that spelling and generating ideas are important but not sufficient for writing. Writing requires someone being in charge of the process – what the goal of the writing is, for whom it has been written, what to include and leave out, what strategies to employ – an executive in other words. They added 'executive function' to the model and called their new model 'The Not So Simple View of Writing' which rather neatly implies that writing is…not so simple?

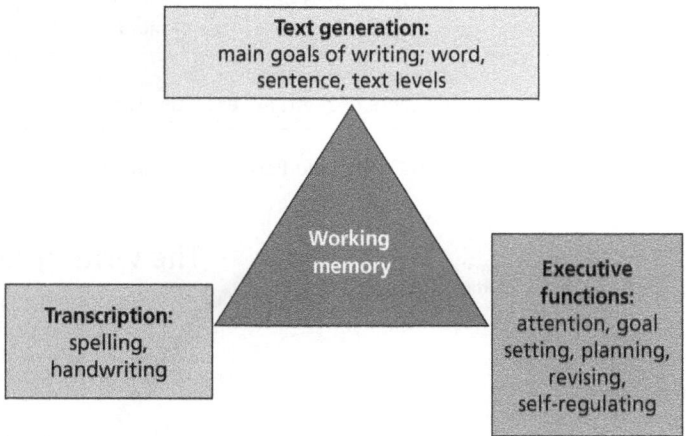

Not-so-simple view of writing. Source: Beringer (2002)

And things got even less simple when Young-Suk Kim and her colleagues (2019) suggested that an understanding of the writing process, motivation and self-efficacy needs along with content and genre knowledge were also vital pillars of any model of writing development. Joan Sedita wove all of these elements together in *The Writing Rope* (2023) wherein skilled writing requires the strands of critical thinking, syntax, text structure, writing craft and transcription interlaced and entwined.

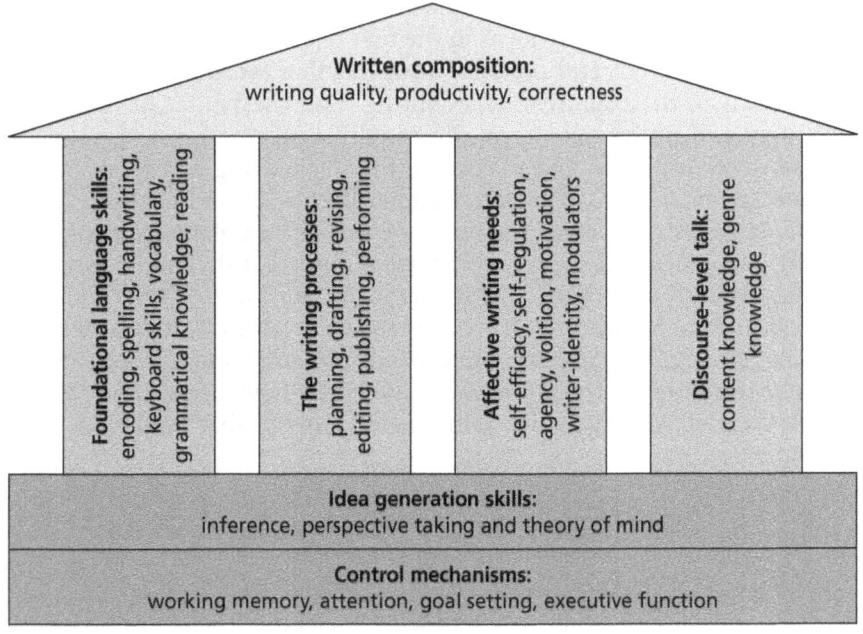

Sources: Kim and Schatschneider (2017); Kim and Park (2019); Kim 2020; Kim and Graham (2022)

Critical thinking
- Generating ideas, gathering information.
- Writing processes, organising, drafting, writing, revising.

Syntax
- Grammar and syntactic structures.
- Sentence elaboration.
- Punctuation.

Text structure
- Narrative, informational, opinion structures.
- Paragraph structure.
- Patterns of organisation (description, sequence, cause/effect, compare/contrast, problem/solution).
- Linking and transition words/phrases.

Writing craft
- Word choice.
- Awareness of task, audience, purpose.
- Literary devices.

Transcription
- Spelling.
- Handwriting, keyboarding.

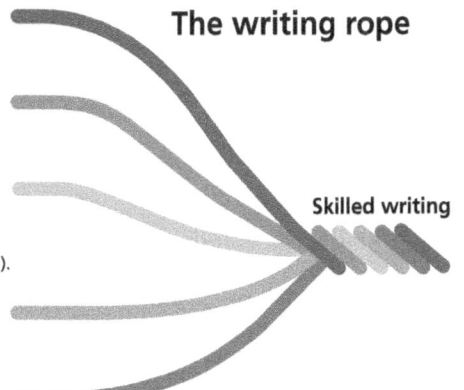

Source: *The Writing Rope*, Joan Sedita (2023)

Phew! Is it any wonder that there is a view that writing is just too difficult to teach when the models are so complex?

However, there is a single golden thread running through all of these models that is crucial, and this is the acknowledgement that the human cognitive system imposes constraints on writing operations. Every single model, however simple or complex, recognises that all of the elements of writing within the framework are dependent upon and militated by the restricted size of a writer's working memory. In fact, pretty much every piece of research into writing acquisition acknowledges the role of working memory.

What is working memory?

Working memory is the brain's workspace. It is a cognitive resource that preserves and processes information. It is linked to higher order thinking skills and heavily correlated with academic achievement. The critical element is that this crucial cognitive resource has a highly limited capacity and because of its limited capacity, it is quickly and easily overloaded. When overload happens, we are unable to remember the thing we were just trying to think about, and we might also not be able to remember stuff we thought we had already understood! Working memory size therefore poses a major limitation on human information processing. Humanity has developed a 'hack' to get around the limits of working memory. This hack is long-term memory which has the advantage of being huge and able to accommodate a near infinite store of previous learned (or prior) knowledge. Even more usefully, some knowledge is stored in long-term memory as an automatised procedure. For example, with practice, decoding of phonics becomes automatised, and we can read words without having to think about them. Indeed, once this automaticity is acquired, it is impossible *not* to read a word, so unconscious is the process. Try not to read this next word – elephant. It's impossible! You cannot *not* read it, no matter how hard you try.

This automisation of decoding frees up working memory to attend to the meaning of the text. If decoding is not automatised, then reading comprehension becomes almost impossible: finite working memory has to attend to decoding and word recognition and has nothing left to use for comprehension. Think about when you come across a long word you haven't encountered before – you probably revert to serial decoding. You then may find yourself rereading the whole sentence again to make sense of how this newly decoded word fits into the sentence as a whole. Working memory is clearly a major factor in cognitive load theory and crucial for the pedagogy of primary education. Inclusive education approaches therefore are ones that consider learning through the lens of working memory, seeking to anticipate, support and reduce working memory demands while strengthening long-term memory.

Working memory and writing

As writing is one of the most effortful cognitive activities, the small size of working memory presents a significant challenge.

Working memory is important for writing for four different reasons:

1. It provides that temporary space for the transient information required as we compose – we need to hold an idea that has occurred to us, before we write it down.

2. Until automatised or fluent, it provides a temporary store for syntax, grammar, spelling and language as we write.

3. Working memory is crucial for enabling us to switch between the phases of the writing process: sometimes thinking ahead as we plan; sometimes thinking back as we review; sometimes making changes on the fly as we edit; sometimes realising we need to go and find something out before we can continue.

4. As we compose, we need to hold the mental representations of our intention and goals as well as a picture of our reader and their perceived needs, knowledge, likes and dislikes. What can we assume our reader already knows and what might they not know and therefore need explaining? What might they find funny or interesting?

And all of this has to happen within a restricted and constrained cognitive space that, once overloaded, makes translating our thoughts into writing very difficult and frustrating and undermines quality.

Is it any wonder that John Hayes and Linda Flower (1980) described the writer as 'full time overloaded'?

You may feel that knowing about the restricted cognitive capacity associated with working memory and writing makes the prospect of teaching of writing even bleaker. However, it is the key. Indeed, Thierry Olive (2002) suggests that the understanding of this restricted capacity of working memory and the heavy demands on it for emergent writers makes the approach to teaching writing much clearer.

His supposition is supported by both Virginia Berninger (1999) and Margaret McCutchen (1995). As children learn to write, Berninger and McCutchen argue, they require significant practice to achieve automatisation of key procedural knowledge. Writing becomes more fluid and less onerous the more automatised and fluent this procedural knowledge becomes. Patricia Alexander, Steve Graham and Karen Harris synthetised this neatly by suggesting that the skills and strategies of writing acquisition sat on a continuum from automaticity to intentionality (1998). Automatic, effortless and involuntary skills supported the effortful and intentional demands of creative expression. Strategy, they noted, often resists automatisation but, crucially, as Rui Alvez (2024) maintains, is enabled by it. Perhaps think of a top tennis player whose opponent comes to the net – they need not consider how to play the return shot (their backhand and forehand are automatic), so they can concentrate on which strategy (cross-court, down-the-line or lob) is going to be most effective given the variables.

Working memory: Ages and phases

Virginia Berninger (1999) identified the role working memory has at the different stages of writing acquisition and across the skills/strategies continuum. Typically, until the age of about eight, writing performance and working memory will be mainly constrained by the demands of handwriting and spelling. As these become automatised, children's working memory capacity is able to attend more to planning, composing and revising. By twelve, as the writing processes become increasingly developed, working memory demands derive increasingly from the use of language and from ensuring coherence within longer pieces of extended text, cognisant of the demands of the specific discipline within which one is writing.

As writers become more familiar with the phases of the writing process – planning, drafting and revising – they can work more easily on linguistic units of increasing size from words to sentences, building paragraphs and finally longer texts (This does not mean that younger children never get to write whole texts; helpfully some picture books are short!). But Berninger stresses that the demands on a restricted working memory capacity remain important across all phases of children's development as writers. No matter whether a novice or an expert, writing places challenges on working memory – back to Hayes and Flower (1980) and the overloaded writer.

Working memory: Capacity over time

Working memory capacity is heavily correlated with academic outcomes, and this is especially evident with writing. Capacity is usually four chunks (or episodes) of information or seven single elements of information (a phone number for instance). Once this capacity is reached, the system becomes overloaded. However, not all of us have the same capacity. In the same way that height varies within a population, working memory capacity follows a normal distribution curve. Some people have greater capacity, and some have an appreciably reduced capacity. Academic outcomes for children with a smaller capacity have been historically poor, particularly in writing, despite the fact that they may have no other cognitive restrictions. This is highly relevant to the acquisition of writing over the primary phase of education and why it is so easy to overload that capacity in earlier years when the working memory volume is developing but is smaller.

Having a smaller working memory is egalitarian in that it is not related to any socio-economic factors. In any primary classroom the span of working memory capacity may be as much as 5 years; 10% of children will have a significantly reduced capacity. Up to 50% of children in lower prior attainment maths and English groups will have below average working memory. A restricted working memory often presents as an attention deficit when the child becomes distracted as a result of overload of instructions and attention drifts – Susan Gathercole and Tracy Alloway (2004) suggest that this can be mis-diagnosed as ADHD.

But while working memory size is not related to socio-economic background, the extent to which any limitations are mitigated by the ready availability of deep funds of knowledge within long-term memory is much more strongly correlated with socio-economic status.

Mediation for working memory restrictions

Although working memory capacity will expand as children mature, it will not expand to the extent that any restriction will ultimately be reconciled with the capacity of other children. In other words, smaller working memory is probably for life. But remember, this is a cognitive restriction not a cognitive disability. The mediation for children with a restricted working memory in the classroom lies with anticipating the heavy memory demands inherent in learning to write and therefore deliberately deploying effective pedagogy, appropriate adjustments and adaptations. Such pedagogy is useful for all children but absolutely vital for those with smaller working memories. Children with smaller working memory will require work to strengthen long-term memory so that they acquire highly automatised procedural knowledge (handwriting, spelling, grammar, punctuation, sentence structure) and significant content knowledge to reduce the cognitive load. They will also benefit from a reduction in the number of instructions given prior to activities, repeated reminders, regular targeted cognitive and metacognitive prompts, the reduction of material to be remembered by the use of scaffolds, matrices, memory aids, worked examples and peer support. Pupils with a restricted working memory will need to develop strategies to support their own facilitation, particularly as they move into secondary school – note-taking, the use of long-term memory, place-keeping, organisational strategies and aide-memoires. There is also research that suggests that children with reduced working memory capacity require more error-free learning as their working memory restrictions mean they are unable to utilise trial and adjustment strategies once errors occur.

Working memory and teaching writing

So, an understanding of working memory and its relationship to the demands of writing affords us a very valuable lens when it comes to teaching writing to children: teach writing in a progression that mediates and supports, but never overloads, a child's growing working memory capacity. We need to anticipate, reduce, manage and support working memory demands while strengthening memory. This means in practice:

- Automatise that which can be automatised through systematic teaching and practice – and automatise to the point of effortlessness.

- Ensure absolute fluency of a process to support movement to the next phase.

- Build automatisation and fluency to support the heavy cognitive lifting required for the application of strategies to achieve quality writing.

- Build a writing curriculum designed to anticipate working memory challenges. Progress from words to sentences and then to paragraphs and finally longer texts as automaticity and fluency builds.

- Plan lessons that are cognisant of and mediate working memory restrictions that come under huge demands when writing.

- Be vigilant for working memory overload – it results in frustration and/or poor quality outcomes.

- Be aware that different children have different working memory capacities.

Throughout this book we will draw your attention to working memory since the research and evidence for effective writing instruction is predicated on the importance of mediating this restricted cognitive workspace.

Chapter 3
Transcription

Tim writes: *I am happy to confess that I love handwriting and spent ages in my early teens designing my own individual script – labouring for many long hours over the perfect 'f'. I have spent a fortune on fountain pens. This all despite the fact that my mother taught me how to hold a pen in an uncomfortable and ugly grip that left a painful dent on my finger – I rectified this at the age of 20 revising for my finals so that I could write faster. I consider my handwriting fast, fluent and really rather attractive – flamboyant, legible and just the right side of bohemian. Compliment my handwriting, and I'll be your friend for life. Paradoxically, I spent little time teaching handwriting to my pupils and when some struggled with this element in writing lessons, I suggested they spend some of their own time 'designing' their handwriting into something more aesthetically pleasing and legible. I certainly never checked their grips or their posture or even timetabled any time for handwriting practice. I am less happy to confess that my spelling has always been poor, and I have had to work hard to improve it. I learned to read relatively easily but was not taught phonics systematically ('Janet and John' – repetition of words) so the orthographic knowledge I developed was through whole word teaching and not grapheme/phoneme correspondences. Spelling tests were lists of random words learned on a Thursday, tested on a Friday and forgotten by Monday. I used this model to teach my pupils – I have no idea why, as I had substantial personal evidence that it was a flawed model – until I decided to organise spelling lists according to synonyms. This improved my pupils' vocabulary but not their spelling. Teaching older primary children, I don't believe that I was alone in basically ignoring handwriting and spelling instruction (and phonics), and I really don't remember there being any strong directives from anyone on how to teach spelling. If I am brutally honest, I was far more interested and excited by the prospect of my charges creating wonderful, creative and inspiring compositions and was happy to gloss over the hard yards of transcription.*

Clare writes: *I too am an alumnus of Janet and John, though Miss Gudgeon in Year 2 went quietly rogue and explicitly taught us the more complex vowel sounds. Handwriting though – no recollection at all about ever being taught anything, ever. My handwriting isn't great – perfectly functional, rather messy, definitely neither flamboyant nor bohemian. As for teaching handwriting, I never received any training about this at all. My first school 'did Jarman' so it was just a case of working through the workbooks and getting children to practise the letter formation. Because publishing children's work was so central to the school's approach, children did a lot of copying work out 'in best' for either display (triple mounted, naturally) or to be made into books for the reading corner. The sheer amount of time devoted to rewriting best copies alongside the sky-high presentational expectations meant that, despite the lack of explicit teaching, children practised their way into producing handwriting that was, as I recall, at least legible. Maybe not very fluent though.*

It's mind-blowing to consider the opportunity cost of hours and hours a week spent copying out and decorating writing as if these nine-year-olds were mediaeval monks illustrating manuscripts, all in the name of unleashing some innate creativity that explicit teaching would irrevocably damage. In case you are wondering how we fitted in the rest of the curriculum, there wasn't really much by way of the rest of the curriculum. You had a topic – the weather perhaps – and would make some stormy pictures, write some stormy poems, make a rain gauge and a rainfall shaker to use in your rainfall dance. Then next year another teacher might also decide that weather would make a good topic and pretty much rinse and repeat. Those stormy poems though – they looked amazing!

But that is a mere trifle compared to our attitude to teaching spelling. We didn't teach spelling at all (what with phonics being the intrinsically evil vile corrupter of motivation and creativity and all that.) However, because writing was always for sharing, best copies had to be error free. Why we thought explicit teaching was bad but rote copying was good eludes me, but it made sense at the time. So I would laboriously correct every single spelling in all children's work so that they could then copy it out correctly spelled – usually onto a blank piece of paper with a line guide underneath – and then make a highly decorated border. Children then stuck this work onto sugar paper, trimmed it, stuck that onto another piece and trimmed that. Whole afternoons passed by composed solely of copying out, decorating a border, cutting and sticking. Meanwhile I sat in a corner furiously trying to 'transcribe' the work of poor Stevie whose 'developmental' writing contained letters of the alphabet chunked together with maybe the odd initial sound possibly corresponding to something or other. Had Stevie been three or four, this would have been fine – and his work would have been little more than a couple of sentences. But Stevie was nine years old and, encouraged by me that having a go was all that was needed, wrote pages of completely illegible text that he couldn't read back. So then he would make up the story or whatever again and I would write his spoken words underneath each written 'word'. Then he would copy my words out. What Stevie needed was phonics – and even then I reckon he would have found spelling hard. What he got instead was vacuous encouragement. Sorry Stevie. We failed you big time.

I left the school and the area a couple of years later so have no idea how Stevie got on later in secondary school and beyond. He was a lovely child and quite good at maths, but literacy was made impossible for him – presumably a dyslexic child – by our fundamentalist beliefs in creativity alone as the key driver of literacy acquisition. Possibly, hopefully, he went on to a life of fulfilment and happiness despite his literacy difficulties. Statistically though, adults who leave school with literacy at a primary school standard – and both his reading and writing were way below that – are much more at risk of not living happily ever after. As the Adult Literacy Trust (2026) writes:

> 'The lack of reading skills can have devastating impacts on a person's life and is a key contributor to an intergenerational cycle of poverty. Those with low literacy skills are twice as likely to be unemployed, and workers with poor literacy earn on average 60% less than those with basic literacy. Adults with low literacy are far less likely to access the health, housing and other social services to which they are entitled, and report significantly poorer health outcomes.'

The luxury beliefs of middle-class teachers have serious real-life consequences for other people's children. 57% of adults in prison in the UK have a reading level below that of an average 11-year-old. Indeed, having a reading level of an 11-year old or below is the biggest single predictor of ending up in prison, bigger even than drug use or having parents who have been to prison. Meanwhile children who are the most engaged with literacy are three times more likely to have higher levels of mental wellbeing than children who are the least engaged (39.4% vs 11.8%) (National Literacy Trust, 2018a) and 'children and young people who enjoy writing very much and who think positively about writing have, on average, higher mental wellbeing scores than their peers who don't enjoy writing at all and who hold negative attitudes towards writing.' (National Literacy Trust, 2018b). This is deeply serious stuff. Transcription skills don't thwart creativity, they make it possible. If you want to comprehensively hobble creativity, frustrate imagination and undermine motivation, then sneer at transcription and deride it as boring and dull and mere mechanics. Then wonder why so many children in your school seem to have special needs.

That said, it is entirely possible that some schools overenthusiastically embrace the arguments of this chapter while ignoring the other chapters on the importance of also developing oracy, composition and writing for an audience, leading to similar deleterious effect. The tendency for teachers to see things as either/or rather than both/and never fails to bemuse me. Frankly, while the 'transcription is dull brigade' infuriate me, I can understand their fear that some teachers might reduce teaching writing to only teaching handwriting and spelling and nothing else. Whenever a particular approach is espoused, there are always examples of people who take it way too far. To be fair, that's exactly what happened to the idea that children should write for an audience. My generation of teachers embraced that as some sort of divine truth that needed to be protected at all costs from heresies such as teaching children how to spell.

Writing is, as we hope we make clear, complex and multi-faceted and therefore needs a curriculum that develops all of the strands, rather than over-fixating exclusively on writing for an audience, or on transcription, or on writing sentences, or on knowing about genres, or on meeting the mark scheme requirements – or on whatever is currently all the rage. Only focusing on transcription, to the exclusion or near exclusion of anything else, would indeed be boring and also pointless. This chapter is not a licence to dull but a rallying cry to take children on a journey where the development of technical mastery turbocharges creative expression. If we focus too much on the allure of the final product without teaching children how to develop technical proficiency, then we risk demotivating children because the whole process becomes impossibly hard. If we only ever over-focus on developing one process at a time, we remove the motivational effects of producing an authentic piece of writing that someone else might find interesting. There is however a sweet spot that harnesses the benefits of both.

If you take a look back over the models of writing development in chapter 2, you will see that in every model sits transcription – handwriting and spelling.

Handwriting

As we explored the research on writing and writing debilities for this book, the most often mentioned and repeated element that supports or inhibits writing, appearing again and again, is 'handwriting'. The importance of handwriting to the writing process and the development of writing cannot be overstated.

This may seem somewhat counterintuitive because handwriting is not writing, and having beautiful handwriting (even when flamboyant and just the right side of bohemian) does not mean that the composition is not of suspect quality. No, handwriting is so important because of working memory. We said that working memory would bleed through this book.

Having fluent and legible handwriting that is automatised, effortless and that requires no thought, enables the working memory to load up with more of the strategic, complex demands of composition. Try composing a limerick using alternate upper and lower case letters and using your weaker hand. If you gave this a try, your working memory probably redirected your attention to letter formation rather than composition. So, the handwriting might just have been legible, but the composition would have been pretty poor.

Fluent handwriting is fast and legible, and a deficit in either area constrains writing. Poor legibility makes writing hard to decipher, both for the reader and the writer (as they revise their writing) and often devalues the content for the readers (and examiners). Laboured and slow handwriting inhibits the writing process by redirecting attention from composition to letter formation, with ideas being forgotten or poorly developed. And perhaps even more importantly, children who experience difficulties with handwriting often develop a negative view of themselves as writers, leading them to writing little or avoiding writing altogether. Note that legibility is not the same as neatness.

The correlation between fluent handwriting and quality writing is significant so we need to attend to it.

Before handwriting

Gerard Van Galen (1991), who spent much time and effort researching handwriting, suggested that the move from scribbling and making marks to writing letters and words is a huge cognitive leap for children. Not only do they have to have an intention to communicate (something to say) they must also engage their language processes (how they intend to say it). This is further complicated by the engagement of the motor programme – selection of the letter, holding a pen, controlling the size, orientation and speed of the writing as well as engaging and coordinating muscle synergies across much of the body. Furthermore, and crucial to the cognitive demands of handwriting, to engage in any early writing, children will need some understanding of the alphabetic principle: that the letters they are forming are representations of the sounds that create the words that enable the language to be written down – graphemes represent phonemes which in combination can form words. Compare these demands to the ease of talking and scribbling in an imitation of writing.

Let us never forget the importance of the phoneme/grapheme principle as a cognitive Rubicon to be crossed by children learning to write – a principle that almost certainly requires a level of expertise to teach.

So, once children start to develop their understanding that letters and groups of letters can represent sounds and thereby words, and they have sufficient skill to form those letters, they are starting on the journey to becoming writers.

Rui Alves (2024) suggests that a child's writing history starts with this cognitive acknowledgement of the alphabetic principle of sound to letter correspondences. But a child has, he argues, a writing pre-history that builds to this alphabetic epiphany. Likewise, Liliana Tolchinsky (2016) asserts that the journey to becoming a writer starts much earlier and that supporting children well before they actually form recognisable and accurate written letters associated with phonemes can help both the development of writing skills and motivation. While transcription skills and procedural and language knowledge are essential for writing, Tolchinsky argues that very young children need to first develop an understanding of the multiple dimensions of print. She maintains that before looking for letter-to-sound correspondences, children establish a set of distinctive formal principles that set writing apart from other notation systems (numbers, music, signage, symbols) and separate what can be written and read from what cannot. Even before gaining full command of phonographic conventions, children will lay out their scribbles differently depending on genre – narrative scribbles will be structured differently to non-narrative scribbles.

Humans appear to have an inherent desire to create meaning through symbols. We can see this through the engravings and paintings found in Palaeolithic caves. Leo Vygotsky (1978) maintained that although these symbols were not writing, this desire to communicate symbolically was the foundation of a child's journey towards writing. Donald Graves (1983) described young children's natural desire to make symbolic marks being linked to their identity and the wish to say, 'I am'. Harnessing this early desire to construct and communicate identity symbolically is, he argued, essential for building a child's motivation to write and must be encouraged with many and regular opportunities to express this need. The vast majority of cave logographs are hands – the link between writing and identity seems hardwired.

Vygotsky built on Alexander Luria's (1983) supposition that for children to develop the complex skills of communicating through the symbols of a writing system, they must first develop an awareness of the symbolism of language, gesture and play. For thoughts to be expressed in written form, they asserted, they must initially be articulated as speech, and this comes long before any alphabetic principle is encountered. So, the importance of language cannot be overestimated, as there can be no writing development without language development, and this will almost always start orally. Therefore, high quality interactions between young children and adults, with adults modelling effective language, will play a vital role, along with shared reading, storytelling and the learning of rhymes, stories, jokes, poems and songs to develop an understanding of the influence, diversity, expressiveness and entertainment associated with language.

One of the major breakthroughs on a young child's journey to writing is the discovery that written words convey thoughts and meaning. Luria (1983) and Vygotsky (1978) both argued that from the moment children grasp the fundamental, abstract relationship that *something stands for something else*, the development of writing becomes one of cultural development. Children's scribbles may still not convey meaning to either an adult or the child, but Tolchinsky found that, as the child develops, they attempt (usually unsuccessfully) to add referential intent to the scribbles – for instance the scribble for 'monkey' includes an exaggerated tail. She maintains that it is at this point that children start to perceive writing as a communicative tool – a vital breakthrough.

The first step for most children to develop this referential understanding of writing is to informally notice that writing exists out there in the world and that it takes multiple forms and has many uses, but is a curious phenomenon bound by many conventions. In other words, as Jeanne Paratore and her colleagues (2011) found, a child has to gain an awareness of print if they are to build literacy domain knowledge. This is important because, as Bonnie Armbruster and her colleagues (2001) noted, 'children who know about print understand that the words they see in print and the words they speak and hear are related'.

Young children can be supported in 'noticing' that writing exists and does so in in many forms, as well as in answering the myriad questions that will occur to them by:

- Early exposure to books and written texts to support that the communicated information comes from the print as well as illustrations.

- Showing and highlighting the direction in which the print is structured.

- Observing and noticing others write down their thoughts as they articulate them.

- Exposure to the letters in their name.

- Noticing punctuation marks.

- Seeing their own words and thoughts articulated in written form.

- Encouraging an understanding that speech can be written down.

- Understanding that much daily communication occurs in written forms.

Tolchinsky (2016) is clear that these developmental changes that occur prior to an understanding of the grapheme/phoneme principle, 'gear' the development of literacy and are 'strongly dependent on the learning activities that children engage in … ' – teaching in other words.

Rui Alves (2024) suggests that much of this understanding of print and curiosity around the associated conventions is essential for building children's motivation to write. He maintains that it is perhaps not surprising that young children attempt to communicate symbolically before they can read – think of the toddler scribbling with a crayon. Although we teach reading before we teach writing, we must remember that writing always comes before reading – there must be something written to read. We only teach reading first because of the motor restrictions of writing – and what little research exists suggests that where writing is taught first, reading appears to develop without instruction. Alves, nevertheless, is adamant that a child can only notice print and pose the associated questions if they live within a literate environment – if not, he affirms, they are at a disadvantage. Building this literate environment at home and school is vital for children to have the motivation to undertake the demands of learning to write and is the first stage of building what Steve Graham (2018) refers to as writing communities. Alves suggests that 'It is a precondition for both humanity and language to be nurtured by another human being and to be welcomed into a language community…' (2019). As children's curiosity and understanding of the world of print grows, so will their desire to join in that world. By 'welcoming' them into this world and encouraging any of these efforts, we help enhance the motivation to become part of a literate realm.

It is worth remembering Alves' warning, which teachers should hold front and centre when teaching writing: motivation to write is fragile and can vanish easily as with any complex task (2024). Once motivation dissolves, it is almost impossible to resurrect because a fundamental barrier has been constructed – it's too difficult, I'm not good at it, so I'm going to put my energy into avoiding doing it.

Last words to Liliana Tolchinsky (2016): ' … the availability of written input and participation in literate experiences are crucial: if there is no *what* to look at, to explore and interpret, if there is no *with whom* to participate, there is no chance of increasing sensibility and interpretation.'

Preparing for the physical demands of handwriting

Handwriting has a language element – the word, letters, sounds – and a physical element – gripping the pencil, positioning the paper, positioning the body, controlling the size and speed of the writing, the direction of the writing and the perception of the line. The requirement of attending to these demands simultaneously should not be underestimated, and children will need considerable instruction, support, time and practice to meet them.

Handwriting is not only cognitively demanding but is also physically demanding. According to Denise Donica (2010), children will be better prepared for the physical demands of handwriting if they have developed some key motor skills and associated muscle growth.

Writing does not only require fine motor skills but also gross motor skills to support good posture and arm movement. As Van Galen (1991) highlights, these will need to be integrated with a child's visual perception for them to be able to control the symbols they produce and develop the hand-eye coordination so crucial for later handwriting success. Creating many opportunities for young children to build their upper body strength as well as their arm, wrist, hand and finger strength along with hand-eye coordination will help build the finger dexterity, muscles and stamina required for early handwriting development. Where these opportunities develop naturally through play and a child's inherent curiosity, their motivation to write and become writers is more likely to flourish. However, children who start school without these skills should not be prevented from beginning transcription learning but may require some explicit exercise to develop key muscle groups.

Gross and fine motor control

The development of a strong body is absolutely fundamental to being able to write.

Before a child is able to write effectively, they need to be able to physically have developed the following. Schools with nursery provision in particular need to ensure they provide rich provision to promote physical development, though continued opportunities in Reception and for some children in Year 1 and beyond are important.

- **Core stability:** Appropriate muscle strength to maintain good, upright posture and balance. This includes stomach and back muscles.

- **Bilateral integration:** Coordination of both sides of the brain to allow both hands to work together. Provide opportunities for hands to do the same thing and also for hands to do different things at the same time, such as mark making with one hand and stabilising the body with the other hand.

- **Crossing the midline:** Being able to cross over the middle of the body to the opposite side.

- **Hand-eye coordination:** Being able to process visual stimuli and control of eye movement with hand movement.

- **Visual perception:** The brain's ability to make sense of what the eyes see. This is different to visual acuity which relates to how clearly the eyes can see.

- **Shoulder girdle stability and strength:** Being able to take part in activities that involve climbing, pushing, pulling, throwing and weight-bearing through their arms, in order to strengthen all the muscles around the shoulder joints and the scapulae. This enables the smaller muscles in the arms and hands to work more efficiently because they have been given a stable base of support.

- **Elbow pivot:** Allows a child to mark make, use tools directing and coordinating from the elbow. At this stage in development, the shoulder becomes more of a support and the elbow starts to do most of the work.

- **Hand division:** Also regarded as ulnar/radial differentiation. Being able to use the thumb, index and middle finger for manipulation while keeping the ring and small finger tucked into their palm to stabilise.

- **Hand and finger strength:** Necessary muscle power for controlled movement.

- **Manipulation:** Primarily using the fingers rather than the whole hand, such as picking, pinching, touching.

Hanging from climbing bars, crawling, lying on the tummy while propping oneself up on the forearms, and activities that require using the whole arm at height, such as hanging things on washing lines or painting on an easel, all help to develop the necessary strength needed for writing. Early years teachers should plan an enabling environment with a deliberate focus on distinct aspects of gross motor control over time. For example, setting a child the challenge of moving across apparatus or the ground by pulling themselves strengthens shoulder girdle strength. Moving across the same apparatus by shuffling strengthens pelvic girdle strength.

Forearm, wrist, hand and finger strength also need opportunities to strengthen in order to make the physical act of writing easy for children. These can be developed through activities such as building with blocks, climbing, rolling, squeezing or kneading play dough, playing with construction materials such as Lego, scooping and pouring water, threading beads on thick string, using different sizes of tweezers or tongs to pick up objects. For example, using large tongs helps develop palmar strength, middle sized tweezers develop finger strength and manipulation, and tiny tweezers develop the ability to manipulate the thumb, index and middle finger. As well as varying equipment by size, the amount of resistance offered by materials or equipment can be increased or decreased in line with the unique child's developmental needs. For example, malleable materials can be stiffer or softer – clay, home-made play dough and commercially provided play dough all have different resistances, and practitioners should increase or reduce challenge in order to enable all children to be successful. Similarly, adaptive scissors can support children by reducing resistance, increasing size, or both.

Early years staff therefore need to be knowledgeable about how to promote all the different aspects that contribute to gross and fine motor control and plan for this over time and in response to identification of individual need.

Most very young children naturally experiment with symbol and mark making and Carol Trivette (2013) and her colleagues found that this development tends to follow a highly predictable sequence: marks develop into dots and circles and then into more purposeful scribbling that progresses into the production of more defined and sophisticated geometric shapes and drawings and eventually into letters.

These developments are important to support the cognitive leap a child must make to start writing but these marks are not writing. To be able to write an alphabetic script, a crucial discovery that children have to make, according to Anne Castles, Kathy Rastle and Kate Nation (2018), is that of the alphabetic principle – that is, graphemes represent phonemes. And for this to happen, children need to belong to a literate community that is able to explicitly teach them how to make this discovery.

Crossing the Rubicon: the importance of systematic phonics instruction to handwriting

Virginia Berninger (2000) makes it clear that systematic synthetic phonics instruction and handwriting have a reciprocal and highly beneficial relationship. When linked to phonics instruction, handwriting can be taught from the very beginning of Reception. Not only does this ensure a purpose and motivation for children, but the understanding of the alphabetic principle – that the letters they are forming are representations of the sounds of the language – supports the link between the sounds and the letters and helps children form a mental representation of the letter rather than merely copying the letter. It also means that the handwriting/grapheme formation aspect of phonics can be taught in very small steps with lots of practice.

The act of handwriting letters (as opposed to typing) enhances the recognition of the letter forms which in turn supports reading acquisition in young children. It supports phonics instruction and word recognition, so by encouraging children to use their knowledge of phonemes and graphemes and then handwriting those graphemes, teachers are supporting the identification and memorisation of the phonemes and the decoding of words. The research also suggests that handwriting instruction helps children develop their understanding and recognition of letter patterns of the language – thereby supporting the move to instant word recognition enhancing spelling. So, there is a double benefit: it supports both writing and reading.

Systematic Synthetic Phonics (SSP) programmes have been devised to teach decoding and reading so the graphemes are introduced in a systematic and logical decoding order and not in a logical handwriting order. SSP programmes usually start off by teaching the grapheme/ phoneme correspondences SATPIN as these are very different sounds from each other, which makes them easier to learn, and can also be combined to make a host of simple words. However, from a handwriting point of view, learning to form letters in this sequence is a terrible idea as not only do they belong to different letter movement groups, but also some of them involve really complicated movement patterns. Children should first of all learn how to write the letters with the easiest movement patterns before progressing to groups formed with more complicated movement. 'S' and 'a' with their curves are tricky. A sensible place to start would be with those letters that employ a simple down-bump movement: 'l' and 'i' and then when they are secure 't'. After that, teaching could proceed to letters when the down movement is followed by an up movement and then a push to the right as in 'r' 'n' 'h' 'm'. Only after that does it make sense to start to learn the letters whose movement patterns involve the pulls and pushes that create more circular shapes: 'c' 'o' 'a' and then the more complicated 'd' 'g' and 'q' before the really complicated 's'. So, all in all, not via SATPIN!

Often, teachers think about handwriting in terms of reproducing a visual shape by copying a static example, possibly provided with information about a starting point rather than as a motor movement that needs internalising. However, as Florence Bara and Nathalie Bonneton-Botté show in their research (2017), learning to handwrite requires visual-motor integration. Children need to internalise *both* the movement pattern involved in forming a letter and the visual shape the letter makes. According to research carried out by Annie Vinter and Estelle Chartrel (2010), merely copying or tracing letters is not as effective as watching a letter be written, creating a mental image of the letter when it is not displayed followed by practice drawing the letter with significant repetition. The mental image is one of a dynamic process – a series of movements – and not of a static image alone. Digital technology is helpful here as it enables access to short video clips of letter formation being modelled. However, having a mental image of what the visual image should look like is also important to allow the child to check their letter production and ask themselves metacognitive questions such as, 'is the tall part (the ascender) tall enough to be clear that this is an *h* and not an *n*, as if not, what does that mean about what my body needs to do?'

This is an important point that pervades the research into the development of writing: the creation of secure mental representations from letters through to words, sentences, paragraphs and whole texts is essential for building the domain of writing. Furthermore, Vinter and Chartrel's (2010) findings divide handwriting into instruction and practice, which is a useful heuristic for teaching. While letter formation and legibility are developing, the emphasis will be on instruction with practice, but as accurate letter formation and legibility develops, the focus moves to practice improving legibility at speed. Where children's handwriting lacks legibility they require instruction, where handwriting is legible but slow, they require practice.

There is more to learning to handwrite with fluency and legibility than learning letter formation. Handwriting is itself a complex, composite activity that relies on:

- The development of component gross and fine motor skills.

- The adoption of a stable writing position.

- The ability to hold a pencil in an efficient and effective grip.

- Knowledge of letter formation.

- The ability to form letters that are correctly differentiated by their relative starting heights (a key component of legibility).

- Spacing within and between words (teachers often obsess over finger spaces and neglect spacing within words – spacing within words is another key component of legibility).

- Spacing of writing across the line, starting close to the left-hand side and aiming to use the whole line each time (rather than the strange diagonal effect some children produce with each line being progressively shorter!).

- Grounding (writing letters 'on the line' rather than floating).

Only when these elements are in place, and they are different for left-handed and right-handed writers, can children work on writing with flow and at speed. Indeed, the 'rope' metaphor used by Scarborough (2001) to describe the reading process and by Sedita (2023) to describe the writing process is also useful when thinking about the different strands involved in handwriting that at first are learned in isolation and then later woven together. Fluent, automatic handwriting is dependent on the deliberate nurture of these separate strands.

Stable writing position

Children therefore need explicit teaching in and opportunities to practise and self-monitor their use of a stable writing position that supports the forearm, with the paper or whiteboard correctly sloped (to the right for left handers and to the left for right handers). Supporting the forearm – either by writing at a table or when writing lying on the ground – is important as this support frees up the hand to move more freely and better use the tiny movements involved when writing.

Children also need to be taught the importance of stabilising the writing surface with their non-dominant hand, sitting back in their chair, putting their feet on the floor. Adopting this position is not only effective when writing, but also when carrying out other tasks such as using a ruler (stabilising the ruler with the non-dominant hand). By contrast, writing on a mini whiteboard when sitting cross-legged on the carpet provides neither forearm support nor support for the core from the feet, both of which contribute to making correct letter formation harder. Yet such practice is common in many primary schools, particularly in phonics lessons. Using either a table or getting children to lie on their tummies are better alternatives that provide appropriate support.

Grips and joins

The classic tripod grip has become accepted in England as the 'correct' grip for teaching handwriting. This has been in part due to it being included in a number of government publications. The national curriculum, however, merely states that pupils should be taught to hold a pencil 'comfortably and correctly' (it does not define what that 'correct' grip is). Neil Almond (2025) suggests that there is no definitive research that affords the tripod grip the status of 'correct' grip. He maintains that the evidence asserts that so long as a child's mature grip does not impede handwriting fluency then it should not be altered. He gives some useful practical advice to teachers of children learning to handwrite by advising that a single grip is far easier to teach across a class than multiple grips (so teaching the tripod grip makes sense). However, where a child has developed a mature grip that is effective and fluent, it should be left alone.

Teachers can become very exercised over when to teach joined or cursive handwriting to children. The battle lines are drawn between those who feel cursive script should be taught from the start on the grounds that it is confusing for children to learn a skill that they later have to unlearn, and those who feel cursive handwriting is just too demanding for young children. Here the research is pretty emphatic and very helpful: children taught cursive from the get-go write more slowly initially but tend to spell better and have better syntactic awareness. Children taught to print first and then move to letter joins write more quickly initially but need more spelling instruction. You pays your money, and you takes your choice. However, most schools are keen to get children writing faster earlier, so go for the printing first model – the faster track to composition may well be more motivating.

And here's the really big message: according to Steve Graham's (1998) research, we don't reach adult handwriting speeds until well into our early teens, so we need to teach and practise handwriting regularly throughout primary school.

And back to working memory

We mentioned early in this chapter that developing automatic, effortless, fluent handwriting is essential in order to enable our working memory to have space to bear the considerable cognitive load of writing sentences, building paragraphs and translating our ideas into written compositions that readers want to read. This is what makes teaching handwriting so important, indeed essential for writing. But here's where its leverage is even more indispensable: the sooner children have sufficient handwriting fluency, the sooner they can actually write down stuff while thinking about the stuff and not the handwriting. Sentence structure, punctuation, paragraphing and composition can only be *written* when we can actually *write* – prior to that it will all have to be oral. And speaking (although essential for the development of writing) is not writing.

So, for schools and teachers there is one big message from the research: get handwriting sorted as quickly as possible. Then, and only then, can children start giving written composition the mental space it deserves.

Assessing handwriting

Handwriting fluency is relatively easy to assess. Writing speed is usually measured in letters written per minute and most assessments require pupils to copy a standard sentence (usually a pangram) repeatedly for a minute. This produces a letters-per-minute score which can be compared to an average score.

Handwriting speed on a copying task – letters written per minute		
Year group	Left-handed	Right-handed
2	17	19
3	27	35
4	50	47
5	56	64
6	70	73
7	72	86
8	92	100

Source: Graham *et al* (1998)

Legibility is usually assessed either by an overall impression with a three-point score (1–3 if you remember the old national curriculum writing assessment) or by using a five-point scale (like that established by Anna Barnett's team (2018)) that scores overall legibility, letter formation and the layout of words on the page.

And what about typing?

Typing falls under the transcription element of writing and in today's digitalised writing environment is increasingly important. However, handwriting appears to offer unique benefits over typing, particularly early in a child's reading and writing development.

Karin James and colleagues (2016) found evidence from brain research that indicates that the act of handwriting letters enhances the perception of the letter forms, which in turn supports reading acquisition in young children – writing letters helps children recognise letters – which is why writing during phonics lessons is recommended once letter formation is secure. The research also suggests that by activating the motor cortex through the need for sequential finger movements, handwriting instruction helps children develop those important orthographic processing skills that support reading and spelling. For primary-aged pupils, handwriting also appears to enhance the memorisation of new information beyond that of typing, suggesting it is more beneficial for learning according to Eva Ose's studies (2020) and it also appears that handwritten passages correlate with higher quality writing than typed passages.

However, typing is a skill that students in a modern world will eventually need to be competent at. The research is pretty thin here, but it doesn't seem that many children will have developed a sufficient level of motor dexterity, coordination and hand span before the age of nine to engage with typing instruction and that's close to the end of primary school. Furthermore, it seems that a familiarisation with keyboards as encountered in computing lessons and regular engagement with keyboards appears to be sufficient and does not undermine the benefits of handwriting. So, handwriting is important and improves spelling, reading and memorisation more than typing, which can develop more intuitively.

Spelling

The other side of the transcription coin, and equally important for automatisation, is spelling. Spelling has, for many years, been linked to reading – the more we read, the better we spell has been the received wisdom, and we often forget that spelling is writing (the encoding side of decoding) and poor spelling will inhibit writing fluency just as laboured handwriting does. This link to reading is interesting and central to the fallacious argument that English spelling has drifted so far from its phonic roots that English is no longer a phonic language.

The complexity of the English alphabetic code is why it takes far longer to learn to decode English when compared to more transparent orthographies (Spanish for example) and as such takes longer to learn to spell. However, as the American reading psychologist Keith Rayner reminds us (2012), English spelling is not chaotic, inconsistent and random, but has evolved into what Charles Perfetti described as a morphophonemic system. That is to say, letters and combinations of letters express the sounds *and* the meaning. This is highly economic and why words in English tend to be short. This is great once you've mastered reading and spelling, but it means that we have lots of homophones (*made* and *maid*) and different letters representing the same sound and the same letter representing different sounds – we have five vowels and over a dozen vowel sounds. This has made English more demanding to learn to read and thereby even more difficult to learn to spell.

Perhaps that's why we often don't really bother teaching spelling and hope it is absorbed through extensive reading. Actually, this *is* an option…

Rebecca Treiman (2018) argues that much of the spelling skill required to write English words accurately may be acquired through regular exposure to the letter patterns as children read. This 'statistical learning' occurs despite no conscious intent to acquire the skill and builds knowledge of spelling patterns of the reader's writing system, with more frequent patterns spelled more accurately. However, she goes on, if this were the case then all rapacious readers would be great spellers, and this is clearly not true. Steve Graham's research (2014) indicated that spelling improved more effectively through specific instruction rather than through a reliance on the natural absorption associated with statistical learning. We know from cognitive science that merely rereading passages is not an effective revision technique – it's far more effective to test your recall of the material…and write some notes. As such, part of the issue with the natural learning approach is the assumption that when reading, children pay attention to the spelling of words. This is just not the case. Younger children are often attending to the story rather than the spelling, with older children often in metacognition – attending to the ideas being expressed in the text thereby limiting attention on letter patterns. This is why Treiman (2018) concluded that providing children with structured occasions to analyse spellings is a more effective strategy to improve spelling. But what structure?

Traditionally, structured spelling instruction has been based on the notion that the spelling rules of English have so many exceptions that it is more efficient for learners to memorise whole words rather than the patterns of letters, resulting in a reliance on rote memorisation of the word (particularly words with more complex patterns) to acquire the spelling rather than attention to the letter patterns. Akin to ignoring the numbers when calculating multi-digit subtraction, according to Robert Dixon (1993). Or as Lyn Stone suggests in her book *Spelling for Life* (2021), irregular words are irregular until their structure is understood – they are spelled that way for a reason so let's understand the reason. She goes on to dismiss the 'look and say' methods of spelling by pointing out that word storage and retrieval are not functions of the visual memory and, if they were, then blindness would prevent reading (which it clearly does not).

Phonics teaching and spelling

So, if letter patterns are the key to spelling acquisition, then phonics instruction must be the key to spelling. As Lyn Stone (2021) makes clear, it's the sequence of letters that is important for children to attend to. There's strong evidence to suggest that this is the case. The famous and highly influential Clackmannanshire study (Johnston and Watson, 2004) found that the teaching of systematic phonics resulted in substantial progress in spelling acquisition as well as comprehension. This aligned with the conclusions of the wide-ranging US National Reading Panel that systematic phonics instruction, particularly in the early years, improved spelling. This was all reinforced by Sebastian Suggate's (2016) meta-analysis of long-term outcomes of phonics instruction that found clear evidence for benefits to spelling. Genevieve McArthur and Anne Castles (2017) advise that spelling instruction that attends directly to the issue at hand is more likely to benefit the learner than instruction that focuses on other skills. Systematic phonics instruction, with the exclusive intent of articulating links between sounds and spelling, draws learners' attention to spelling in a structured manner, thereby also directing their attention to the patterns rather than the intrinsic knowledge acquisition associated with statistical learning. So, reading widely is important for spelling acquisition, but learning and being taught the grapheme/phoneme correspondences is crucial. Somewhat counterintuitively (unless you think about it really deeply – more on this later) learning to spell well improves reading more than reading improves spelling). Does that mean that as long as phonics is being taught systematically, spelling is being taught systematically? Job done? You won't be surprised to learn that it's not that simple.

Orthographic knowledge: Spelling is more than just phonics

SSP programmes are reading development programmes designed to teach children to decode quickly enough to cultivate instant word recognition. Once children are decoding sufficiently quickly and accurately, the programmes become redundant – the Phonics Screening Check is a *de*coding and not an *en*coding assessment. So, they are not spelling programmes by design. Thus, they are taught for a restricted period – usually to the end of Year 2 – to enable decoding to occur automatically. However, spelling acquisition, particularly of multi-syllable words, continues well beyond this. Furthermore, when we are reading, we are processing (decoding) letters into sounds to read words – so we can read and make sense of 'he stormed off in a huf'. The fact that we notice that 'huf' should be spelled 'huff' is down to our knowledge of our English orthography – the accepted spelling patterns associated with our language. The allowable sequence of letters in English expect the double 'f' at the end after a 'u'. We also need to know that 'pouf' does not require the double 'ff' – that's all down to our orthographic knowledge.

The correspondence between the grapheme and the phoneme is enough to read but not enough to spell. So, Treiman (2018) argues, phonics instruction is an effective spelling strategy. But it stops too early to be comprehensive. Lyn Stone (2021) adds to this by warning against merely grouping by sound, as this misses out on much of the other generalisable information held within words. Again, she insists that as letters appear in words in sequences, taking attention away from sequences interferes with efficient and crucial orthographic mapping. Subsequently, children then need to be taught and to practise what the allowable sequences of letters in English are and how to apply these sequences of letters – this application is known as *graphotactics* – how English words are written, not how they are read – you read 'huf' but you spell 'huff'. The focus is then on the probabilities of the orthography rather than rules and their exceptions. So much of the focus should be on the different spellings of the same sound – when is the 'ay' sound spelled with an 'ai' or 'eigh' or 'a'.

Dictation

If you are as ancient as Clare and Tim, this may send shivers down your spine as you recall the dreaded French *dictée*. Every word you spelled correctly gained you one mark. But every word you spelled incorrectly incurred a subtraction of one mark. *(**Clare and Tim write:** Both of us often scored negative scores and Clare remembers the whole class cheering* *when she finally attained the dizzy heights of scoring zero for the first time.)* Clearly, this is not what we are advocating.

However, Virginia Berninger and her colleagues (2002) found that spelling words in context in the form of dictated passages helped embed not only the phonological connections, but, more importantly, the orthographic associations. Not only that, it is also the most effective tool for assessing orthographic knowledge development, and, perhaps even more importantly, spelling correctly in a dictated passage is a far greater indication of mastery than a spelling test, according to Michel Fayol (2016) – it guards against the learning it on Friday and forgetting it by Monday syndrome.

What's more, regular dictation helps pupils with developing handwriting, sentence structure and grammar automaticity and there is even research that indicates it supports fluency when pupils write independently. And all this while efficiently helping with working memory management. What's not to love? (**Tim writes:** *Perhaps this is why I write French far better than I speak it.* **Clare writes:** *It's probably more to do with the working memory intense nature of transient speaking and listening – see chapter 4!)*

Morphology and spelling

Remember Charles Perfetti's assertion (1997) that English has developed into a morphophonemic language with words delivering sound cues as well as meaning cues? That means that spelling is not only enhanced by teaching phonics (grapheme/phoneme correspondence) and orthography (allowable sequences of letters) but also by teaching morphology – the units of meaning contained in a word.

So, knowing that the word 'uncomfortable' has three morphemes helps us to spell it correctly. By being aware that the prefix 'un' in English means 'not' and the suffix 'able' makes the word an adjective, the reader can deduce that the noun being described (a chair or an atmosphere perhaps) produces *negative* 'comfort'. When writing the word, having an understanding of the three morphemes makes it more likely that the writer will spell it correctly. Kathy Rastle's (2019) research suggests that this morphological knowledge appears to give children a tactical advantage when mapping between spelling and meaning and improves spelling. Teaching children the most common affixes and how to spell them will, therefore, enhance not only their spelling, but also their reading.

Making time for more spelling instruction in schools where timetables are already constrained may seem a step too far. However, spelling excellence has far wider implications beyond accurate writing. The benefits of spelling proficiency are not solely related to encoding and effective writing but have significant benefits for reading proficiency. Charles Perfetti (1997) maintained that a knowledge of the precise representation of a word (its exact spelling in other words) enabled the reader to quickly differentiate a target word from a similarly spelled word, thereby developing their mental representations of a word. His conclusion that spelling helped reading more than reading helped spelling and had a significant beneficial effect on orthographic processing development may seem counterintuitive but was supported by Gene Ouellette and his colleagues (2017). Their research confirmed that greater proficiency at spelling was directly correlated with higher reading rates. As mental representations of words build and words are identified more quickly, this then frees cognitive resources to attend to the heavy cognitive demands of reading comprehension. When our mental representations are low, much of the cognitive resource (working memory) must be applied to word recognition.

Etymology

Etymology is the study of the linguistic and historical origin of a word. It has been argued that studying words' roots promotes spelling through the knowledge of the foundation of words and their language (usually Greek or Latin) origins. The research into the usefulness of etymology instruction for spelling improvements is fairly thin, and what there is suggests that it is only effective for children in upper primary who read and write well. There is more robust research for its use in promoting vocabulary. For example, the argument goes, knowing that the Latin word 'tract' means 'drag' and that 'ex' in Latin means 'from' makes it easier to spell extract…and to know what it means. The argument for vocabulary does appear stronger in this example. Tim Rasinski, a fierce proponent of etymology for promoting vocabulary, suggests that the study of etymology promotes word curiosity for pupils and an awareness of English being a living language (2008).

The message is very clear: the importance of transcription for writing development cannot be overstated.

Key messages

Handwriting

- In the early stages of writing, handwriting places a significant load on working memory to the exclusion of other writing processes.

- Difficulties with handwriting constrain children's development as writers.

- Gross and fine motor skills underpin successful handwriting and development of these needs to be understood and planned for, even more so where schools have nursery provision.

- An element of writing in phonics lessons supports and enhances both the decoding and encoding component of phonics.

- Separate, discrete and regular instruction in handwriting is necessary from the start of Reception.

- Learning to form letters involves learning both a dynamic movement pattern and a static visual shape. Copying a shape is not effective.

- Handwriting instruction (not only practice) is essential for writing development and should continue into KS2 with regular opportunities for regular practice continuing throughout KS2.

- Handwriting fluency is a significant predictor of positive writing outcomes.

- Children who are specifically taught handwriting improve their overall writing quality compared to children who do not receive specific instruction.

- The sooner handwriting starts to become automatised, the sooner cognitive attention can be focused on composition.

- For developing writers, handwriting has significant cognitive advantages over typing and promotes spelling and reading more effectively than typing.

Spelling

- Spelling, along with handwriting, forms the transcription element of writing. Difficulty spelling, like difficulty handwriting, places a cognitive load on children and restricts their ability to attend to other elements of writing like sentence structure and composition. The sooner children handwrite and spell more fluently, the better they are able to attend to the increasing demands of composition.

- English has a complex alphabetic code that makes learning to spell more challenging as one sound can be spelled in many ways and letters can represent more than one sound.

- English has a morphophonemic structure – letters indicate not only sound but also meaning.

- Regular and wide reading will have a positive effect on children's spelling but is seldom sufficient to promote consistently accurate spelling.

- Systematic phonics instruction promotes good spelling, particularly where the writing of letters is regularly incorporated into instruction.

- Structured and systematic spelling teaching should continue beyond systematic phonics instruction and continue throughout primary years. When pupils have a comprehensive knowledge of the alphabetic code for decoding, the emphasis can focus on encoding, with increasingly greater emphasis on legitimate letter patterns.

- Structured and systematic spelling instruction should integrate phonology, orthography and morphology, and should be regular and timetabled, with opportunity for both learning and practice.

- Dictation should be used along with regular tests to improve and assess orthographic development.

- Improvements in spelling help increase reading rates.

- Handwriting needs to be easily and quickly legible by the pupil for them to be able to reinforce reading correct spellings, or to edit those that are incorrect. If it is only the teacher who can 'translate' the pupil's writing, it is only the teacher who will correct the spellings.

Chapter 4
Talking and writing

Tim writes: I like talking. I talk too much. I always talked a lot to my pupils, particularly around writing. It felt important to discuss what we were going to write about and what we had written about. I was even keen to encourage opportunities when we could break from writing and talk about where we were in the process and what might have been bothering us or what worked particularly well. I actually based this approach on what I had heard about the writing approach on the US sitcom Friends *where groups of writers dissected and analysed a draft script in a forum, with the view to improving and honing it. Very cutting edge and relevant, I thought. And actually, it was effective…in a way. What I never thought about, and never addressed were the differences between speaking and writing. Oh, there was lots of 'oracy' and lots of talk about writing but never any thought, analysis or acceptance that talk and writing may have been different. They are both communication, so I felt that writing was merely an extension of spoken communication, and I viewed writing as a transcriptional system for converting spoken language into a written modality.*

Clare writes: For once I can start a chapter without a mea culpa about how badly I taught a particular aspect of writing! While my understanding of the mutual interactions of oracy and writing has developed over time, this is one area where I actually did something right. A couple of years into my teaching career I specialised in supporting children who were in the early stages of learning English as an additional language; most of what I did was scaffolding and supporting talk. For almost 30 years my teaching career was based in Tower Hamlets, a local authority with a very high percentage of children who speak English as an additional language and where, despite very high levels of economic deprivation, standards of attainment are high. We had a fantastic local authority school improvement team who provided excellent training within which approaches that promoted spoken language acquisition were second nature. For example, the use of talk partners was routine and unremarkable there decades ago. A document by the Tower Hamlets English as an additional language team (Tower Hamlets EMA team, 2009), outlines progression in language structures across various different communicative functions: argument, comparison, deduction, description, evaluation, explanation, hypothesis, prediction, retelling and sequencing. The idea being that first of all children should be taught to express themselves verbally using these academic language structures as a precursor to being able to do so in writing. Even back then, we were thinking about sentences. The work was based on the early work of Cummins (1979) who contrasts BICS (Basic Interpersonal Communicative Skills) used in conversation and CALP (Cognitive Academic Language Proficiency – the language of decontextualized academic situations). Children who are learning English as an additional language at school may within a couple of years develop conversational fluency necessary for function, yet social use may take five to seven years or longer to achieve a level of academic linguistic proficiency comparable to monolingual English-speaking peers. This gap may indeed be the case, but I was convinced that the monolingual English speakers weren't that proficient in the language of CALP either.[2] What was vital for beginner bilingual learners was also really useful for their monolingual peers. After all, cognitive academic language is not the language any of us tend to use very much in everyday conversation and needs to be explicitly modelled if children – bilingual or otherwise – are to acquire it.

It was rather a shock when I started doing school improvement partner work outside London to realise that embedding talk was not a routine component of teaching that everybody automatically used. It was weird to have to suggest using talk as a school improvement strategy that benefitted all learners – not just those new to learning English – as if this were some revolutionary new-fangled invention. Indeed, I now appreciate more fully what I then vaguely intuited: the language of academic English is no one's natal tongue and something that every child has to learn, primarily at school. Growing up in a family where you are read stories certainly will introduce you to a certain genre of sentence-based idiom and this clearly helps. But the more analytical, non-fiction forms of academic English – very few of us grew up immersed in this language in quite the same way we are immersed in the conversational. For sure, in some families there may be a degree of environmental exposure to it – maybe the family watches lots

---

2   Indeed this study showed that many English monolingual children 'failed' an assessment purported to assess the fluency in English of English as an additional language learners.

of documentaries, news programmes or reads lots of non-fiction to their child or has a child with an insatiable appetite for non-fiction audio media. Maybe they belong to a faith community or political group where the child hears sermons. But while some children may have greater exposure to the receptive use of sentence-based idiom, very, very few children routinely use it to produce speech, outside of school.

The difference between spoken and written language

'Speech, the universal way by which humans communicate and transmit experience, fades instantly: before a word is fully pronounced it has vanished forever. Writing, the first technology to make the spoken word permanent, changed the human condition.' So wrote Denise Schmandt-Besserat (1992) in her seminal work *How Writing Came About*. It implies that the purpose of writing is transcribing speech. Originally it most certainly was.

However, Martin Nystrand (1986) argues that a significant difference between the two has developed but that the difference is not the purpose. All communication is purposeful, he posits, whether it be writing, speaking, painting, gesturing or signing, so the difference between speaking and writing cannot be the purpose. It cannot merely be that spoken thoughts are oral and written thoughts are textual. But a difference has developed that extends beyond merely the form or format of the communication. Speech does not become writing merely by switching the communication format.

Writing is something different from speech

Speaking and writing have very different communication conventions. The differences are starkest when we analyse casual conversations in both formats. When actual spoken conversations are transcribed, they appear to ramble, have numerous false starts and digressions with very little cohesion, and are disjointed, repetitive and difficult to follow because they are being blown around by the winds of emotion, attention and curiosity. When a playwright creates a spoken conversation for a drama, they employ cohesive devices throughout to ensure the audience has clear, conventional and regular signposts. Great actors will make the words *seem* like a conversation, but analyse the text and it will be clear that something else is going on. Real conversations are difficult for others to follow because the participants share integral, interdependent and personal knowledge. Staged conversations on the other hand must be clear for an audience of strangers.

[3]The obvious difference between talking and writing that profoundly influences the nature of what each is able to communicate and therefore shapes conventions is that talk is transient, fleeting, ephemeral whereas writing is durable; it has permanence. Since working memory is fairly limited, the transience of speech means that it is challenging to articulate and organise complex thoughts or to revisit the complex thoughts of others. The development of the technology of writing effectively extended working memory by outsourcing it to an external memory field – the written word – giving humans the ability to store and retrieve ideas efficiently and accurately. This had vast implications for human thought. By circumventing some of the limits of working memory, the technology of writing enabled humans to think differently.

Preliterate cultures had their own ways of hacking the limits of working memory. Through rituals, folktales, song, ballads, chants and poems, the transience of talk was captured and became memorable and transmissible via mnemonic tools such as repetitive and rhythmic language patterns. However, with nowhere to store information outside of human minds, huge amounts of energy had to be devoted to keeping the oral culture alive. Socrates was opposed to writing because he could see that once culture could be stored externally, it would be evicted from human memory.

The development of the technology of writing removed the limits on information storage and enabled information sharing across cultures and generations. As a result, human consciousness was now able to devote more energy to thinking about what was remembered rather than to keeping the information alive. This shift from the wetware of the human brain to the hardware of tablet, scroll, page (or latterly – screen) enabled knowledge to be shared, contested, refined, elaborated and refuted at scale and across time and space. This had profound implications. Writing, it could be said, over delivered.

The very fact that writing could store and enable retrieval of ideas resulted in a new type of communication related to, but different from, the spoken word. Because everyday speech and writing are produced in very different communicative situations, there are differences in how they are structured. Both types of communication involve trade-offs. Because writing is durable and has permanence, unlike speech, it does not usually

---

3   This section taken from Clare's chapter in *The ResearchED Guide to Primary Literacy*.

involve live interaction with a listener. This has the advantage that it is possible to communicate across time and space – through writing even the dead can communicate with us! However, this distancing comes with drawbacks. Whereas with face-to-face speech, the speaker receives immediate feedback and can add in more details should their listeners appear confused, writers don't. There is no possibility of on-the-spot interaction to clarify meaning. In face-to face-spoken communication, our listeners are bound by social conventions that are difficult to break – leaving a conversation or talk before the speaker has finished is not easy if we don't want to appear rude. When we write, not only can we not see the reader, but we may also not even know them, and they can stop reading our words without any fear of social condemnation. They may not even be bored by our words; they may simply be distracted by something more alluring like social media or a custard cream. We, as writers, have no literal oral voice. We can't read our text to them and if we could, perhaps we'd be better off just having a conversation. We have to influence our reader's inner voice so that they 'hear' our inner voice as closely to our original as possible. We can only influence the reader's attention and understanding through the language we use, the vocabulary, imagery, sentence structures, punctuation and paragraphs we employ in the hope that we write something suitably entertaining, informative or useful to keep them on board. It's a tough gig!

This places a responsibility on writers to explain things much more clearly, explicitly and compellingly than when talking. We also have to be aware of the reader (a reader whose subject knowledge we don't know) to avoid potential confusion, misinterpretation and indifference. Since everyday conversation usually takes place between people who share a context, the speaker can make assumptions about what the listener already knows. A writer cannot and should not make such assumptions. They need to have in mind at all times how the non-present reader will understand, or fail to understand, what they have written. The potential for differences of culture or history between author and audience has structural implications for writing as a mode of communication. Vernacular ways of speaking work in a local, immediate context. But for written material that may be read by a reader at some remove in time or space from the author, standardised ways of writing need developing that mitigate linguistic differences.

Spoken language has its own drawbacks. Its transient nature places burdens on the working memory not only for the speaker but for the listener. Spoken language therefore includes characteristics that work around the limits of working memory, helping the listener understand what is being spoken and giving the speaker time to formulate their next thought. For example, when speaking, we build in thinking time both for ourselves and our listener by using voiced hesitations such as 'um' and 'ah'. We pause, repeat and rephrase so that listeners have time to absorb the spoken message and to give ourselves time to plan our next utterance. These hesitations are not only acceptable, they are necessary as buffers of oral communication. The fixity of writing means these working memory workarounds are not necessary. The written word does not vanish once uttered. The reader can revisit written utterances. It is the reader who hesitates, who pauses, who rereads. Because writing is an asynchronous mode of communication, the reader can 'rewind' the communication stream. The writer is expected to have *already* rephrased their thoughts into the clearest utterance possible prior to publication. Repetition, so necessary in spoken language, is generally frowned upon in writing. Writers deliberately try to use synonyms rather than repeat the same word within a sentence.

Speaking involves thinking on the spot. Writing gives you take-up time to monitor and edit your thoughts. You can write a sentence, pause, reread it, reword it, change the order, extent it, abridge it or delete it. You have time to think about word choice, literacy devices, removing repetition, adding in rhetorical devices, changing sentence length. Writing is *expected* to be polished in ways that conversation speech is not.

In spoken communication, tone of voice, timing, volume, stress and timbre communicate not only meaning but also attitude and emotion. There is no direct written equivalent to a speaker altering their pitch, their volume, or making eye contact and smiling.

These have no direct correlate in writing. Instead, both punctuation and typeface (the use of italics, bold, underlining, capitals, font size) play a crucial though not entirely straightforward role in communicating meaning and emotional intent.

Adverbs and adjectives are also much more common in writing, since emotion and intensity cannot be inferred from tone, stress or volume. A written text may include charts, maps, illustrations or a list of characters.

Having begun as a way of communicating at a distance, formal academic writing adopts language structures that assert this detachment through removing the grammar of the personal. Far from perceiving the absence of social interaction as weakness, formal academic writing sees its deliberate impersonal stance as underpinning objectivity. The focus is on what is written rather than the writer. Academic thought is – or at least should be – an ongoing truth quest untrammelled by group loyalty or personal circumstance. It therefore explicitly rejects tell-tale signs of social interaction, codifying detachment from the sphere of social influence by such devices as writing in the third person, deliberately impersonal using passive voice constructions and nominalised forms of verbs (invasion rather than invade, decision rather than decide). Modal verbs convey the provisional, tentative and challengeable nature of written thought. The reader is guided through extended prose via headings, subheadings, chapters and page numbers, sometimes with glossaries and footnotes to give further explanation or to back up a claim by referencing the writing of another.

Ros Fisher and her colleagues (2010) noted that the syntactical structures of writing tend to be longer and more complex than talk. Writing, they suggest, draws on a vocabulary repertoire which extends beyond that of spoken vocabulary and requires mastery of spelling and punctuation conventions which we don't need to master when we talk (we need to master other syntactical, physical and structural skills to be good conversationalists). So, vocabulary selection for writing needs to be more specific and deliberate. Writing uses syntactical structures that are quite different from those used in conversation. Fragments abound in conversational speech. In writing, the sentence rules. Try conversing in full sentences only for the next five minutes. You will see how unnatural and stilted it sounds. The sentence-based idiom of academic language developed out of the trade-offs involved in making a durable, asynchronous way of communicating with non-present others.

The permanence of writing resulted in not just sentence-based idiom, but a whole host of complex sentences, including those with subordinate clauses, adverbial phrases (fronted or otherwise), past or present participles, relative pronouns, chains of adjectives or verbs, appositives, prepositional phrases, alliteration, similes, metaphor and comparative clauses. These structures allowed us to communicate with greater precision and complexity and to think more abstractly and analytically. David Didau (2026) describes them as cognitive levers which shape how students think and write. For example, if we introduce the word 'since' into a sentence, this heralds the introduction of either a causal reason or a time reference. If we introduce the phrase 'at first glance', this signals the rest of the sentence will reconsider initial impressions. These cognitive levers are integral in shifting writing from knowledge-telling into knowledge-transforming (Bereiter and Scardamalia, 1987; more on this in the composition chapter).

This is not to say that none of these structures ever feature in conversational talk. They are not, however, typical. But conversational talk does not consist of a series of coherently connected sentences of varying and diverse complexity, so (most) children are not going to learn how to communicate in sentence-based idiom through environmental osmosis, but through the explicit modelling of these structures and plenty of opportunities to practise them.

To recap, writing needs to be clearer, more explicit, more standardised, less repetitive and more polished than spoken utterances. Writing, and the sort of presentational talk that uses the idiom of writing, is a very different way of communicating compared to conversational talk. Developing the ability to speak in sentence-based idiom is the gateway to thinking in sentences – both necessary precursors to academic writing.

The decision to express ourselves in writing or in speech is not a neutral decision. It is dependent upon the functional potential of the preferred mode. We could of course transcribe our conversations or orate our dissertations...but we don't. We trust the function and potential of our chosen format...or switch to a more appropriate format. However, while we ask children to express themselves in writing and learn all the associated conventions that this involves, so that the non-present reader can understand and engage with what has been written, in the vast majority of contemporary classrooms, the non-present reader isn't, in fact, present anywhere! The reader is sadly often only an imaginary construct, a non-existent non-present reader, or possibly, an examiner paid (albeit poorly) to engage with and make sense of our work. If we are very lucky, our teacher reads our work with genuine interest, and not as some professional chore.

Clare writes: *The obsession with writing for an audience at the start of my career went too far to be sure, but now it's gone too far the other way. The non-present reader is non-existent!*

What this means for teaching writing is that although speaking and writing are both forms of communication, they serve different functions. This is something seldom conveyed to pupils and yet we have seen in the previous chapter that children, even those who can't yet write, have an understanding that writing is something different. Because speech and text are so related and interdependent we must not confuse them as being merely the transcription of one form into another or the vocalisation of text into speech.

We can whistle an invented tune, but we need to write a symphony.

Developing spoken language into written language

Although writing and speech are different dominions, the ability to communicate through spoken words will be the foundation of the language that develops into written communication. Debra Myhill wrote that, 'Becoming a writer means extending your language repertoire from spoken forms to written forms,' because we learn to talk before we can learn to write (Fisher *et al*, 2010). Speech patterns will heavily influence children's writing development, particularly at the outset. However, merely using the model for speech and applying it to writing poses challenges for pupils learning to communicate through writing.

One of the key challenges for pupils learning to write is that, unlike learning to speak, it requires a good deal of conscious effort. Learning to speak depends to a large degree on the process of statistical learning. Through listening to speech in their natural environment, infants are evolutionarily primed to pick up statistical probabilities. For example, they may notice that certain syllables or sounds or words are more or less likely to occur next to each other. If this sounds very like the way in which AI learns through probabilistic pattern spotting, this is because it is. We might have a romantic notion of babies learning through some mystical process of consciously discovering and making meaning – and yes, babies do also do this too, and there is also a good deal of social input required as well in order to understand social conventions around when to talk, turn taking and so on. But the deeply unromantic fact of the matter is that much of how babies learn to speak is through the acquisition of statistical regularities that just happen through being immersed in an environment, without the need for the baby to consciously decide to pay attention. Not so much lighting a fire within as filling a pail with statistical probabilities. Sorry Plutarch. Possibly this process is effortful in the sense that it is exhausting for the young infant. But it doesn't require deliberate and conscious direct application of one's cognitive capabilities. Unlike learning to write, where conscious effort is very much the thing.

This means that the formal structures of written language will need to be taught in order to bridge this gap between spoken language and written language. It is the building of this bridge that should exercise the focus of pedagogues.

Liliana Tolchinsky (2016) agrees that writing cannot be merely a transcriptional system of recording spoken language so is not therefore unidirectional (speech to print) but multidirectional with constant interactions between language and text. Thus, she maintains that writing is not simply an ability added to linguistic development but a transformational part of the development. This may sound all very esoteric, but it adds considerably to the complexity of teaching writing and so to our understanding of the task we are charged with. We are not merely showing children how their spoken words can be recorded in print for permanence and transfer. We are developing a whole new sphere of language development. And this goes well beyond mastering the differences in syntax between spoken and written communication.

Nowhere is this clearer than the gap that occurs between learning how to write words and sentences and how to compose texts. Children do not move smoothly and naturally to composition once they know how to transcribe their words accurately. So, it cannot only be about mastering the syntax of writing as opposed to speech. There is more to writing than this. There are all of the macro-structural features of text that have to be learned, understood, managed and controlled, along with those local decisions and choices.

Bridging the gap between spoken language and written language

Reading aloud to pupils and retelling stories

Children will initially experience orally the more formal and precise structures of writing through hearing books and stories read to them. This is the first link between spoken and written language structures and is not dependent upon pupils having developed transcription skills. As Sam Leith (2024) suggests in his book on the history of childhood reading, this is where we first understand that written words and sentences carry a style and tone of voice (a voice different to talk). While transcription skills are developing, drawing pupils' attention to these different structures in stories read aloud to them will help them develop an awareness of not only print and its conveyance of meaning, but also of the differences between spoken and written syntax. Learning and repeating the patterns of written words builds this written syntactic knowledge. Children enjoy this learning and repetition and often do it naturally without instruction. What they are repeating, of course, is written syntax.

This can be further supported by:

- Explicitly drawing attention to the written structure of language. Indicating to younger children that the words they are hearing from books have been written down and that there is a structure to that process will help bridge the gap between spoken and written language. This can be as simple as indicating words with a finger during reading rather than attending only to the illustrations.

- Encouraging pupils to retell stories orally using the more formal structures of written language. By learning stories prior to retelling them, the cognitive load associated with recall and composition can be better managed and pupils can focus on the vocabulary choices and syntactic patterns associated with written language. As children retell the story, visual cues and simple pictures can support memory and indicate where sentences can be marked. Pie Corbett's[4] emphasis on helping children internalise the language and structure of stories through learning to retell them together is one powerful way of internalising the structures of written communication. Picture books can be particularly powerful (and popular with children) with their inherent dual coding. Digital technology can also be used to make transitory speech more durable and hence repeatable and revisable. This could be by giving the child access to a recording of an adult retelling a story or a way of capturing – and possibly revising – their own retelling. The app *Chatta*, for example, provides a way of recording sentences alongside six pictures or photos, allowing children to compose orally in a format that can be shared with classmates and family.

- Highlighting sentence structure being studied when we read aloud to older pupils and reading with prosody that clearly indicates demarcation of phrases and clauses can support the embedding of written language structures and how the writer's inner voice can be coterminous with that of the reader.

Structures of written language used in talk

Encouraging pupils to use more formal written structures when speaking in class will support the use of these structures when writing.

---

4   Pie Corbett developed the Talk for Writing approach.

This can be done through:

- Explicit modelling of more formal language structures by the teacher.

- Providing sentence openings for answering questions and discussion feedback and linking these to written structures ('How would we say this if we were writing it?'). Sentence builders, a technique borrowed from MFL teaching, are helpful here in that they provide both a sentence opening and various different sentence endings, with children choosing which ending they want to use.

- Providing opportunities for exploratory talk between partners or in small groups which start off using a more conversational tone and are then recast into 'speaking like an author/scientist/historian, using full sentences, technical vocabulary.

- Encouraging pupils to rehearse spoken answers internally or with peers prior to answering and putting them into written structures.

- Using voice pitch and gestures to indicate sentence boundaries and sentence types as well as key punctuation – speech does not use punctuation.

- Using sentence frames to build oral sentence structure and linking it to the written structure.

Oral rehearsal prior to writing

Writing has the distinct advantage over speaking in that it can be revised before it is shared. We do this through rehearsal and editing in internal or external voicing of the words to be written.

As adults we rehearse our written words almost without thinking about them before we commit them to print. Our 'inner voice' enables us to 'hear' the words prior to writing them (try just writing whatever comes into your head and see what happens). Being explicit about using and expecting children to use this oral rehearsal prior to writing is extremely helpful for young writers who will otherwise have to discover it for themselves. It is even more useful when we teach them initially to vocalise this rehearsal so that they (and sometimes others) can actually hear the words they are potentially writing and assess their appropriateness. This enables pupils to hear the syntax they are using and facilitates some initial editing in the moment. Ros Fisher and her colleagues (2010) conclude that rehearsing written text in spoken form is particularly helpful in supporting pupils to develop their understanding of the differences between speech and writing and is a key structure in developing a bridge between the two.

The use of full sentences by pupils when speaking in class is sometimes objected to on the grounds that it ignores differences between spoken utterances and written communication – the sentence being a convention within writing and not speech.

However, asking pupils to speak 'like a writer' is a way of providing scaffolding to support working memory. Remember that writing puts a significant strain on working memory that requires management. Rehearsing what we are going to write helps us manage this load. David Lobina's research (2020) suggests that when we read, the load on working memory is at its greatest until we read the verb and can then decide just what the sentence is about. Conversely, he suggests that, when we write, we manage the load by initially composing the words using our inner voice and then concentrating on the transcription of those words. For young writers without fully automatised handwriting and spelling this is crucial. Trying to compose and transcribe simultaneously is just too demanding. Vocalising the phrase or clause to be written frees the working memory to attend to transcription and helps develop the inner voice. But like most things in teaching, it can be done badly. The concepts of exploratory and presentational talk may be useful here. These are categories first proposed by Douglas Barnes and then expanded upon by Neil Mercer (2008). Exploratory talk is, as you may think, more tentative and closer to conversational idiom than presentational talk, which uses the structures of writing. Using exploratory talk, without having to simultaneously translate initial thought into neatly packaged sentences, allows cognitive space for thoughts to roam. If we try to get children to use the formal, academic idiom of presentational talk during the initial stages of exploring an idea, this could overwhelm working memory and thwart proper exploration of ideas and the transformation of knowledge that we want, as children are thinking too much about how to say it rather than mulling over ideas. It is therefore often preferable to start discussion off in conversational idiom, possibly jotting initial thoughts on mini whiteboards. Working with a partner, these thoughts are then recast into more formal, presentational idiom. Sentence frames, sentence builders and word banks can provide useful models to scaffold this translation from one idiom to another. But being able to transform a fleeting thought into a sentence is cognitively empowering. Answering in full sentences helps develop the capacity to do so.

Furthermore, oral rehearsal is a proven and effective writing strategy. Rehearsing and testing ideas before committing them to paper is a staple strategy of professional writers. Explicitly teaching this strategy, modelling it, encouraging it and highlighting its successful adoption will support pupils in their journey to competence in composition.

For oral rehearsal to develop successfully it requires:

- Regular, intentional and articulated modelling by the teacher.

- Regular practice by pupils and monitoring by the teacher and an expectation that it is used as part of the writing process.

- No more than single sentences rehearsed before writing and initially phrases or clauses.

- That once written, the words should be reread to ensure they comply with the oral rehearsal – they can be revised and edited after rereading.

The ultimate aim is for the process of oral rehearsal to be silent, automatised and internalised. Teachers, through modelled writing, can exemplify the strategy of rehearsing sentences and editing them orally before committing them to written text. This can be further enhanced by using the strategy for spoken answers in class. Encouraging pupils to orally rehearse answers, and edit and refine them prior to sharing, further develops the link between written and spoken language.

Talk to support writing

Few writers write in a vacuum; just read the acknowledgments list in the front of any book. Even great writers consult with other people, and publishers will almost always assign an editor to work with an author. Stephen King (2020) talks about writing his first draft 'with the door closed'. This is where he writes and revises and edits alone. He then writes 'with the door open' where he confers with trusted friends and colleagues to hone his script and iron out any of the creases and identify and untie any knots. This of course is essential with our future readers never having access to any clarification. What may seem very clear to the writer may be far opaquer to a reader and having someone point this out can be very important. Wilkie Collins probably wished he'd had a few more eyes on *The Woman in White* when, after publication, it was pointed out that a crucial event happened at a date that undermined all of his intricate plotting. The novel had to be withdrawn and revised.

So, although drafting requires the writer to create text alone, collaboration, discussion, support and encouragement are a crucial part of the composition process and can enhance written outcomes. By building this into the pedagogy of the classroom and systematising the process, children can develop an understanding of the importance of discussion with trusted collaborators as part of the writing process at all stages. Digital technology that allows several authors to work on the same text simultaneously, or peers to easily access and comment on one another's texts, makes collaboration much easier than previously. It also gives teachers a window into the quality of the collaboration taking place – as they too can see comments and track changes and so on, minimising the risks of social loafing.

Debra Myhill and her colleague (Fisher *et al*, 2010) s identify three main areas where using talk during the writing process can support pupils' written work:

1. Talk can be crucial for children prior to them writing. The opportunity to share ideas and build knowledge, when structured and planned with intentionality and purpose, can develop rich ideas, deep knowledge and appropriate vocabulary prior to writing. Some children will know more about a subject. Some may have a more mature grasp of the structure needed to convey the ideas and others may have richer language and greater vocabulary knowledge. Bringing these together in a supportive and coherent forum can help all young writers to manage some of the cognitive demands of writing. Equal importance lies in the generative learning power of explaining one's ideas orally. Leonie Jacob and her colleagues (2020) suggest that oral explaining as a learning activity has a strong research base which triggers deep cognitive and metacognitive processes. Cohering one's thoughts and explaining complex ideas orally not only has a positive effect on the speaker but also indicates to less confident writers how they might approach the writing task. Ideas can be stimulated by talking about relevant artefacts and images as well as engaging in drama activities to develop character insights. But remember that the point of the artefact and the drama is to promote writing, so ensure the insights and ideas are recorded and then developed for the domain of writing.

2. Although writing should take place in a calm and quiet environment with minimal distractions, talk can be useful at any point during the writing process if well-planned and strategic. This can be particularly important to support children to generate ideas for elaborating the

main idea of a paragraph during drafting. When revising a draft, focused and intentional talk can support the restructuring and accuracy of sentences and is particularly useful when assessing the inclusion of cohesive devices, improving vocabulary and rhetorical devices and monitoring grammar and spelling accuracy. During the writing process is often the perfect moment to teach and revise the use of writing strategies as well as identify where strategies have been used successfully. Just as important, encouragement from peers and teachers can be highly motivating, particularly in the middle of the maelstrom of composition when young writers encounter the problems, knots, frustrations and joy of the 'messiness of writing' – Steve Graham and Karen Harris's (2019) lovely phrase.

3. After the writing process has concluded, explaining one's ideas and choices, as well as the issues encountered, develops metacognitive processes. This also encourages young writers to put themselves in the place of the reader, further developing the concept of writing coherently for someone who is not present. At this point pupils can be encouraged to orally assess and evaluate their own and others' writing against agreed goals and plans (one of the most powerful strategies that writers use) and to offer opinions and encouragement. And remember it is often the child feeding back who gains the most from the encounter. Again, digital technology can assist with this process.

In order for pupils to use talk as part of the writing process, it is essential that they are taught how to use it as a successful strategy. Clear structures, protocols and goals will need to be put in place and modelled by teachers. There is little benefit in allowing children to just 'have a chat' about their writing.

Key messages

- The ability to communicate through spoken words is the foundation of language development into written communication.

- Writing, however, is not talk written down. It is not a developmental addition to, and extrapolation of, speaking: it is a domain in its own right. The decision to communicate through spoken or written words will depend upon the function and expected outcome.

- The syntax of writing differs from that of speech and must follow the 'rules' of writing.

- Children require support to bridge their knowledge of spoken syntax and develop their knowledge of the rules of written syntax. This will be done initially through exposure to the new syntax in books read to them, teacher modelling and explicating of written syntax in speech. Direct and explicit instruction of written syntax will be necessary. Children will need support navigating between the two domains.

- The development of oral rehearsal prior to transcription is an essential skill for the management of working memory capacity during writing.

- Drama activities can support writing but should focus on their contribution to the writing process and ultimately help produce higher quality text.

- Well-structured and focused opportunities to share thoughts, ideas, opinions, knowledge, vocabulary and language will enhance writing at all stages of the writing process.

- Teacher modelling of all strategies for using talk to develop writing will enhance and support children's progress.

Chapter 5
Reading and writing connections

Tim writes: *It felt like 'a truth universally acknowledged' that reading and writing were intrinsically linked. The two elements even sat side by side in the timetabled subject 'Literacy'. Often it was up to me whether I taught 'reading' or 'writing' as part of that timetabled subject. However, I certainly taught more 'reading' than 'writing' and my pupils did more reading than writing. The two felt so interlinked that I felt that they were pretty much the same thing – just different sides of the same coin. I even suggested to my pupils that if they could read and successfully comprehend and analyse a text then they should be able to write one…merely through the osmosis of reading. What I was suggesting to them was that reading and writing were inverses. Which of course meant that while I was teaching reading, I was also teaching writing. Nice. Yet I would never have suggested that because they could read an Ordinance Survey map, they could construct one…or that if they could read the music of the* Moonlight Sonata *they could compose a sonata. So, I am not sure that I ever really 'taught' writing. Oh, we did lots of writing – often inspired by what we had read. We explored writing through texts, making observations and assumptions and then applied them to the written form. But did I actually teach it?*

Clare writes: *I can trace three different phases in how I taught writing. The first – well, I've already banged on about that – so focused on creativity it denied pupils the tools out of which creativity is fashioned. Writing wasn't taught as such as it was assumed immersion in high quality literature was all that was needed.*

Next came the National Literacy Strategy which was a breath of fresh air. It was very focused on the explicit teaching of genre and the text structures and sentence types that were their defining features. Different genres of non-fiction featured a fair bit, which was a major shift from the previous overwhelming emphasis on fiction. Sue Palmer (2006) produced a useful set of books with skeleton planning structures of the various genres. The National Literacy Strategy produced the brilliant Grammar for Writing (2000). Plus, children now had to learn phonics (sort of). Things were looking up. However, the link with high quality literature took a hit.

This could have been redeemable were it not for the introduction of the writing SATs paper which rewarded tight fidelity to hallmarks of a specific genre. As there were so many genres that might be tested, teaching became a broad and shallow attempt to ensure children could reproduce any of these genres to order rather than being able to use a couple of genres really well. Although there was always a story on the test, this gave rise to its own problems that disrupted further the cross-fertilisation of reading and writing. Because a test is short, any story written would of necessity be brief – far, far briefer (and less satisfying) than books studied in class. So either the teaching of reading became reduced to very, very short stories – there was a book of short stories we used to tackle this exact problem – or learning to write a short story became completely divorced from real reading. Learning to write shrunk to a technical exercise in learning to get marks in a test.

Eventually the writing SAT was abolished, and the new national curriculum was introduced. This new curriculum did away with the expectation of children churning out genre specific pieces to order – which was a win. Getting rid of the writing SAT was also a good move, though its successor, moderated teacher assessment of writing, spawned equally problematic though different problems. Now we had tick lists of features that needed to be included, leading to ludicrous situations where children revised their writing in order to shoehorn in their use of hyphens and the passive voice. We always used to recommend writing a two-digit number (as that would cover the hyphen requirement) and saying that someone was born or married or buried (as that would get a tick for the use of the passive).

In these latter two, it was not the curriculum that was the problem per se, it was the high stakes assessment that warped the curriculum into weird, unnatural shapes.

What the abolition of the genre requirement and timed writing assessment did do was enable a richer exchange between reading and writing. Pieces of writing could now be longer. They could now be revisited and improved. They might actually be worth reading! They might even be shared with other members of the class! However, the strictures of the teacher assessment regime encouraged a very specific type of sharing. The writing that was included in the portfolio of teacher-assessed and levelled writing had to be done independently but could be edited. In order to be deemed 'independent', the teacher could not directly teach the child how they might improve their work. However, other pupils could. So those children who excelled at writing spent a lot of time reading their peers' work and suggesting improvements, functioning as a quasi-teacher. If I told a pupil to add in an adverbial phrase, then that wasn't independent work. But if 10-year-old Nadira made the same suggestion, that was entirely legitimate! And by improvements, let's be clear, this meant features detailed in the mark scheme, with scant regard for whether they genuinely improved the experience for the non-present reader (or for Nadira). At the time, I was aware that this was a bit mad, but thems was the rules. Now working at a remove from this crazy English context, I see quite how bonkers the whole thing was.

But with the need to spew out genres to order gone, like many schools, we shifted to linking our writing to our reading. So, for example, we might read the novel Holes and then as part of this write a persuasive speech arguing against the harsh conditions at Camp Green Lake and an explanation piece describing the features of the notorious Yellow Spotted Lizard. Or read Podkin One-Ear then write a letter to other burrows warning them to flee before the Gorm arrived. Which were certainly motivating contexts that children were fired up to write about. However, do you see the fatal flaw? They read a novel yet wrote a persuasive speech or factual explanation. They didn't read any real-world examples of either. We might have produced lists of success criteria, but they didn't see any examples 'in the wild' as it were. This would have been easily remedied if we had accompanied our main reading text – almost always fiction – with satellite texts (shorter, non-fiction, real-world examples of the genre we wanted children to use in their writing). When teaching reading, we tend, with good reason, to choose novels with compelling plots and characters. However, we are not going to get children to write their own novel, so if we want to link the teaching of reading and writing together, this will need more thought than merely having the book provide a motivating stimulus for writing. Children need to study mentor texts that share the same structure and language features as the writing we then expect them to produce. If we want children to be able to write coherent, cohesive texts then they need to study how real authors do this. In many schools, despite the focus on curriculum – in England at least – there is no properly thought-out curriculum for writing beyond riding on the coattails of a text chosen for teaching reading.

And as an aside, high stakes assessment regimes are the death knell to schools investing much time in getting children to write poetry. Poetry writing is just not amenable to producing reliable results to order. Once again, the high stakes assessment regime becomes the de facto curriculum, whatever the *national curriculum might say. Measure what you value, as the saying goes, or you will end up valuing what you measure, and that alone.*

Steve Graham (2020) says, 'There is no reading without writing, and no purpose for writing without readers.' He suggests that the two are connected in the most fundamental and intimate ways. Readers and writers apply many of the same cognitive properties, such as background knowledge and understanding of text structure, language and semantics. And both reading and writing are fundamentally about communication, about a social interaction or metaphorical conversation. But are they merely reflections of one another?

The difference between reading and writing

They are indeed interrelated, suggests Martin Nystrand (1986), but they are not the same – close siblings but not identical twins. Reading, he suggests, is a process whereby the reader gains information by *eliminating* possible meanings and thereby gradually refining understanding. By discerning what a text is *not* about, the reader works their way into it, processing each layer in terms of the expectations that have been set up by the previous layer. In doing this, the reader fine-tunes their expectations and understanding, and all previous texts that a reader has read become context for texts as yet unread.

Conversely, Nystrand goes on, if reading is the elimination of interpretive possibilities to construct meaning, then writing is the reciprocal process. The writer is intent on focusing the reader to construct meaning through elaborating the possibilities and understanding layer by layer. Each layer built by the writer narrows the reader's focus into a tighter and tighter fovea of anticipated understanding. The writer does this by loading the communication to the reader in the direction of prospective possibilities and contexts that encourage and influence the reader's interpretative potential.

This understanding that reading and writing are not symmetrical has important practical implications for teaching. That reading and writing are asymmetrical means that pupils must receive instruction in both and the teaching of one alone is insufficient for the other to fully develop (***Tim writes:** Rats!*).

Clearly reading does affect writing. It is possible to learn to write an adventure story by studying adventure stories. So, how does reading influence writing and what is the reciprocal effect and how does this affect novice writers? Most of the research has tended to be unidirectional – the effects of reading on writing and vice versa. This has resulted in models and research that suggest one is more dominant than the other.

Reading to writing

We tend to be taught to read before we are taught to write and there is a body of theory and research that indicates that reading is the prime lever in writing development. We saw in the earlier chapter on transcription that the development of grapheme/phoneme correspondence is crucial for handwriting and spelling and that much written syntax is experienced through being read to and through reading. We learn orthographic patterns through reading, which enhances correct orthographic accuracy when we write. Children who are frequently exposed to written texts tend to learn to write and spell words with greater accuracy. Higher levels of reading are associated with higher scores in writing tasks, and improvements in reading comprehension directly influence our ability to express ourselves in writing. In other words, the better a child is at evaluating a text, the more likely they are to apply this knowledge to their writing.

Yusra Ahmed and her team (2014) found in their longitudinal study that for primary school children, reading tended to have a greater influence on writing outcomes than writing had on reading. However, this influence tended to be more pronounced the younger the children were and dissipated as composition and comprehension became influenced by more complex cognitive elements as students matured.

Clearly, our ability to write is interrelated with our ability to read. But this is not a one-way street.

Writing to reading

We know that frequent exposure to a word does not guarantee that we will be able to write it. Writing, the research indicates, needs to be taught and taught discretely. Donald Graves (1983) suggested that the development of writing in fact precedes that of reading, so reading, he suggested, is also dependent on writing. He posited that children want to write before they want to read, leaving messages in mark form on many surfaces (anyone with small children will have ample evidence of this on their walls). But when they arrive at school, they discover that a higher premium is placed on receiving messages (reading) than sending messages (writing). The repetition of others' ideas appears more important than the expression of one's own ideas, Graves suggests. He even describes this anxiety about reading as a national neurosis in anglophone countries whereas elsewhere in the world the view of literacy is more focused on communication.

This suggestion that writing is central to reading development was supported by Uta Frith (1985). She showed that the order of transference from writing to reading is real – the methodical nature of writing letters is co-opted for use in decoding. So, children may actually be learning to spell the word and then applying that knowledge to read the word. Handwriting letters and letter patterns have been proven to embed the mental representations and so support reading. We know that improvement in spelling ability improves reading speeds and that proficiency in written sentence structure also improves reading fluency and comprehension. The development of sentence structure competency seems particularly sensitive to instruction and application rather than mere analysis and noticing through reading. Furthermore, written vocabulary is a far sturdier indication of mastery than vocabulary comprehended when read, given the associated contextual cues to support understanding. And recently, Adi Elimelech and his team's research (2020) into pre-schoolers being taught at home by parents to write the spellings of Hebrew words found that this resulted in the effective promotion of word reading despite them not explicitly being taught to read words.

Perhaps more convincing for the influence of writing on reading is this: you can probably think of many children who have both excellent reading comprehension and writing composition. You can probably think of a number who have poor reading comprehension and writing composition. You may even know some children whose reading comprehension is good but who struggle to compose well. But have you encountered many children whose reading comprehension is poor but whose written composition is excellent?

Tim writes: *Having suggested this scenario at a conference, I was approached by a teacher who felt he fell into this category. He explained that he was dyslexic and still found reading comprehension effortful. He found his slow pace made creating meaning from large amounts of text demanding. Nonetheless, he was a published author so clearly wrote well. This was because, he explained, writing did not have to occur in the moment. He could take as much time as required to compose his texts – this benefit of writing is seldom shared with children.*

Clare writes: *I remember a teacher who helped children understand the inferences authors make about how a character is feeling by asking them to write a paragraph about a character that contained a secret emotion* *that their partner had to guess. They couldn't name the emotion or use a synonym. Instead, they had to describe bodily changes 'his heart beat like a drum', and so on. This worked really well.*

So then, much of our ability to read is enhanced by developments in our writing.

A multi-directional process

The research indicates that teaching reading promotes writing skills and strategies (as well, of course, as reading skills), and teaching writing promotes reading skills and strategies. They indisputably share many of the same elements so, when we teach reading, we are indeed supporting writing and when we teach writing, we are supporting reading. However, only teaching one element is not sufficient for the other to develop. As Timothy Shanahan (2016) advises, 'That reading and writing are not just reverse images of each other is one reason students must receive instruction in *both* reading and writing.' It appears that it is therefore essential to teach reading and writing discretely to secure all of these reciprocal benefits.

That sounds straightforward – teach reading but also teach writing... separately and probably for equal amounts of time.

What about teaching them together?

You may be surprised to learn that although there is a fair body of research on the effects that the discrete teaching of reading has on writing and the effects that the teaching of writing has on reading – unidirectional effects – the research on the effects of teaching them together as a multidirectional and interactive process is fairly thin. This does not mean we should not do it. Timothy Shanahan's research (2016) does indicate that this is a potentially powerful model, and this is partly supported by Yusra Ahmed's meta research (2014) which suggested that the relationship between reading and writing becomes more interactive as pupils become older and the focus of instruction moves away from skills and becomes more a function of the complexity of language. As language features become more multifarious and subtle, explicit instruction that blends the writing with the reading and noticing of such language becomes more useful.

Perhaps more profound is the meta-analysis by Steve Graham and Michael Hebert (2010) that showed that a combined use of reading and writing during study can have a powerful impact on the learning of content. They concluded that teachers could enhance their pupils' understanding of a text by getting them to write about it. They recommend that the practice starts in a more atomised form with short summaries and notes, but can develop into longer expressions of opinions, critiques and points of view. They also warn that writing will enhance reading far more profoundly when pupils receive direct instruction on how to write and when they write frequently and practise frequently. Or as Timothy Shanahan (2016) puts it, 'There is little possibility that writing will impact reading if there is no writing.'

However, we should be wary of turning 'writing about reading' into answering SATs type reading comprehension questions, which helps develop neither reading comprehension nor writing. Instead, teaching of complex sentence structure can be embedded within analysis of character and plot. Let us return to the novels *Holes* and *Podkin One-Ear* mentioned previously.

When we first meet Podkin, he is lazy and spoilt. In the course of the book, Podkin is transformed into a legendary warrior. This could be used to teach and experiment with a variety of sentence structures as outlined by Didau and Cole (2026).

For example, the use of the subordinating conjunction *although* to signal the redemption of Podkin which is the central theme of the book:

- Although Podkin initially appears lazy and spoilt, through his adventures he is transformed into a legendary warrior.

- Although at first Podkin is only interested in himself, by the end of the story he confronts his own weaknesses and discovers an inner strength.

- Although Podkin initially resisted responsibility, the Gorm invasion forced him to protect his family.

Similarly for *Holes*:

- Although Stanley Yelnats is initially timid and awkward, through his struggles he develops self-confidence and resilience.

- Although Stanley Yelnats starts the novel as a physically and mentally weak character, his experiences at Camp Green Lake develop his strength, determination and grit.

Past participle sentence starters could be practised through writing sentences such as:

- Forced to flee with his brother and sister, Podkin's journey involves danger and hardship.

- Faced with danger, Podkin discovers for the first time an inner strength.

- Confronted by his own weakness, Podkin transforms into a brave protector of his family.

- Wrongly convicted, Stanley blames the family curse.

- Forced to dig holes, Stanley develops physical strength.

- Nicknamed Zero, Zeroni is viewed by others as worth nothing.

- Thought to be stupid and worthless, Zero is revealed to be fiercely intelligent.

Through using complex sentence structures to analyse plot and character development, children begin to understand how themes of power, ambition, redemption and responsibility – the thematic mainstays of much literature – are developed. (Didau and Cole, 2026)

Clearly this would involve a lot of modelling by the teacher and practice by pupils. But how much richer than SATs paper questions. How good a preparation for the sort of textual analysis that forms much of the secondary English curriculum.

Developing an understanding of the concept of 'the non-present reader'

When we read, we may or may not have an explicit sense of the author, and when we do it may be because the author is frustrating us with a lack of clarity or writing in a manner that annoys us. But we all have favourite authors. There may be many reasons we like them, from the genres in which they write to the characters they create. So, when we read, we often have a sense that someone else is in our heads.

Whether we are aware of an author will often depend on whether the author wishes to be visible and how visible. If they write in the first person, authors are clearly making themselves more visible and they may even address the reader directly – 'Reader, I married him.' When writing about a contentious and sensitive subject, writers often wish to be less visible to mediate readers' mindfulness of author bias.

Charles Bazerman (2016) suggests that, as we develop the ability to read with an awareness of the author, we read more than their words and ideas and gain a sense of 'what the writer is doing.' Gaining a sense of what a writer does is clearly going to be very useful for children's development as writers. Developing this metacognitive perspective – awareness of thinking as we think – will help children become better writers.

But again, this metacognition does not merely apply to our reading. There is a similar reciprocal perspective when we write.

In chapter 4 we noted that the bridge between spoken language and written language supports children to develop control of the different syntactic structures of writing. Just as importantly, it also supports in developing an understanding that writing involves communicating with someone who is not there, and whom the writer may never meet. Martin Nystrand (1986) suggests that 'When readers understand a text, an exchange of meaning has taken place. The writer has spoken to the readers.'

As we have seen, when we actually speak to one another, we usually know the person to whom we are speaking and are also present in the conversation, which means we can adapt to the responses of the listener. We can also receive instant feedback regarding how clearly our message is being relayed and so are able to modify and mediate any misconceptions or use of language. These vital clarifying opportunities support the coherence of our message but are not usually available to the reader when they read our writing. They may be reading our writing long after we wrote it (the author may well be dead) and/or may be many miles away – personal clarification from the writer is usually just not possible.

So, not only is it useful for readers to be aware of the writer, but it may also be useful for writers to be aware of the reader. In fact, it appears to be more than merely useful; if we want children to develop quality writing, an awareness of the reader may be essential.

Debra Myhill (2020) suggests that this requires a reflective effort by the writer related to an increased awareness of the reader. A writer must therefore, she suggests, concern themselves not only with their intentions as they write, but also with the imagined response of the reader to the text. This results in developing the key communicative concept of 'writing like a reader'.

Writing like a reader

This means that when we transform our thoughts and ideas into written text, we have to maintain an image of our potential readership in our minds (we write differently for academic supervisors than we do for our work colleagues or parents or children). It also means that we have to make our writing very clear and coherent as there is no opportunity for clarification in the moment of reading.

We have to make assumptions about the knowledge that our readership already possesses to avoid over-simplification and explaining elements that they already know and understand but, conversely, we need to be clear and coherent with ideas that will potentially be new to them. It is much easier for a reader to disengage with a text than it is for a listener to disengage with a speaker – remember that distracting custard cream. As C.S. Lewis (1959) advised, 'Take great pains to be clear.' Your reader doesn't start reading aware of what you know, even if you do. Choose just one wrong word and your reader might completely misunderstand. 'The whole picture is so clear in your own mind that you forget that it isn't the same in his.' (Lewis, 1959)

This move from the 'here and now' language of speech to the 'there and away' language of writing appears to be a key developmental Rubicon crossing for children learning to communicate their thoughts and ideas through writing. Central to this consideration, suggest Debra Myhill and Susan Jones (2015), is metacognition. Only by having an awareness of our thoughts and reflections can we apply how these might affect the reader. Although this is by definition explicit (we have to think about it), when we write, we are also influenced by the implicit knowledge we have gleaned about how authors get writing to work from our reading. This is why children who read a lot tend to write better – they have an idea of how writing works. But many pupils, Myhill and Jones argue, will not have read widely so will lack this implicit knowledge, and many children, although they read a lot, will not have absorbed this knowledge either. So, this will have to be taught explicitly. We can't merely rely on lots of reading (*Tim writes: Mea culpa ... again*).

Clare writes: Whereas at the start of my career, the emphasis on writing for an audience was emphasised at the expense of everything else, the pendulum has swung so far in the other direction that the idea of an actual, living and breathing reader has been eclipsed. Instead, in England at least, and maybe this distortion is also present in other locations, children write to fulfil the dictacts of the mark scheme or assessment rubric. This is a very, very poor substitute for an actual reader. Instead of thinking about whether or not a turn of phrase or shift between paragraphs is clear enough or interesting enough for this non-present reader, the child, and possibly the teacher, thinks about whether or not they have included particular features that become an end in themselves. And instead of reflecting on whether or not a child is able to make writing clear by identifying when a reader might need to know the reasons why something has happened, the teacher notices they have used the conjunction 'because' in three different pieces of writing, ticks off that objective and turns their attention to hunting for 'so'. A superficial splattering of language features replaces a genuine ear for what a non-present reader might need to know.

Building awareness of the reader

Although keeping the reader in mind adds greatly to the cognitive load of the developing writer and adds further pressure to their restricted working memory, pupils can be supported to manage this load. Pupils need to bear in mind two golden questions: Is my writing suitably clear? Is it suitably interesting? The challenge being that clarity and interest can sometimes pull in different directions, with too much of a focus on clarity – via endless caveat or description sabotaging interest. It is worth exploring with pupils what the author has *not* said. Is the meaning still clear? If we added more detail to make it even clearer, would that help or hinder interest?

Myhill and Jones (2015) suggest four main pedagogical strategies to help develop this awareness of the non-present reader. In terms of grammar and introducing new grammatical forms they suggest making explicit *links* between the grammar being introduced and how it works in the text type being taught. This is further elucidated by identifying its use in short and clear *examples* from a text, followed by high-quality *discussion* on the effects of the grammar. This is then further embedded by using examples from *authentic texts* written by established authors.

Building awareness of the disciplinary reader

Clare writes: When attempting to teach KS2 children persuasive writing, I would try to find contexts that gave children something they might actually want to persuade someone about. So, I reached for that old hoary chestnut, wearing school uniform. My reasoning being that their dislike of school uniform would be a sufficient spur to awaken their inner persuasiveness. However, the problem was that they didn't actually know why they disliked it – beyond 'my own clothes are nicer/more fashionable'. Neither did they appreciate why schools might have reasons for inflicting uniform upon them in the first place. Ironically, on non-uniform days, many children came to school proudly wearing a uniform...of their favourite sports team. So, it wasn't uniforms per se that were disliked, but a school uniform and all that it represented. The semiotics of uniforms was, however, lost on them.

To be properly persuasive, writing not only needs to be compelling in presenting its case, but also in dismantling the counter argument. This is somewhat challenging if you have no clue as to what the counter argument might be, or even what the arguments are for your own case – beyond mere stating of preference. And so, alongside teaching children the features of persuasive argument, we also had to teach them the arguments for and against uniforms in general. This, as well as eating into valuable teaching time, also rather undermined the notion that writing about uniforms would be motivating.

Meanwhile, in other lessons, children were learning about volcanoes and Vikings and Varjak Paw. They already knew about these. So why not use the knowledge base of other subjects as a meaningful context within which to write persuasively or to explain or present a balanced argument? We will see in our chapter on motivation that writing about what children already know can be highly motivating. This does not only mean writing about their interests outside of school – though it could include these – it also includes things that children know about because they have been learning them in other areas of the curriculum.

This is not to advocate for the kind of tenuous 'links across the curriculum', vacuous forms of cross-curricular links that grasp at connection as if 'linkiness', of itself, enjoyed an inbuilt and incontestable superiority with things that were not (however tenuously) linked. It is to understand that we may first learn to write in English lessons, but writing is a tool that can then be deployed within other areas of the curriculum.

If we have achieved one thing so far in writing this book, it is that writing only has any meaning insofar as it serves the needs of the non-present reader. Somewhere around Years 4 or 5, we need to begin to alert children to the fact that not all non-present readers are the same. Up until this point, this non-present reader will be fashioned in the image of the reading child, a proxy for the non-present reader in general. Is this story interesting to me? Is it clear or confusing? Could I follow these instructions? Has this persuaded me? The next step on the journey is to understand the non-present reader, not so much as an extension of individual preferences, but as informed by the academic and social norms of the different subject communities. Upper KS2 is the right place for children to begin to learn how the subjects differ and how these differences shape writing – what is known as disciplinary writing. Disciplinary writing also provides a meaningful context for developing the richness and power of children's expression as they develop command of more complex sentence structure in meaningful contexts.

When scientists read science, they are expecting the writing to concentrate on the research, not on the researcher. They expect the codification of objectivity. For example, the use of the passive voice to emphasise the action or process, focusing on the result and effect (with no mention of the one doing the experiment). Modal verbs may be used to acknowledge the tentative status of some conclusions. Accurate, technical language ensures clarity and reduces ambiguity. Conjunctions – those useful cognitive levers – are used to contrast, explain, emphasise or qualify. When scientists read, they don't expect much by way of adjectives, hyperbole or figurative language. This is very different from when writing fiction.

Since history involves arguments about interpretations, when we write like historians, modal verbs acknowledge that some statements are not absolute facts, but contested claims. Since much of history involves discussion of causation and consequence, the use of causal conjunctions will need practice, as will fronted adverbials of time. Confident use of the past perfect tense enables more sophisticated use of chronology, enabling descriptions of actions completed before another past action or time point. Appositives enable the writer to add useful detail into a sentence in an economical yet informative manner.

When writing like a geographer, fronted adverbials of place are extremely useful, as is secure command of prepositions. Understanding when to use the passive or active voice is linked to appreciation of factors beyond or within human control. Abstract nouns – climate change, urbanisation, renewable energy, rising sea temperatures – allow the writer to say a lot with a little.

In contrast, when writing in an expressive discipline – the arts or when giving an opinion about a piece of literature – grammatical structures which codify subjectivity get their moment in the sun. The use of the first-person singular pronoun is welcomed. Qualifiers, adjectives and prepositions allow for rich description. Expressive disciplines also provide a context for children to begin to go beyond giving opinions in terms of liking or not liking something and to begin to use analytical language. Once again, conjunctions are our friend here, acting as cognitive levers that enable contrast or juxtaposition or causality.

Since we will want to teach our children to write non-fiction, instead of manufacturing artificial contexts for explaining or persuading or describing, why not use the authentic contacts of what children already know from other subjects? Describe the features of the tundra, persuade me that the transportation of food over thousands of miles has consequences for climate change, explain how the lungs work, analyse character development or musical dynamics. And in the process, learn how different subjects make truth claims in different ways.

Steve Graham and Karen Harris (2019) have shown the importance of modelling and articulating writing strategies to children. Explicitly demonstrating the strategy of acknowledging the non-present reader in teachers' modelled writing, further draws attention to the pupils that the reader is always a consideration – essentially, we are modelling metacognition. This can be at sentence, word and structural level. Isabel Beck and her colleagues (1996) recommends that during reading, teachers question the fallibility of the author when there may be ambiguity and lack of clarity, thereby connecting the writer to the reader. This develops an understanding of the need for clarity and coherence when writing. If the author were present, what might we say to them? How might they make their writing clearer, more interesting, less difficult to read?

Clare writes: And this is why we need an explicit writing curriculum, to make sure that these things are identified in real texts, modelled, discussed and practised!

Aside from the teacher (whose modelling of strategies is one of the big pedagogical levers of teaching writing), one of the greatest resources in primary classrooms can be other children. When writing is well structured and peers are well trained, using present readers can act as a simple bridge to the non-present reader. Peer-to-peer review of writing in class encourages young writers to understand that the purpose of writing is for it to be read. By having a reader close at hand, the writer can receive feedback close to the drafting task but develop the idea that their writing will be read *after* drafting. This not only improves the clarity and coherence of the written work for the writer receiving feedback, according to Martin Nystrand (1986), but adds a more powerful, reciprocal benefit, with the effects of giving feedback improving the writing of the feedback provider. By receiving feedback from peers, developing writers can be challenged on the clarity and cohesion of their compositions, make suitable revisions and develop an understanding of why clarity in their writing is so important for their readers. Giving feedback increases pupils' awareness of readers and the concept of the non-present reader by manifesting that audience. Furthermore, when teacher feedback on children's writing explicitly references the reader, this makes the connection between the writing and the reader.

And the reason we have cohesive devices as writers, is to make our texts more coherent for the reader – much more on this in chapter 7.

Evidence of growing awareness of the reader's needs

As children mature as writers, we can expect them to exhibit greater awareness of their readership's needs and how, as writers, they can affect them. These positive signs of metacognition are important and although they may be evident in their texts as cohesion and the use of tone and language choices, we cannot know for sure that the young writer is using them because that's what they've been taught (and this is good), or because they are exhibiting an awareness of the reader (even better). One of the most effective ways of knowing which is the case is to ask them.

Younger writers often concentrate on *what* they are writing, focusing on the content and the information they have communicated. This is to be expected as they develop, but it is when they start to notice and articulate *how* they have written something that suggests an awareness of the way that their writing may influence the reader. This may reference the reader explicitly – 'I wanted them to be frightened … I wanted them to feel pity for the dog' or through the selection of language – 'I think that word explains it better … I liked the image that those words conjured up.' *(Clare writes: And not, 'I've used a fronted adverbial because Miss likes that sort of thing.')* And even if children are unable to articulate these decisions unprompted, by encouraging them to think about their decisions ('Why did you use this particular vocabulary/sentence structure/image?' 'Which version do you prefer?'), we can encourage them to consider the choices they made and make some of these deliberate in the future.

Developing this awareness of the reader appears to have an important influence on the quality of composition according to psychologists Carl Bereiter and Marlene Scardamalia (1987). They suggest that the synchronisation of two points of view (the writer's and the reader's) elevates a text's quality – much more on Bereiter and Scardamalia in chapter 7.

An awareness that our writing is for a reader we may never meet is a concept that pupils will need support developing on their journey to this achievement. Like everything in writing, it will not happen instantly in a fully formed developmental package. However, by encouraging it through our language, our modelling and frequent spotlighting we can spark the metacognitive ignition that drives the development of children's written expression.

One of the most important elements of both having a motivation to write and being able to appraise our writing is the setting, adapting and evaluation of the goals of the writing. These goals will range from global (what I want to achieve by writing this) to more finessed (what I want this paragraph to achieve). One thing is certain though: without a clear idea of how we wish to affect the reader, it is impossible to establish any goals.

Key messages

- Reading and writing are intrinsically interrelated; they are not inverses. They need teaching separately.

- Teach reading to influence and improve writing by explicitly drawing attention to writers and authors at work, along with the written structures they used during reading – thereby helping to cement the link between the two.

- Develop grapheme/phoneme correspondence early as a crucial skill for both reading and writing.

- Teach writing explicitly to influence reading by teaching spelling to improve reading rates. Teach and practise sentence structure regularly through writing, thereby improving reading fluency.

- Teach composition as a means to improve reading comprehension.

- Ensure children write during and after reading to enhance reading comprehension.

- Ensure children write after reading to improve their recollection of content and understanding of concepts.

- Teach reading and writing together to improve content knowledge and develop language. Use authentic texts to exemplify writing structures as a model for high quality writing.

- Develop the concept of a non-present reader to improve writing goals and children's writing quality by:

  - Referencing the reader during goal setting prior to writing.

  - Referencing the reader during the modelling of writing.

  - Referencing the reader during teacher feedback.

- Using peer-to-peer feedback to create an instant readership.
- Encouraging children to articulate writing choices during conferencing.
- Questioning children as to their writing choices during conferencing.
- Teaching the use of cohesive devices with reference to clarity and coherence for the reader.

Chapter 6
Grammar and sentences

Tim writes: *I was taught grammar at school. I was taught it explicitly, ritually and at times maliciously – or so it felt. I was taught it in English lessons, French lessons and Latin lessons. I can't say that I enjoyed it – I still remember the class sigh in unison as the little blue grammar books clattered on our desks and we were given the exercise numbers to complete – but I never had much trouble with structuring and punctuating sentences when writing. I could concentrate on my composition. When I started teaching, I was disconcerted by the almost wanton disregard for the application of sentence structure across the school. The quality of children's vocabulary was excellent and their creative ideas and expression uplifting but trying to make sense of their writing was at times a trial. It was only when the headteacher was so dismayed at the school's KS2 writing test results which had been dragged down by the low sentence structure scores that I was charged with addressing the issue. We devised a sentence structure programme based upon subject and verb and the application of appropriate punctuation. It was pretty dry with very few bells and whistles and was based on the research on sentence-combining, but it worked (it became my MA project), and KS2 sentence structure scores improved exponentially. The children were fairly ambivalent about it, but what surprised me the most was that the teachers warmed to it – not because it worked, but because their own understanding of sentence structure developed – it seemed that most hadn't experienced the regular clattering landing of the little blue grammar book and wished they had.*

Clare writes: *Tim and I are close in age and were probably among the last of those to have been taught grammar, until its recent resurgence in England courtesy of the SPAG test. Though I mainly learned grammar through Latin and French, rather than in English lessons. The tide was already turning against grammar teaching even in my staid boarding school. The parallel class in my year group had a more 'old-school' English teacher who taught* *them about subjects and predicates whereas my more groovy teacher eschewed such things. I don't remember being taught how to write at all at secondary school. We just read lots of works of literature and then were expected – somehow – to be able to compose essays and stories – presumably by osmosis. I was most put out when my friends in the other class talked about the fun subject/predicate game they had played (less old school than Tim's teachers apparently – games indeed!). I was affronted that my peers had acquired knowledge that I had not. I led a delegation to complain about groovy teacher's groovy ways and demanded that we too were let in on the secret, foreshadowing perhaps preoccupations of my later career!*

The Romans taught grammar – ruthlessly. Quintilian had an entire stage assigned to it. There was no getting into the more expressive stage of Rhetoric unless the pupil had mastered the Grammaticus stage – and mastery meant just that, no mistakes, complete proficiency, parsing every word in every sentence correctly. This approach to teaching writing changed little for hundreds of years. It was how Shakespeare learned to write (he attended a Grammar school – the clue was in the title) and most of Europe adopted the approach. The systematic teaching of grammar continued into the modern era. The Czechs are obsessed with it, the French love it, the Spanish have entire research groups exploring how to teach it more effectively, teachers in the Netherlands have explicit instruction in it, Brazil embed it in their curriculum. There was one exception – the major anglophone countries (and that included Britain) who started to drop the systematic instruction of grammar in the 1960s and 70s.

Clare writes: *So while Tim – only a few months older than me – received full-fat grammar teaching, I received a grammar-lite version, and my younger brother received none at all. Within maybe five years, the practice of centuries had been overturned.*

This was not done as a malicious attempt to undermine children's ability to write, but teaching grammar takes time and that time, it was felt, could be better directed towards the more expressive (and enjoyable) elements of writing. Grammar, it was felt, could be absorbed through reading widely and integrated into composition – back to statistical learning here. Remember, this was the era of whole language instruction for teaching reading – learn to read by doing lots of reading. *(**Tim writes:** It was also the era of the Brits being useless at tennis – learn to play tennis by playing lots of tennis.)*

Many British private schools eschewed this approach to grammar and continued to drop those little blue books onto pupils' desks thereby infusing grammar knowledge with a large spoonful of Bourdieu's habitus as well as adding a political perspective – the use of grammar indicated class. *(Clare writes: Or even if grooviness had spread to the English department, you learned it in Latin, accompanied by huffing and puffing from the teacher, who made no secret that she did not see why she should have to teach stuff we should already know.)*

Of course, in England, the introduction of testing of grammatical knowledge for ten and eleven-year-olds from 2013 onwards has resulted in the return of grammar teaching…but more on this later in the chapter.

What is grammar?

Grammar is the structure and common system of a language. By following that system, we are able to communicate with greater consistency and clarity both as speakers and writers.

Pupils develop their spoken grammar through speaking to and listening to other speakers. When children start school, their understanding and experience of language and grammar will be mostly through speaking and listening and from hearing stories read to them.

We saw in the previous chapters that although writing is usually dependent on the development of spoken communication, the two are different. The structure of writing is different from that of speech. When we write (as opposed to spoken communication) we have a different set of rules that our readers expect us to abide by. These structures and accepted systems are more prescriptive for writing to ensure consistency, so tighter structures developed to help the putative non-present reader negotiate intended meaning. This includes not only the accepted and expected forms of structuring sentences, but also the use of punctuation to ensure that the reader has clarity over meaning and indication of the boundaries of sentences. This consistency will need to be learned (and therefore taught) for pupils to write confidently and fluently, see themselves as authors and be understood by their readers.

Why should grammar be taught?

Let's return to working memory. As Thierry Olive (2002) helpfully explained, understanding working memory and its restricted nature explains the necessity of breaking down the teaching of writing into a progression of smaller steps. If working memory becomes overloaded, writing will stall, slow and potentially result in frustrated and demotivated writers.

So, let's view grammar on the continuum of writing – with working memory needing managing throughout the continuum. At one end we have the elements that can be automatised – handwriting and spelling. At the other end we have our creative ideas and expressive desires and intentions. As we move further along the continuum, elements become more difficult to automatise because we need to think more about them and make choices.

Applying grammatical rules may require some cognitive attention – we often stop to consider the structure of our sentences and revise them as we write – but for the most part, as we move along the continuum, these elements become more fluent (not entirely automatic, but they require less effort). The more this fluency develops, the more it supports the next more complex components that sit on the continuum. So, fluent application of grammar will not ensure you can write the great European novel, but you will not be able to write it without significant fluency of grammar when writing. And fluent sentence structure will be essential as you start to develop your ability to create paragraphs (which you'll also need for your novel).

In her book *The Writing Rope*, Joan Sedita (2023) is clear that poor grammar skills increase the cognitive demand when writing. Sedita is American so the dubious joys of England's Year 6 SPAG test are presumably unknown to her. When she speaks of 'grammar skills' she does not mean the ability to distinguish a relative clause from a prepositional phrase at 100 paces. She means being able to form a range of coherent and sophisticated sentences without breaking (too much of) a sweat. She maintains that if pupils struggle to form effective sentences, this will reduce their ability to attend to writing down the ideas they want to express and may lead to some ideas being forgotten. Pupils who struggle with grammar tend to write sentences that are shorter, lack complexity, contain a greater number of grammatical errors, contain simpler vocabulary and represent poorer quality ideas. Compositions that lack effective grammar are more difficult to read and are often unclear – and they receive fewer marks. The creative ideas that a pupil wants to express may become unclear or confuse the reader, leading to the communication failing. Furthermore, pupils who are unable to write their ideas clearly and whose readers stop reading their work, may become disillusioned with the writing process, thereby inhibiting their motivation to write.

We saw in chapter 5 that grammar and sentence structure knowledge is also important for improving our reading. Not only does it support our reading fluency, but it also helps us cope when we encounter more complex syntax in texts. Ngoni Chipere (2003) found that complex syntax is far easier to read for pupils after some explicit instruction. He determined that it was necessary to provide instruction in grammar throughout the school years. This is because, he concluded, 'Indications are that being a native speaker of a language does not automatically mean that individuals will be able to construct linguistic systems which enable them to understand, at a syntactic level, all the sentences of that language.' *(Clare writes: Probably because being a native speaker does not usually involve speaking or hearing all the sentences in a language – because we don't usually talk in sentences and rarely in complex sentences.)* Perhaps more importantly for us as teachers, his research indicated that instruction in this area enhances linguistic performance. His research helps to square the circle between statistical learning and explicit instruction by surmising that the teaching of our native language should incorporate both rules-based and experience-based approaches. So, we need to learn the rules but also apply them. This 'both, and' approach appears to be rather hard for some teachers who seem to oscillate between focusing only on one or the other, either all application and no rules (as both Tim and Clare recall from their early careers) to all rules and no application as in the SPAG test inspired teaching of grammar. (Though apparently the test is about to be reformed to include more application.)

Acquiring grammar knowledge to improve writing

If grammar appears to be so important, how should children acquire it?

Most teachers reading this were probably taught grammar by a 'grammar in context' model whereby grammar was only taught when it was directly relevant to a writing task, if at all. There was no systematic teaching of grammar, and it was up to the teacher to decide when teaching was relevant and what teaching was relevant. Whether and how that new knowledge related to your existing knowledge was very much a matter of chance, so you will have ended up with an unstructured bank of haphazard, accidental and arbitrary grammar knowledge. You will also have been very dependent upon your teacher's knowledge of grammar which, if they had been taught like you, was probably pretty thin. The grammar-poor decades of instruction produced a grammar knowledge deficit for a generation of English teachers, according to Richard Hudson (2016).

It is perhaps unsurprising that this model resulted in pupils acquiring grammar knowledge that had little effect on the quality of writing.

The alternative model goes something like this:

Teaching grammar introduces the ideas and terminology of grammar and teaches them as a system. This will include the understanding of terms like *noun, verb, relative clause, subject* and *object*. Developing this **knowledge of grammar** seeks to establish a conscious awareness of the patterns and definitions of English grammar that promotes children's **knowledge about grammar**. Having this **knowledge about grammar** should then develop children's **awareness of grammar** and it is this awareness which can then enable them to apply their knowledge and so improve their writing.

Those of us who have taught in England over the past few years will recognise this model. It is what the English national curriculum has been embedding. It appears to suggest that once a knowledge of grammar exists, that knowledge builds an awareness that can be applied to writing. It is this knowledge that is then tested at the end of primary school.

It seems a reasonable theory with a strong intuitive logic.

However, the mass of research from the twentieth century refutes the model and indicates that teaching grammar knowledge, in itself, does not improve writing. The dominoes do not fall in the seemingly logical way resulting in grammar being used in writing. Richard Andrews (2004) and his team of researchers went even further, suggesting that the teaching of grammar 'had virtually no influence on the writing quality or accuracy of 5 to 16 year-olds.'

You probably had an inkling that this was the case. It's why many very competent writers cannot score full marks on a grammar paper. Their knowledge of grammar may be thin, but they can still apply the rules. (***Clare writes:*** *And why when I was a headteacher we were able to teach many children enough grammar to achieve greater depth in the SPAG test and yet some of those children achieved 'working towards' in their writing assessments. They learned the – very teachable – rules, but couldn't (yet) apply them.*) But this really is not very helpful for those of us who have to teach writing. What on earth are we meant to do? Grammar is important to improve writing but there's no point teaching it. Thanks!

Well, there is hope (you knew there would be).

Applying grammar knowledge to improve writing

Richard Hudson (2016) agrees that the research shows that it is not enough to teach the grammatical system and hope that writing will magically progress. For grammar teaching to be effective at improving writing, it must be *explicitly applied to writing* (remember Chipere earlier?). Hudson cites Debra Myhill and her team's research (2012) which demonstrated significant improvements in writing quality when specific grammatical patterns were *taught* and then *applied* directly to writing tasks. Reassuringly for all of us, in this case neither students nor teachers started with much grammatical knowledge.

When we teach writing, we need to teach both substantive *and* disciplinary knowledge. Substantive knowledge is the teaching of technical knowledge about what things are called, when they apply, the ability to spot them as well as technical prowess in their use. Disciplinary knowledge is about awareness of the reader; what do they need of us authors so that our writing is clear and sufficiently interesting, useful or informative? How can we put our substantive knowledge to creative use? The teaching of writing goes wrong when it does not harness both forms of knowledge together. So, it either becomes dry and meaningless or a well-intentioned journey into impossibility, where the writer, lacking the requisite technical tools, cannot, in fact, make anything meaningful either (we will see in chapter 7 that this is what Bereiter and Scardamalia (1987) are driving at). Education fashion waxes and wanes in emphasising one or other aspect, when, to state the tiresomely obvious, children need both and need them taught in a way where the technical enables the creative. Teaching the technical without it feeding into the creative is pointless. Teaching the creative without building technical competence is futile. Clare wrote about this in more detail in her blog (Sealy, 2025).

The importance of sentences

And here's a thing...much of the research into grammar teaching does not include studies into the teaching of sentence structure. Hudson (2016) remains bemused at this omission and is adamant that it should count – it's an important omission.

But why is it so important? The research is significant and emphatic. Sentence manipulating activities (often referred to as sentence combining) improve writing and particularly improve sentence structure. When Richard Andrews and his team (2005) at York University carried out a meta-study of all grammar teaching going back 100 years, they again found that grammar teaching had little effect on the quality of writing but one of the main conclusions was that the findings 'suggest that the teaching of sentence combining may be one of the more effective approaches.'

They went on to recommend that it was included as part of the National Literacy Strategy as a matter of urgency. This was back in 2005. It seemed to fall on deaf ears despite continued research emphasising its positive effect on pupils' writing. Instead, in 2013, pupils in England got the SPAG test. This rewarded the ability to name and identify grammatical features – underline the relative clause for example. There was some basic application – e.g. replace the noun with a pronoun – but nothing that required children to make deliberate choices to improve clarity or interest for the reader or to understand why a pronoun or a relative clause might help. It was all substantive knowledge and no disciplinary knowledge.

In 2022, research by Dominic Wyse and the teams at UCL and the University of York (2022) once again emphasised the importance of sentence combining as a strategy for enabling children to generate sentences, particularly when compared with grammar knowledge instruction. (**Tim and Clare write:** *Including sentence combining in the DfE's Writing Framework means we can die happy!*)

So, it seems that if we want children to learn to write well, then they need to be able to compose written sentences well. And if we want them to compose sentences well, then they need to develop an understanding of syntax.

Syntax

Syntax is one aspect of grammar and refers to the system we use to consistently organise words, phrases and clauses that make up a sentence. When composing, we draw on our knowledge of syntax in order to craft sentences. To compose coherent, cohesive texts pupils will need to develop a deep understanding of sentence structure and how to apply it.

We also draw on our knowledge of punctuation to ensure these sentences are clear and make sense to the reader. Punctuation and syntax work in tandem to ensure the reader can infer the meaning of the text easily and with the greatest clarity.

Developing familiarity with these conventions of sentence structure and punctuation, and how words are structured into sentences, is crucial for pupils to convey their ideas in writing. Syntactic awareness enables pupils to recognise when their (and others') sentence structure is effective or less effective and helps them to remedy or improve the structure. As pupils' syntactic awareness deepens, they become more familiar with the availability and use of more complex sentence structures that enable them to create more cohesion in their texts. Cohesion is one of those words bandied about when talking about writing that could do with a little unpacking. It really just means connectedness. When a piece of writing lacks cohesion, it reads like a horizontally presented list, a random assortment of disconnected sentences laid out one after the other, who knows why. It is difficult to see where the writing is going and why we, the reader, should stay around to find out.

Talking of getting the reader to stay around (the custard creams beckon, after all), writing needs variety if it is to be interesting. A procession of sentences with similar rhythm is stultifying, as this clever piece deftly illustrates.

Gunter Kress (1994) maintained that one of the most significant features of language development in young writers is learning about the sentence. Much of this syntactic awareness is developed orally at first, and learning to apply this different syntactic awareness to writing is more difficult because the rules are stricter. But it starts with the sentence.

According to Bruce Saddler (2012), one of the major difficulties that children encounter when they write is the challenge of constructing sentences that convey their intended meaning but also conform to the conventions of grammar. Without knowledge of these conventions, it is extremely difficult to conform to them and apply them in their written work.

> This sentence has five words. Here are five more words. Five-word sentences are fine. But several become monotonous. Listen to what is happening. The writing is getting boring. The sound of it drones. It's like a stuck record. The ear demands some variety.
>
> Now listen. I vary the sentence length, and I create music. Music. The writing sings. It has a pleasant rhythm, a lilt, a harmony. I use short sentences. And I use sentences of medium length. And sometimes when I am certain the reader is rested, I will engage him with a sentence of considerable length, a sentence that burns with energy and builds with all the impetus of a crescendo, the roll of the drums, the crash of the cymbals—sounds that say listen to this, it is important.
>
> So write with a combination of short, medium, and long sentences. Create a sound that pleases the reader's ear. Don't just write words. Write music.
>
> – Gary Provost

Teaching sentences

Debra Myhill (2016) suggests that sentences are the building blocks of writing. The vast majority of texts are written in sentences. (There are obvious exceptions such as lists, notes and some poems.) Being able to write sentences will not turn children into compelling authors, but there is no writing of extended text without a strong grasp on the sentence. And there is no rule-breaking for effect a la John Updike, ee cummings or Rebecca Watson without first knowing the rules that you are considering breaking.

Judith Hochman and Natalie Wexler (2017) in their book *The Writing Revolution* are unwavering in their belief in the importance of teaching sentence structure: 'The importance of spending plenty of instructional time working with sentences can't be stressed enough. Sentence-level work is the engine that will propel your students from writing the way they speak to using the structures of written language.'

Yes, children will be able to absorb some concepts of written syntax from reading, but many will not. By being taught a range of sentence structures and then applying them and practising them regularly, revisiting them and practising them again, they will become more and more fluent. This should be done both through drills and through authentic attempts at communicating to an audience – albeit probably just one's classmates most of the time. The former hones the skill, the latter reveals the skill's usefulness. And let's labour the idea of repeated, spaced and deliberate practice here. We have just seen that grammar teaching alone is almost useless unless those skills are *applied*. So, it makes sense to apply them and keep applying them.

What is a sentence?

Although English has a vast vocabulary and writers have many words from which to choose to express their ideas, sentences are built around nouns and verbs – *something* has to *do* something, *be* something or *act* in some way.

We can select from myriad options of the word or words we use to name that thing, and we can describe at length what that thing is up to, adding all sorts of descriptions and images, but if something (the noun) isn't up to something (the verb) then it ain't a sentence.

It's as simple as that.

A sentence has to have a subject (the actor – the noun) and that actor has to be acting in some way or be in some way (the verb).

So…The doctor ran. I ate my lunch. Elvis left the building. Jesus wept. He felt sad. Love sucks. She was amazing. I think therefore I am…are all sentences. Even if the actor (as in 'love') is intangible or the action is mere existence (am). Some verbs do and some verbs be, but you gotta have a verb! In fact, you can have a sentence where the subject is implied such as 'Go away!' (the invisible, implied subject being 'you') but not one where the verb is implied. Remember David Lobina (2020) saying that when we read, it is only when we hit the verb that the sentence makes cognitive sense.

But sentences can also include other types (classes) of words.

For example, this is a sentence:

'The dog barked in the garden.'

It has a subject (The dog) and a verb (barked). But it also adds some extra information – in the garden. That's a preposition (in) and an object (the garden). But 'barked in the garden' is not a sentence (no subject) and neither is 'The dog in the garden' (no verb).

Using scaffolds for children to develop their speech into written structures can be useful throughout school. This will begin in a simple form:

SUBJECT	VERB	OTHER INFORMATION
The dog	barked.	
The dog	barked	in the garden.
The dog	barked	loudly.
The dog	barked	at me.
The dog	barked	yesterday.

And can become more complex:

SUBJECT	VERB	OBJECT	OTHER INFORMATION
Animal cells	contain	a nucleus	where chemical reactions take place to keep the cell alive.

And then there are a couple of additional conventions to help the reader. First, the writer lets the reader know that the sentence is starting by capitalising the 'T' of 'The' and the writer also lets the reader know when the sentence ends by putting a stop mark – in this case a full stop. This may not seem that necessary when there is only one stand-alone sentence, but in a text with hundreds of sentences it's going to be really helpful. Originally in Latin they didn't even separate the words, just ranthemalltogether – really not helpful for the reader (but remember the Romans were much more concerned with oration than writing). Once again, the writer's awareness of the reader is crucial and needs sharing with children who are learning about sentences and punctuation. It's the reason we are learning all these rules and conventions. In terms of substantive and disciplinary knowledge, the process can be broken down as follows:

	Substantive knowledge	Disciplinary knowledge
Conceptual ... know that ... because ...	We start off sharing examples of simple sentences, explaining they always have a subject and a verb and identifying these.	While also explaining the reader can't make sense of what we are writing unless both are included.
Procedural ... know how to ... and be able to ... (Skills: involves a verb)	We then help children identify subjects and verbs and where they are absent. We then help children expand fragments into complete sentences.	Then children write simple sentences to describe a picture or animation to someone else who may not have seen it. Then children evaluate the sentences they have written to check that they make sense (because they include both a subject and a verb), making changes where necessary.

The journey is one of developing technical proficiency as an enabler of creative communication (Sealy, 2025).

You could even publish these simple sentences, using digital technology, if the children are working orally, or by making simple books. It is not necessary to do this all the time, but neither should it never be done. This non-present reader we keep on banging on about needs to be more than a fictional construct.

Of course, sentences can relay huge amounts of additional information to the reader as writers become more confident with controlling their structure:

'Shortly after midnight as the moon rose above the distant moor, the colossal hound, teeth glinting in the moonlight, sinews stretched to breaking point, mouth foaming with rage, let rip a bellow of such ferocity and intensity that the very trees in the garden shook and trembled and seemed to recoil in a state of utter terror.'

And possibly, this is too much information, all at once. But it is still essentially, 'The dog barked.' So, let's start with that.

The early stages of teaching about writing sentence

Joan Sedita (2023) suggests that pupils who are learning to form complete sentences benefit from understanding that there are two basic parts (fragments) of a sentence:

- The naming part (the subject).

- The action/feeling/state of being part.

This is sometimes referred to as the **subject** (the naming part) and the **predicate** (all of the rest) and this is a useful way of children understanding the two essentials of a sentence – the main actor and the action. And they can improve their syntactic awareness by practising forming sentences out of the two parts and identifying the two parts.

Objects

Not all writing that has a verb and a noun is a sentence. 'Walked to the shops' has the verb 'walked' and the noun 'shops' but it is not a sentence as it still has no subject. No one is doing the walking. So, the noun 'shops' is the **object** – the thing that the verb is acting on, not the thing doing the acting. 'Robin walked to the shops.' now has a **subject** (Robin) who has acted (walked – the **verb**) with some added information as to where Robin walked (the shops – the **object**). This is different to how we use language when we speak. If someone asked us what we did this afternoon, we might well say 'walked to the shops,' 'went shopping' or perhaps, if we are feeling particularly monosyllabic, 'shopping'. But this is not how written communication works and hence needs explicit teaching. Learning the syntax of the written sentence involves a degree of *unlearning* of conversational modes of communication.

One of the issues for pupils starting to write sentences is to understand the concept of sentence boundaries. Marking these boundaries by a capital letter at the beginning and a full stop, question mark or exclamation mark further enhances their understanding of what a sentence is by introducing the concepts in context.

Children should experience sentences orally at first. Using fragments of sentences and then building them orally with a class into complete sentences is an effective way of developing syntactic awareness. The fragment might be the noun or noun phrase – 'Elizabeth II' – or the verb and the acting/feeling/state of being part of the sentence – 'reigned for seventy years'. Orally combining these fragments into a sentence supports an understanding of how sentences are constructed and can develop into the writing of sentence fragments into written sentences, suggest Hochman and Wexler (2017).

For example, activities where children take sentence fragments of nouns and noun phrases and actions (these can be in card form or digital) and form them into full sentences can support their understanding of these two parts of a sentence. This can be extended by offering pupils sentence fragments that they then turn into full sentences.

Pupils can also be offered a collection of sentences and sentence fragments and sort them into these two groups explaining why they have identified them as a sentence or a fragment.

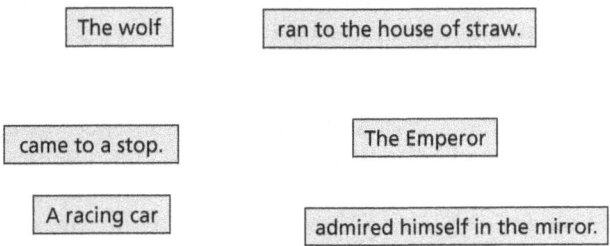

Steve Graham (2006) recommends that teachers focus on building syntactic awareness and suggests they achieve this through explicit teaching of sentence structure during writing lessons – with plenty of practice. He recommends particular attention to pupils checking sentence structure during the revising phases of composition – checking our sentence structure is one of the reasons we revise our writing (we dare not tell you how many times we have reread and revised this chapter – and we continue to find sentence errors – thank God for sub-editors!)

Hochman and Wexler (2017) advocate that pupils should be encouraged to identify sentences in their own and others' work. They should also be encouraged to identify writing that is not in sentences and repair the writing. And they should be exposed to high quality examples of good writing. Explicitly drawing pupils' attention to the sentence structure being studied in books will further embed the learning of these structures.

For example, in their reading, pupils may encounter the line:

'*The old woman* didn't say anything for a long time.'

and they can break the sentence into two fragments.

Giving pupils pictures and animations with a clear subject and a clear action and asking them to form a sentence is a good way to start developing an understanding of sentence structure. For example, a picture or animation of a woman digging a hole gives the teacher the opportunity to ask, 'Who is the subject? What is she doing? What is the verb?' Further pictures can promote further exploration of sentence structure. A picture of the woman planting a tree in the hole for example can lead to the use of a conjunction 'The woman dug a hole *and* planted a tree.' The animation also helps children manage their working memory load as they can attend to the sentence structure rather than the composition.

Developing sentence structure further

As pupils develop more knowledge of sentence structure, activities where pupils identify incorrect sentence structure in text or identify sentence boundaries where none are indicated helps them develop the habit of noticing and remedying this when rereading their own work.

In other curriculum areas, a teacher can write a text with sentence fragments missing that include content knowledge. The pupils identify the fragment and add the missing fragment.

For example, when studying Van Gogh in art:

> born in the town of Zundert in the Netherlands in 1853. He is now considered. His early paintings. Subject matter mainly focused on. sold for $117 million in 2022.

This not only promotes syntactic awareness but also enables pupils to apply content knowledge, thus supporting with working memory demands while also strengthening knowledge.

Introducing sentence types

Hochman and Wexler (2017) recommend introducing students to the four sentence types. This, they suggest, will pay dividends when it comes time for them to write paragraphs with varying sentence structures.

There are four main sentence types: statement, question, exclamation and command.

1	Statement	the most common type of sentence	*Elizabeth II reigned for seventy years.*
2	Question	asks a question and ends with a question mark	*For how long did Elizabeth II reign?*
3	Exclamation	expresses a heightened emotion	*I adored Queen Elizabeth!*
4	Command	expresses a requirement or command	*Describe the importance of the reign of Queen Elizabeth II.*

Pupils will need practice distinguishing between the four sentence types and then practice using them. Simple identification activities introduce them to the types:

> I want an ice cream.
> Do you want an ice cream?
> Buy me an ice cream.
> I hate ice cream!

Pupils can then be encouraged to alter sentences to different types:

- Turn this statement into a question: 'The Thames is the longest river in England.' → 'What is the longest river in England?'

- Turn this question into a statement: 'Have you ever seen a dolphin?' → 'Dolphins can be spotted off the coast of Devon.'

Pupils can then be encouraged to write the four types of sentence. This can be an effective activity in other curriculum areas:

> When water freezes it becomes a solid.
> What happens to water when it freezes?
> Add frozen water.
> This water is freezing!

Pupils can also find examples of the different sentence types in the texts they are reading and when sharing writing with their peers. Much of the learning from these activities comes not specifically from identifying and using sentence types but in the manipulation and control of sentences, identifying the subject and verb.

Teaching the four sentence types not only supports pupils with developing punctuation and using it in context but can be used to enhance the understanding and application of new vocabulary and as part of teaching spelling. When pupils use new vocabulary in the four sentence types, they have to consider its meaning more carefully. Writing the word supports the spelling of the new word.

For example, if pupils have learned the word 'extract', they can apply its use in the four sentence types:

> The engineer extracted the metal ore.
> Do you need the ore extracted?
> We must not extract the ore!
> Extract the ore.

Developing sentence structure

If sentences are the building blocks of writing, then, Geoff Barton (2005) (his book *Grammar Survival* is one of the clearest, though unfathomably out of print) maintains, clauses are the building blocks of sentences. Clauses can be either finite and can stand on their own – *she eats vegetables* – or non-finite – *eating her vegetables*. Younger writers tend to use single **main clause** sentences (one subject and one verb) that deliver pieces of information one at a time. These are known as **simple sentences**. These are used to effect by confident writers but in the hands of emergent writers often open with the same noun or pronoun repeated, creating little cohesion. The writing reads like a disjointed list. As a reader we tend to find reading through a list of episodes rather dull. To the reader, it feels jerky rather than smooth and isn't very satisfying.

> Little Red Riding Hood set off. She went through the forest. She met the woodcutter. She went to her grandmother's house.

As pupils become more confident using single clause sentences, they can be encouraged to link those single clauses to create greater cohesion.

One of the most effective ways of developing greater cohesion in pupils' writing is to teach them to extend their single clause sentence into a multi clause sentence by using a conjunction to link two main clauses together. When **simple sentences** are linked using coordinating conjunctions, they become **compound sentences**. The progression from simple to compound sentences can transform children's writing from staccato, repetitive and list-like, to far more fluid and interesting.

Encouraging them to hear, notice and appreciate these improvements can be very motivating:

> Little Red Riding Hood set off **and** went through the forest. She met the woodcutter **and** went to her grandmother's house.

Merely by the addition of two conjunctions, the writer has been able to remove two pronouns and reduce four sentences to two. Perhaps not Henry James but so much easier to read as it flows more. The jerkiness has gone and there is the beginning of linking – of purpose – between actions. It isn't just one seemingly random thing after another. She set off and went through the forest. The two things exist in some sort of relationship to each other. *(**Clare writes:** If I were teaching this to young children, I might use the metaphor of Lego blocks. Two Lego blocks are just two separate Lego blocks, no matter how closely together they are placed. Yet put a third Lego block on top, joining them together – we have a joined structure. **Tim writes:** I wish I'd thought of this!)*

Coordinating conjunctions

So, connecting clauses and phrases with conjunctions helps make writing clearer – in this instance because the reader now understands that setting off and going through the forest are related, at least in terms of time, and possibly causally too. It also gives the reader more information in a single sentence – disrupting jerkiness and providing a smoother reading experience – and mediates the overuse of the same pronoun. For instance, 'I went to the shop. I bought an apple.' Becomes, 'I went to the shop and bought an apple.' The writer has dropped one of the pronouns making the one sentence much more cohesive – the going to the shop and the buying of an apple are now linked with less intrusive and clunky repetition. As a result, the message is much clearer and more enjoyable for the reader (remember them…and their distracting custard cream?).

The skilful use of conjunctions within sentences is an essential part of disciplinary writing. Conjunctions change the direction of a sentence. Before, the sentence was heading in one direction and then – bam – it ran into a [con]junction, and had to shoot off in another. 'Because' introduces cause, (imagine a right-hand fork in the road), 'so' introduces consequence, (imagine a left-hand fork), 'but' paves the way for exceptions, alternatives and differences (imagine a U-turn!). Becoming fluent in compound sentence formation through using these and other conjunctions correctly is an integral part of learning to write with greater fluidity and interest.

An effective activity to build understanding and application of greater cohesion in pupils' writing is to use these basic conjunctions to develop the same sentence stem:

> The pupils were happy because …
> The pupils were happy, but …
> The pupils were happy, and …
> The pupils were happy, so …

By using a [con]junction, the very sense of the sentence stem changes. Meaning takes off in a new direction. The two parts of the sentence – the two clauses – now exist in a relationship of tension with one another. And this brings the writing alive in a way a serial list of sentences cannot. Conjunctions allow us to express ideas or events in parallel, not in series.

The activity can be used in other curriculum areas where pupils will have content knowledge. It can help to embed awareness of sentence structure but also to develop content knowledge and further thinking about that knowledge:

Plants need water because …
Plants need water, and …
Plants need water, but …
Plants need water, so …

Using the activity orally in feedback can help develop pupils' understanding of sentence structure, cohesion, and the importance of developing ideas. For example, responding to a pupil's writing by saying. 'I like your use of the adverb 'skilfully' **because** it lets me know that the character has been practising.' Alternatively, responding to a pupil's answer, 'Yes, you are correct, plants do need water. Can you extend the sentence with **'but'** to give me an example of plants that survive with little water?'

The following rule is very robust:

Every time some new action or idea occurs, either start a new sentence or link the actions with a conjunction.

We could probably write effectively and clearly by using only simple and compound sentences. Paul Jennings, the Australian children's author (*Tim writes: And writer of the best, funniest, most perfect children's book ever written* – The Gizmo Again.) writes almost exclusively in simple and compound sentences. And pupils need to be very secure in both sentence types.

However, pupils will be aware of more convoluted and different sentence structures in speech and may try to replicate them in their writing.

Once pupils are secure with using these coordinating conjunctions to extend their ideas and cohere their sentences, they can be introduced to **subordinate conjunctions**. These offer the opportunity to add further information into sentences in a far more effective and economical way, adding significant cohesion to the writer's message.

Subordinating conjunctions

Developing the use of **complex sentences** will greatly extend children's ability to include more information in their sentences in an economical and coherent way. Furthermore, it will extend their options for opening their sentences by pushing the subjects and verbs deeper into the sentence. This helps them avoid the repeated use of nouns and pronouns opening their sentences, which can be unattractive for readers (and verbs pushed deeper into sentences are associated with higher quality writing). It will also support their reading as they encounter more complex sentences in texts.

Compound sentences are made up of clauses that are coordinated (they have equal weight):

> The dog barked and ran away but came home.

The clauses are linked by the coordinating conjunctions **and** plus **but** (plus the others from the familiar **FANBOYS: for, and, nor, but, or, yet** and **so.**)

Complex sentences, on the other hand, are made up of a **main clause** and one or more **subordinate clauses**. Whereas in a compound sentence the clauses have equal weight (they give main information), in a complex sentence the subordinate clause adds background information.

For example, in the sentence, 'The dog stood its ground, although it felt threatened.' 'although it felt threatened' is the subordinate clause. It adds some extra detail to the main idea that the dog stood its ground.

This may sound unhelpfully vague for teaching children, but you will have noticed the conjunction 'although'. It is this conjunction that reduces the weight of the second clause – it is a **subordinating conjunction**. So, as Geoff Barton (2005) recommends, a very effective way of teaching subordination is through the identification and use of these **subordinating conjunctions**.

The most frequently used subordinating conjunctions that open written sentences are either to do with time, *before, after, when, while, as*, or to do with cause, *although, since, if*.

Temporal subordinate clauses are easier to understand, so it makes sense to start with these and then progress to **causal subordinate conjunctions**. The labelling of subordinate conjunctions as **temporal** or **causal** is useful when planning a curriculum. However, when teaching, the emphasis for the pupil should be on understanding the *function* of the conjunction, rather than its label.

By providing opening subordinate clauses and the main clauses, pupils can connect the two and start to understand the nature of this more complicated sentence structure. They can then experiment with shifting the subordinate clause to the end of the sentence.

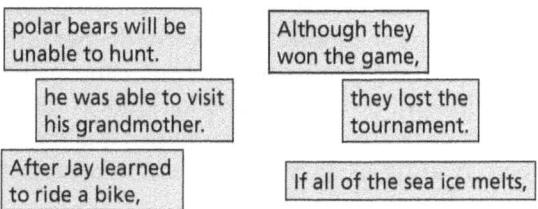

Geoff Barton (2005) suggests pupils only start to 'get' the difference between coordination and subordination by seeing and working with lots of examples. It is a matter of seeing what can make sense on its own but also a matter of feeling. The tension between the main and subordinate clause *feels* stronger than that between two clauses in a compound sentence. This tension, this stored energy, propels the reader through the story, argument or exposition. It heightens the sense of connectedness.

The above activity can be used across the curriculum and can help embed content knowledge. It can be particularly useful to assess content knowledge by giving pupils a question along with the subordinate clause. They then complete the main clause.

For example:

Why did the Iceni lose the final battle with the Roman army?

Although the Roman army was heavily outnumbered, ...

Once pupils have become more familiar with this structure then they can be given only the subordinate clauses or the main clauses. This can be made even more challenging by giving pupils only the subordinating conjunction and the noun.

For example:

Since a triangle ...
If a triangle ...
Unless a triangle ...

Using subordinating conjunctions helps pupils to add cohesion and interest to their writing by adding variety to their sentence structure and giving them alternative ways of changing sentence order and opening and closing their sentences. Returning to our junction metaphor, when using a subordinating conjunction at the start of the sentence, the reader travels some way along a sentence before encountering the verb and finally understanding what is going on. This slight delay, this small deferment of gratification, this anticipation of full understanding is pleasurable. In their wide-ranging corpus study of what elements appear in 'quality writing', Phillip Durrant and his team (2021) found that higher quality writing was associated with the main verb appearing deeper in sentences. Subordinate clauses at the front of sentences do exactly this!

Relative clauses

These clauses are a specific type of subordinate clause. They are a particularly economical and effective way of adding some more detail about a **noun** within a sentence. They always refer back to the **noun, noun phrase** or **clause** to which they are adding the information by using one of the following pronouns: *that, which, who, whose, where, when.*

For example:

> The prize *that* he was awarded was a book token.
> The boy *who* lives near the farm.
> The girl, *whose* father abandoned her, became a successful entrepreneur.
> The river, *where* we learned to swim, flows into the North Sea.

Adverbials

Pupils who have a good understanding of subordination can be introduced to adverbials. These are encountered infrequently in speech. It is understanding of the function of an adverbial that should be the primary focus, though knowing the term **adverbial** avoids the need for clunky circumlocutions.

By using **adverbials** writers let the reader know *when, where* or *how* the action indicated by the **verb** happened, and again add cohesion to pupils' writing by neatly embedding additional information within the sentence rather than in a new sentence.

These are often subordinate clauses but can be phrases.

For example, take the sentence:

> The Romans won the battle.

Pupils can be encouraged to add adverbials answering the questions *when, where* and *how.*

> **How?** By holding their positions, the Romans won the battle.

And consider how much better this is than the alternative.

> The Romans won the battle. They did this by holding their position.

By using an adverbial, we have that energising tension, that strong sense of connection and causality, injected into the sentence.

We will leave you to do the same exercise with these next two.

Where? The Romans won the battle....

When? ..., the Romans won the battle.

Once again, it is worth noting that adverbials at the front of the sentence push the main verb deeper into the sentence – an effect associated with higher quality writing. When we do this, we have a **fronted adverbial**, a term that for some reason outrages people on social media. But remember the adverbial can also go at the end of the sentence – a sign of a young writer growing in confidence.

Appositives (embedded clauses and phrases)

Appositives are clauses or phrases that add information to a noun. Pupils who are confident with subordination can find this an effective way to add information about the noun directly into the sentence, affording them an efficient way of creating more cohesion.

For example, take the sentence:

London is a major tourist attraction.

Pupils can add additional information directly into the sentence.

London, **the capital of the UK**, is a major tourist attraction.

Compare this with the alternative.

London is a major tourist attraction. It is the capital of the UK.

Without the appositive we are back to horizontal lists of stuff, which sound so much more immature and boring than the alternative. The appositive also introduces a pleasing change of rhythm to the sentence, with the inserted extra information being read much faster and more staccato than the rest of the sentence.

Appositives are particularly useful across the curriculum where large amounts of content knowledge needs to be included in compositions.

By encouraging pupils to use both subordinate clauses and appositives we encourage them to elaborate upon their ideas *within* the boundaries of the sentence. This not only encourages them to think more deeply about the ideas they want to convey but also encourages the fluidity of their written expression. This will need teaching, practice and encouragement.

Active and passive voice

Although the use of passive voice may often feel like an irrelevant assessment-style step too far for primary school children, it can have a relevant place in the teaching of sentence structure. This is because it encourages children to identify the subject and object of a sentence and then invert them.

So:

> The doctor took my temperature.

becomes ...

> My temperature was taken by the doctor.

The subject 'the doctor' moves to the end of the sentence and the object 'my temperature' moves to the front.

The classic way of teaching this is to see if the phrase 'by zombies' can be added after the verb and still produce a meaningful (if daft) sentence. Hence, 'my temperature was taken by zombies' makes sense (so is passive). The use of the passive voice to disguise the subject from the reader is a deliberate stylistic choice. For example, it can be used to heighten objectivity in scientific writing, 'the solution was heated to 100°C until a colour change was observed,' to create mystery when writing fiction, 'the message was erased before it could be read,' or to evade responsibility, 'mistakes were made'.

Using the terms **relative clause**, **adverbial** or **appositive** provide a useful shorthand, but accurate identification of one kind of subordinate clause rather than another is not the main point here. The main point is that pupils have internalised a range of different ways of making their writing clearer and more interesting. That's the whole point of the enterprise. Using technical terms when teaching avoids the need to continually resort to unwieldy explanations – so they *are* useful. But it is understanding function that is key.

David Didau and Rikki Cole (2026) have written an excellent book that unpicks how different subordinate clauses act as cognitive levers that shape our thinking. For example, 'although' prompts the reader to think about different perspectives, 'unless' leads them to look at exceptions to rules, 'in order that' implies intention, and 'at first glance' makes the reader look more deeply and think again about first impressions.

Sentence combining – extending and contracting sentences

We mentioned earlier that, according to a large body of research, one of the most effective ways of developing children's understanding and effective use of sentence structure is the activity known as *sentence combining*. It is a pedagogical device that enables teachers to instruct children how to combine two or more sentences to make one grammatically correct sentence. It has the significant benefit of being both adaptable and adjustable by teachers and pupils so can include almost all of the pupils in a class. It can be done orally as well as through transcription. It can begin from smaller more manageable sentences, growing to more complex structures and include writing practice as part of the activity.

Perhaps even more important, is Bruce Sadler's (2012) observation that it encourages children (and teachers) to develop a playfulness with language. He also emphasises its power as a part-to-whole pedagogy that enables atomised practice of smaller elements of a far more complex whole.

Sentence combining can be done discretely as a short, regular starter, but is easily integrated into English lessons and across the curriculum as a pedagogy or may be used as an effective intervention activity for struggling writers. It is particularly effective during rewriting and revising after composition. This shouldn't need to be said, though experience in education tells us that someone, somewhere is bound to take this too far: it is not the only thing that children should ever do!

Sentence combining can be done orally with children from Reception. This helps develop an understanding that spoken and written language have different structures. Teachers can support this by showing how the sentences are written. Even when children cannot read and write, exemplifying the difference between spoken and written language will support them when they move to writing. Inexperienced writers can experiment with combining two single clause sentences – remember the Lego? Rehearsing this orally exemplifies the concept of spoken and silent rehearsal and starts to build the mental models of text construction required for writing.

For example, the teacher might say:

> The drink is good. The sandwich is good. How could we make these two sentences into one sentence? We might say, 'The drink is good, and the sandwich is good.'

This can be explored further to produce:

> The drink and sandwich are good.
> The sandwich, and the drink are good.

The pupils can try some further examples, discussing their choices with reference to how it makes their writing more interesting or informative for the reader. The teacher might write some of these on the board to show that how it is punctuated and where the capital letter is used – emphasising yet again – will help our reader understand our writing.

This could develop into written work with two sentences:

> Goldilocks was hungry.
> Goldilocks ate the porridge.

This could become:

> Goldilocks was hungry and ate the porridge.

Or:

> Hungry Goldilocks ate the porridge.

Discussion of which of the two children prefer helps develop an ear for the effect of sentence structure on the reader. Sometimes we don't know why we prefer one of two equally grammatical constructions yet have a strong preference. Clare is strongly team 'Goldilocks was hungry' for example, but can't really say why and has a visceral dislike of 'hungry Goldilocks.' Learning that in English, sometimes there are many right answers, and that people express themselves in different ways and have different preferences is part of learning the subject, after all.

Using content learned in lessons will support sentence structure as well as embed the content knowledge. For example, combining the answers to quizzes not only embeds the learned knowledge, it improves sentence structure knowledge.

Sentence combining can be made more challenging as pupils develop their sentence construction skills and are able to use subordinating conjunctions, appositives and relative clauses.

For example, pupils can be given these sentences:

> It was summer.
> The bees were buzzing.
> The bees were in the air.
> There were big ones.
> They were black and yellow.
> They were landing on flowers.
> They flew away.
> They had pollen on their legs.

This might become:

> It was summer and bees were buzzing in the air. There were big ones, and they were black and yellow. After landing on flowers, they flew off with pollen stuck to their legs.

Or:

> It was summer and big, yellow and black bees were buzzing in the air, landing on flowers and flying off with pollen on their legs.

Or:

> Buzzing in the summer air, big black and yellow bees landed on flowers, flying off with pollen on their legs.

Similar activities can be used in other curriculum subjects to create sentences from learned knowledge.

Sentence combining can be used to help pupils develop extending sentences into paragraphs.

For example:

> Walking to school is good for children.
> It is good in many ways.
> Children get exercise.
> They get healthier.
> They don't use cars.
> Walking helps stop pollution.
> This helps the environment.
> Children can meet friends.
> They can speak with friends.
> They become more sociable.

This might become:

> Walking to school is good for children in many ways. Children who walk to school get more exercise, so they become healthier. Furthermore, by not using cars to get to school they help reduce pollution, which is better for the environment. As children walk to school, they can meet up with friends, talk with them and become more sociable.

Sentences and punctuation

Punctuation is crucial to sentence structure and so should be taught in the context of forming sentences. Punctuation indicating sentence boundaries is particularly important for pupils when first encountering sentence construction and when forming the four different types of sentence. Pupils omitting full stops is the bête noire of many a teacher way beyond primary school. Yet we do not put the work in to secure this vital enabler of readability early on, quickly progressing to routinely asking children to compose texts of multiple sentences and then being baffled at their lack of command of the full stop. This is not to say that we should never do extended writing until the full stop is secure, but that extended composition as the mainstay of our teaching before pupils can punctuate a sentence is like learning to drive on a busy dual carriage way before mastering clutch control. You might have some scaffolded practice – the instructor has a dual control car no doubt – but you won't spend most of your lessons there early on.

As pupils start to learn and use more complex sentence structure, they will need to learn how to use an increasing array of punctuation. Developing pupils' understanding of clauses is a very helpful way of building their understanding of internal sentence structure, particularly the variety of uses of commas, colons, semi-colons and parenthesis.

Commas

Commas for lists: A comma is used in lists if it can be replaced by the word 'and' or 'or':

> At the shops we bought some wine, a banana, a large cigar, an onion and some peanuts.

> For a starter we could choose from soup, melon, bread and butter or avocado.

However:

we ordered some French white wine ...

contains no commas as it is not French *and* white *and* wine. There is no intention to form a list.

Commas for joining: Commas are used when two *complete* sentences are joined with the conjunctions 'and', 'but', 'or', 'while' or 'yet':

The teacher wanted the class to be quiet, but the children had eaten chocolate for lunch.

It may be beneficial to teach the joining comma during lessons on the use of conjunctions to join sentences.

Commas used with speech: A comma should be used before speech when the speech appears within a sentence:

He swaggered into the room and announced, 'this is the most beastly day.'

A comma should also be used at the end of speech when the sentence continues:

He swaggered into the room and announced, 'this is the most beastly day,' before vanishing in a puff of smoke.

Commas with connecting adverbs: A comma should be used after the following connectives: 'however', 'anyway', 'on the other hand', 'for example'.

Commas with opening adverbs: A comma should be used after an adverb when the adverb opens the sentence:

Suddenly, John's smile fell from his face.

Silently, he crept down the winding staircase.

Commas that come in pairs (appositives and relative clauses): Commas are used to indicate some additional information. The information can be 'forked' in or out with no loss of meaning to the sentence:

Norman Bates, the young man who ran the motel, always offered guests a shower.

Commas that mark subordinate clauses or non-finite clauses at the beginning of sentences: when a subordinate clause begins a sentence it should be followed by a comma:

> Although it was cold, we didn't wear our coats.

> Striding into the room, Jack was surprised to be faced by his nemesis.

This can be taught when encouraging more complex sentence openers.

Semi-colons, colons and full stops

Semi-colons, colons and full stops are different from commas in that they express a relationship between two sentences (as opposed to clauses.) The choice of which of the three depends on intended effect.

Semi-colons link clauses with the same subject:

> I enjoy playing football; I am just as happy to watch it.

They can also be used to create contrasts:

> Hamlet seems sane at the beginning of the play; by the end he seems deranged.

Notice how swapping the semi-colon with a full stop would not be incorrect but changes the meaning slightly by de-emphasising the connectedness between the clauses. Often the semi-colon indicates a sort of typological 'but'.

A colon reveals what has just been alluded to. It is a way of preparing the reader for the concluding and vital piece of information and then revealing it. Think of it as a typological drum roll:

> He turned the corner and saw the most amazing sight: the Martians had landed.

> For centuries historians have been attempting to answer one question: who murdered the Princes in the Tower?

A colon can also be used to introduce a list or an example:

> I went to the shops and bought the following items: a loaf of bread, a large hat, a sausage and some jam.

A colon is also used to introduce speech in a playscript:

> NORMAN: Would you like a shower?

Parenthesis

We use this when we want to add information to our sentence without interfering with the meaning of the sentence. It is usually achieved by using pairs of **commas**, **dashes** or **brackets**. An economical way of adding detail to a sentence:

> The death of King Harold (1066) marked the end of Saxon rule in England.

> The space shuttle – the first reusable spacecraft – had been NASA's priority after the moon landings.

> Norman Bates, the young man who ran the motel, always offered guests a shower.

Key messages

- Grammar is the common system that organises language communication.

- It is particularly rigid for writing so that readers can expect a consistent approach from all writers.

- Teaching grammar by itself is fairly pointless. It will increase children's knowledge of grammar, but it will not get them to use that in their writing unless they have regular chances to apply that knowledge in their writing. It's about feature use, not just feature spotting.

- The application of grammar is key to improving children's use of it in their writing.

- Improvements in grammar enable children to write with greater clarity and ensure their readers understand what they are trying to say – link it to the non-present reader.

- Syntax is the system we use to organise our words into sentences. It is different for spoken and written communication.

- Becoming adept and fluent at constructing sentences is essential for children to be competent writers. This will take teaching and significant practice.

- Starting by constructing sentences orally, but using the syntax of writing, will develop children's ability to write sentences.

- Children need to understand that a sentence requires an actor and their action – a subject and a verb.

- By building their knowledge of simple and compound sentences and applying this to their writing, children can prepare for developing an understanding and application of complex sentences.

- Compound sentences use coordinating conjunctions to link ideas of equal weight, and complex sentences use subordinating conjunctions to link a main idea with an additional but less important idea.

- Developing a knowledge of subordinating conjunctions helps children understand this difference.

- Elaborating their ideas within a sentence using subordinate clauses, non-finite clauses, appositives and relative clauses encourages children to write with greater fluidity and cohesion.

- Sentence combining activities develop children's competence with the different sentence types, helping them write with greater economy and clarity.

- Sentence combining should be integrated into the teaching of writing and should be regular.

- Punctuation should be taught as part of sentence structure.

Chapter 7
Composition

Tim writes: I learned to write and structure narrative through short stories. I have no idea whether my teacher, Mr Bayfield, had any notion what he was doing. He may have stumbled across a simple, low-effort method of teaching writing, but it worked. He would read us a short story from a vast tome entitled Great British Short Stories. *They were all written by one of the great short story writers – Saki, Du Maurier, Kipling, Sayers, Wilde – and we would then have to write our version of it. He would expect us to change something – the setting, the ending, the characters, the twist – but we followed the same structure as the original. Some turned out better than others, but when we read them out to the class (this was an expectation) they all worked in terms of the plot and narrative – I can still remember my version of* The Monkey's Paw, *and I wrote that over fifty years ago. Perhaps Mr Bayfield was a genius. What he gave us was the highest quality exemplar of a particular narrative as well as a secure (and proven) framework for us to write our stories. And because they were complete stories, we had to plan and write the entire narrative from beginning to end, but because they were* **short** *stories we were able to manage this. When I started teaching, there seemed to be no framework to teach children to write stories (there may have been, but I was pretty clueless), so I used this model for teaching narrative writing almost immediately and even used some of the stories. It seemed to work. I was not so fortunate when it came to non-narrative texts. I always found these difficult to write and even more difficult to teach children to write. There were frameworks (in those enormous and unwieldy books) but there were just so many different structures and models and diagrams for all the different text types. I knew it was confusing for me and even more so for young writers. During one SATs writing test I remember my heart sinking when I helplessly watched a child planning their text using the wrong 'spider diagram' – they were using an explanation text plan rather than a persuasive text plan. They didn't do well despite being a competent writer. My epiphany* *came when someone in the school suggested we just use one planning format for non-narrative text types. We adopted a single, simple structure that worked for all non-fiction text types. We taught it across the whole school, so the only question the children had to ask themselves was 'is this narrative or non-narrative?' rather than 'which of the many planning diagrams am I meant to use?' And when they had to write their first geography essay at secondary school, I knew they would at least be able to structure it well.*

Earnest Hemingway suggested (in his 1932 book *Death in the Afternoon*) that writing was more about architecture than interior design. If no amount of stylish scatter cushions will compensate for an ill-conceived construction, then a well-structured text is, according to Hemingway, probably more effective and readable than a poorly structured text strewn with beautiful language and images. This focus on the overall structure, much of the research suggests, may well get to the heart of teaching children to compose effectively. That is not to say that language and style are not important, but they must support the whole. It seems that as teachers we can often become distracted and enticed by captivating turns of phrase rather than well-formed texts. This being the case, we need to be somewhat modest in the types of text we ask children to compose – think small but well-structured shed (enhanced by scatter cushions) rather than badly designed palace. Which brings us back to the need to share mentor texts as models for writing of the same length as those we want children to write. Which, as we discussed in chapter 5, means that a novel studied to teach reading will not be a good model for teaching writing composition. The scale is all wrong.

The construction analogy appears a lot in the language of writing research and instruction. We saw in chapter 6 that clauses *build* sentences and that sentences are the *building blocks* of writing. However, teaching children to write is not merely a question of placing one block of learning onto another – or joining one sentence to another. As we learn, we encounter gaps in our knowledge and knots in our understanding. Children will naturally attempt to fill these gaps, but it is far more effective if we know where and when many of the gaps are likely to appear. We can then construct relevant scaffolds (more construction analogy) and bridges to cross the void.

As mentioned, one of the most clearly evident gaps appears when children move from developing competence in transcription and sentence construction and start to encounter the complexities of composing longer texts.

As children start to transcribe with greater automatisation and are able to form sentences with more fluency, the demands these elements place on working memory reduce. You would imagine that this enables children to bring more cognitive attention to bear on composition. However, according to Liliana Tolchinsky (2016), this does not seem to be borne out by the research. They can certainly produce *more* text, but the overall *quality* does not seem to improve. She suggests that this is a structural issue. There is a qualitative gap between writing letters, words and sentences, and composing texts that are able to satisfy the vast array of communicative purposes required when we write – in other words, they can put lots of bricks together but end up with a large wall rather than a house. It may be helpful to draw a parallel with art: there is a significant difference (gap) between being highly proficient at the skills required to draw and paint, and the ability to apply those skills in the construction of an affecting composition.

Tolchinsky highlights the dilemma for children learning to compose written texts and teachers teaching this: the features of the whole text have to *gain control* over the more local elements of language choices, sentence structure and grammar. What this means is that writers have to *gain control* over the **macro structure** of their texts because it is this structure that will inform the **micro-structure decisions**. So, to extend Hemingway's analogy, the interior design decisions in every room must be subservient to the overall purpose of the building and the room…the scatter cushions have to be an integral part of the room informed by its purpose and structure and not an attractive distraction from its poor design.

But of course, we have, necessarily, taught the micro structures first.

Once again, we can see the cognitive load that writing exerts. Not only must the writer consider the words, the sentences, the grammar and the language they are producing, but they must also relate all of these choices to the overall structure and purpose required for any specific text… and all at the same time. And it is the macro structure that informs the local decisions.

What this means for us as teachers is that we must provide emergent writers with very clear, reliable and flexible macro structures that will serve the purposes and goals of the text types that they will be composing. But attending to these structures and goals while composing must inform local decisions and not overwhelm the writer. We are in essence (once again) supporting the management of the cognitive load by reducing the burden associated with managing that macro structure.

We do this by building secure but adaptable mental representations of structures – if we know the structure of a two storey, two-bedroom house, we can probably adapt that structure into a two-bedroom bungalow. What we will find more difficult, is to modify the model into a temple or mausoleum.

Mental models and writing

Philip Johnson-Laird (1983) suggested that much of our understanding of the world is assisted by the mental models we develop to help us make sense of complex, changeable phenomena. Helping children build mental models of written communication is key to developing their ability to manage complex text structures. So, we not only need to promote automaticity and fluency in transcription and sentence structure, but we also need to build mental models of how whole texts work and are adapted to achieve different purposes. If we don't do this, we risk children not bridging that gap between writing sentences and composing texts; the local structures dominate the whole and we end up with a long train of sentences – that long wall of bricks!

Ruth Berman and Bracha Nir-Sagiv (2007) found that pupils' progress in developing mental representations of text structures is different for different structures. Although by the age of nine most children can include all of the functional elements of narratives, it can take until adolescence for pupils to have developed the same competency for non-narrative texts. This is due in great part to the greater complexity of language and syntax required for expository writing. It is, therefore, important that we expose children to a balance of narrative and non-narrative text types both in their reading and writing with a growing focus on non-narrative as they move through primary school (without losing narrative writing).

A focus on the goal and purpose of a text not only supports conceptual understanding of different text structures but helps develop the concept of the non-present reader. Within a primary writing curriculum, the majority of texts fall within one of four categories: to entertain, to inform, to persuade or to discuss. Merely by categorising texts we are supporting children's concept of different macro structures and decisions about purpose and goals.

Categories of text structure by purpose

To inform

- Simple recount
- Report
- Letter
- Instructions
- Explanation
- Biography
- Blog/article

To discuss

- Discussion
- Argument
- Balanced argument

To entertain

- Stories – fiction and non-fiction
- Play
- Poetry
- Characters/settings

To persuade

- Letter
- Speech
- Advertisement
- Campaign

It is not necessary or even desirable for children to have written texts in all of these different text types by the end of primary school – that is where the National Strategy went wrong with its mania for genres. Children learned so many that they never got the opportunity to become good at any of them. They do need to have studied them in their reading curriculum though, laying the ground for secondary school when they can be challenged further. There will be overlaps between these purposes and it is important that the concept of engaging the reader (entertaining or informing them in other words) is a thread that runs through all writing and not just narrative writing. When pupils enter secondary school where disciplinary writing and a focus on genre have greater emphasis, having strong mental models of text structured by purpose will support this memory demand – lots of scatter cushions leaning against a wall.

So, it is important for primary school teachers to be aware of the tension between local and macro structures. If we focus solely on the local elements of writing (transcription, grammar and sentence structure), children will not develop the mental representations of the macro structures on which these local decisions depend.

The writing process then becomes dominated by writing words rather than crafting texts.

The importance of the early years of education in developing mental models of written structures cannot be overstated. Prior to the development of transcription skills, young children can still compose – try stopping them creating narratives! This will mainly be done orally, for example, through the kind of story telling advocated by the Talk for Writing approach or through helicopter stories or using digital apps such as Chatta. Alongside oral work, transcribing some elements of their spoken narratives for them to see that their words can be written and become permanent is vital for print awareness. We know that children develop stronger mental models of narrative structures because they experience them more. Experiencing non-narrative structures in the early years will support initial mental model building. Recording both spoken narrative and non-narrative communication into more formal written structures and being explicit about these structures will support these mental models once transcription has been sufficiently mastered.

The writing process

It was, for a long time, felt that writing was a linear process – a series of stages that were undergone to produce a text. The writer had an idea that they wanted to communicate in print, they planned out what they wanted to write, wrote it down and then read it through and made some edits and revisions. That is certainly how it was taught…and often still is.

In the early 1980s, psychologists John Hayes and Linda Flower (1980) proposed a radically different perspective. They acknowledged that planning and drafting and revising were all parts of the process, but they submitted that the process was not linear. They suggested that writing is a distinctive set of thinking processes that interact during the act of composing. We start with a writing goal but as we write, our goals change as the macro interacts with the local. These may be changes in the overall goal or changes to the smaller supporting sub goals. We may, as a result of what we have learned as part of the writing process, establish a whole new set of goals.

If you think back to any of your writing at school or university, how often did the final piece reflect the original idea or plan? We are often drafting small pieces as we plan; replanning as we revise and edit as we discover some new and relevant information; and editing as we write. Sometimes we just start over again – back to the 'messiness' of writing. What this means for the teaching of writing is that we cannot merely encourage children to follow a linear path – plan your text, follow the plan then revise it and check it – a nice five lesson sequence. We have to help them to develop an understanding of this messiness and teach strategies that help them cope with but embrace it. Remember back to chapter 2 where we explored the phenomenon that the mere act of composition is a cognitive phenomenon that helps solve many of the problems we may face, and have set ourselves, while we were planning.

So, the writing process looks more like this:

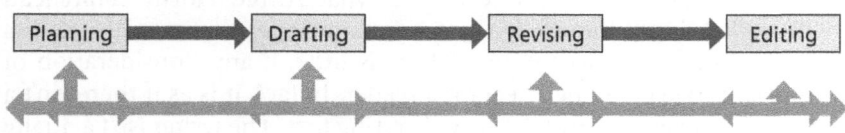

But even this is a little too neat and linear. If you mapped the thought and process lines of a writer composing it would probably look like a Gordian knot with those golden macro threads of 'purpose' and 'goals' running throughout it all.

You may be thinking that if you were able to get your pupils to plan a piece of writing, follow the plan and then check what they'd written for accuracy and grammatical correctness then you'd be pretty happy. Certainly, for early attempts at composition this is no bad strategy. And it is important, according to Ronald Kellogg (1994), that each phase will need to be completed for a written outcome to be produced. It is also important that our pupils are aware of these phases when they are considering and producing written compositions. But you can't fight the cognitive processes. Even novice writers will want to adapt their goals as they write – it's one of the beauties of writing…we just can't help thinking when we do it. The process is never going to be linear because thinking is not linear. And there is one big reason that writers are constantly reviewing their goals.

The reason we've rewritten, revised and edited this page (and every other page) so many times is you…the reader – that non-present presence that is the reason we write. We have to make sure it's clear, coherent and unified – that is our overall goal, and this goal throws up many problems we have to solve. We have been backwards and forwards. We have revised, changed and changed back again. We have taken out bits we love but that were just pretty flannel scatter cushions and replaced them with less fancy sentences that are just much clearer.

We have mentioned, in earlier chapters, the seminal work of psychologists Carl Bereiter and Marlene Scardamalia (1987). They argue that novice writers adopt a simple 'knowledge telling' approach to composition. Essentially, the novice writer merely writes down the knowledge they possess on a subject in an attempt to communicate that information and knowledge (you will see this in many of your pupils' work). The knowledge they are communicating is what Alfred North Whitehead (1929) called 'inert' knowledge – that is knowledge that we can express but can't transform into any use. There is little, if any, consideration of appropriate style or of the effect on a reader. In fact, it is as if there isn't a reader; it's just writing stuff down, generating text. The writer isn't actually doing anything with their knowledge other than expressing it.

In other words, they are considering only what to say.

Bereiter and Scardamalia give an example of a child who follows this approach:

I have a whole bunch of ideas and I write down until my supply of ideas is exhausted. Then I might try to think of more ideas up to the point when you can't get any more ideas that are worth putting down on paper and then I would end it. (Bereiter and Scardamalia, 1987)

Remind you of any of your pupils? This child is making decisions at a local level. There is no consideration of the macro structure and no consideration of the purpose or the reader. Bereiter and Scardamalia (1987) suggest that many writers never get beyond this approach to composition. What they urge us to do is to help our pupils develop a 'knowledge transforming' approach to writing.

Knowledge transforming, in contrast to knowledge telling, is a problem-solving process whereby the writer establishes a series of goals and then solves the problems associated with achieving these goals as part of the writing process. So, the knowledge transforming writer develops a mental model of the assignment (the macro structure) and will consider the style required, the major content points that need to be communicated, the amount of time they have to write it – and all this with a focus on the reader. Their knowledge is synthesised into achieving the goals.

In other words, why they want to say something (macro), what to say (local), how to say it (local) and to whom to say it (macro). Not a bad checklist for approaching any written undertaking. However, consider how this actually plays out in a classroom where statutory assessment requirements rule the roost. Why do I want to say something? Because Miss/Sir has told me to write it. What am I going to say? Whatever it is my teacher has told me to write. How am I going to say it? In a way that ticks off stuff on the mark scheme. Whom am I saying it to? My teacher, duh!

Bereiter and Scardamalia (1987) do not separate the two approaches but see one building on the other as writers develop. We all tend to use knowledge telling at the beginning of an assignment as we collate our understanding and data before we consider how to relate it to our goals. Many competent writers do a 'knowledge dump' as a strategy for getting going. Importantly for teaching, Bereiter and Scardamalia (1987) are adamant that a knowledge transforming approach to writing is not the preserve of the great literary genius. Their research suggests that it is more to do with mindset than literary merit. Perfectly ordinary but adequate writers can adopt the knowledge transforming mindset, while writers with great turns of phrases and vocabulary don't necessarily achieve it – Hegel was accused of slapping together sense-less, raving tangles of verbiage. What the knowledge transforming writer asks themselves is, 'What do I want to say, have I written what I want to say, and do I believe it?' These writers will consider changes not only to the text (local) but also changes in what they want to say (macro). Their writing plays a role in developing their own knowledge, solving the problems of communicating their message to their readers and thereby achieving the goals.

Because we as teachers are in the knowledge business, Bereiter and Sardamalia (1987) believe we should be explicit about developing knowledge transforming approaches to writing. They argue that it is helpful if we make our pupils aware of the full extent of the composition process and help them to ultimately manage the process independently. This will lead them away from seeing writing as merely putting words on paper and towards seeing it as a process driven by goals and overcoming problems and gaining and communicating knowledge. So, if we're going to make the writing process more explicit for our pupils, let's go back and take a closer look.

Planning

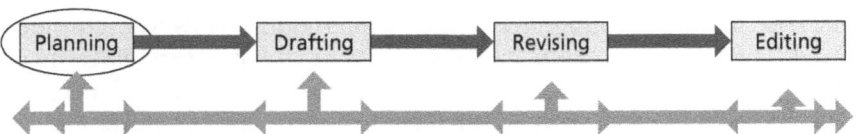

It may surprise you to learn that the research around the effectiveness of constructing a deliberate, physical plan prior to writing is not conclusive. In fact, psychologist Mark Torrence (2016) suggests that much of the research indicates that writers who make substantial and methodical plans prior to writing end up incorporating significant amounts of content that they never included in the plan. There is even some evidence to suggest that too much deliberate planning can inhibit the creative 'flow' identified by Csikszentmihalyi and Csikszentmihalyi (1988).

But here's the rub…and it's an important one: these are experienced and competent writers. Steve Graham and his colleagues' research (2012) was very clear: novice writers improve the quality of their writing when they have been supported through a thorough and structured planning phase and produce a physical plan.

Teaching children how to plan texts develops an essential writing strategy: the understanding that planning is one of the phases of the composing process (whether this is a physical plan or a mental plan). It also develops the important concept in writing of self-regulation (managing one's own goals) by ensuring the writer considers the writing purpose and goal at the start of the process. Steve Graham (2012) is adamant that considering one's writing goals is one of the most effective strategies for writers to produce quality work. A plan provides less confident pupils with a basis from which to start writing rather than staring at a blank page.

Perhaps most importantly, it develops mental models of the macro structures of the whole composition because the structure of the whole composition can literally be viewed in the plan. But it is important to remember, and to remind children, that the plan is not the text. As philosopher Alfred Korzybski (1933) famously stated, 'The map is not the territory, but …', and this is important for planning writing (and often left off the quote), '… if correct, it has a similar structure to the territory, which accounts for its usefulness.' Or to put it more prosaically, the recipe is not the dish, but it's pretty difficult to make the dish without the recipe, especially if you've never made it before and you're not Michel Roux.

It is also important, Mark Torrence (2016) reminds us, to remember that the planning phase is not only about planning a structure for the whole text at the *beginning* of the process. We plan *throughout* the writing process. Sentences are planned and rehearsed prior to transcription. Paragraphs are planned in detail prior to their composition (more on the importance of this later). These planning sub-processes keep acting and interacting throughout the whole writing process – hence its non-linear nature.

When children start to engage with written composition, they will need support collecting and recording the relevant information and personalising that information in a form that they can use in their writing.

We can support children with collecting by:

• Accessing relevant experiences and information through shared talk.

• Directing children to sources of relevant information, such as books, illustrations, images and media.

• Banking and displaying collected knowledge and ideas.

• Encouraging the personalisation and ownership of the knowledge and ideas to build strong mental representations.

So, a teacher might use children's sensory experiences and photographs to collect ideas and details to be used in the composition of poems inspired by a season. Sounds are recorded, smells logged and colours from photographs of autumnal scenes charted, and temperatures, feelings and weather conditions are discussed and noted by the teacher. Objects are collected. Much discussion and collaborative talk adds language ideas and vocabulary to the collection. The collection of all ideas and sensory records is stored both digitally and in written form. By explaining that the collected ideas and resources are to be used for a written outcome, the teacher is helping to link the collection element to the process of composition and begins creating mental representations. Working memory is managed by the use of physical, written and digital stores. Planned, directed and structured talk further supports the management of cognitive load and the harvesting of language by the teacher models note-taking as part of the process. The use of a variety of collection opportunities models the rich variety of sources that experienced writers access prior to planning and translation.

But collecting information, although important for writers, is not sufficient for a plan. Generating ideas, organising those ideas into a structure and creating goals and purpose are all part of planning. For children, learning how to plan offers a place to record ideas. It should also offer a structure to organise their writing, thereby providing a macro scaffold for when they translate these ideas into written text. It helps develop vital mental models of different writing forms and purposes and how to structure them, building more secure mental representations for the future. Children have to build mental models across a number of text types, not only for applying throughout their academic life, but also for their personal use. Planning structures can support this.

Teachers can support children's planning by:

- Providing a model for the recording of the ideas generated in the collecting stage of planning.

- Exemplifying how a model plan relates to a model text and supports writing, such as through guided writing by the teacher and purposely retrofitting a text into a planning structure.

- Providing a model plan outline and supporting children to complete a useful structure for their writing.

So, a teacher might write a model text recounting their own visit to a museum. They might include cohesive chronological devices and time adverbial phrases throughout their text. They would then highlight and draw out the devices and create a planning structure from the text. By extracting the plan from the text, the teacher deliberately links the drafting element of the writing process to the planning element, highlighting how the plan translates into text – how the composition became manifest as part of a process. The teacher has thereby created a model for planning for the pupils, highlighting the separate elements (often paragraphs) that form a cohesive macro structure for when they start to plan their own chronological recount of their class trip – how the map relates to the terrain.

Narrative planning

Children have better developed mental representations of narrative structures than non-narrative. They still, however, need to go through the planning phase and have a sense that they have planned the macro structure. The plots of stories can be very complex. If, however, we are to build a strong and flexible mental model of story writing for children we need to follow Mortimer Adler and Charles Van Doren's mantra (1972) of 'clarity, coherence and unity'. This can be supported by the use of a single macro narrative framework that can be applied across a whole school. It can flex to incorporate more elements as pupils become more confident, but the principal structure can be maintained.

The particular model selected is not important (the story mountain, the story box, the story hand) as long as:

- It is taught consistently across the school (clarity).

- It includes the main elements of narrative (some form of orientation for the story, a problem or complication that creates a conflict for the protagonist and a resolution).

- The elements of the narrative structure link together (the orientation sets up the complication/problem/conflict which is ultimately resolved in the end – coherence and unity).

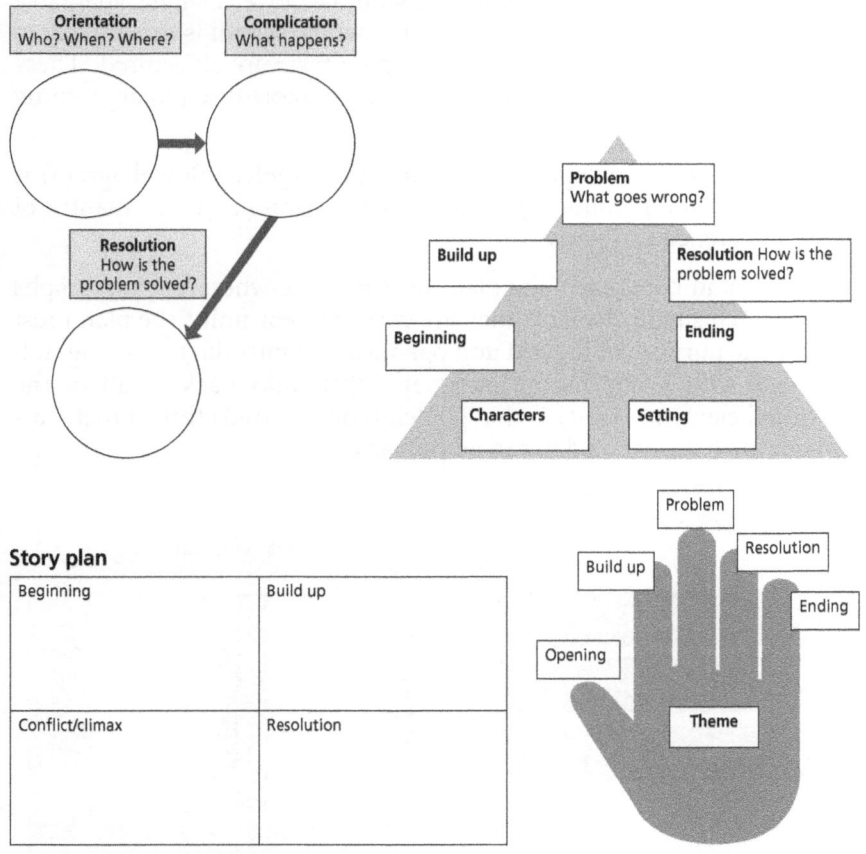

At the early stages of composition, each single element will probably be a sentence or two. As pupils become more confident and have more detail they want to add, this will develop into single paragraphs and then perhaps more paragraphs. Each paragraph will need planning in detail to ensure each element is fully developed.

Non-narrative planning

Not only will pupils have less well-developed mental models of non-narrative texts, but non-narrative texts are more complex, perform many different purposes and apply to different disciplines. Selecting from an array of non-narrative planning frameworks can be confusing and unhelpful for novice writers. Again, as with narrative, a single, adaptable framework used and developed across the whole school is more likely to develop secure mental models of how these texts are structured. These models can then be adapted as pupils encounter more disciplinary writing in secondary school.

Which framework is adopted (the burger, the temple, a flow diagram) is not as important as following Adler and Van Doren's (1972) mantra of clarity, coherence and unity.

For clarity and coherence, the plan must indicate where the paragraphs fit and which single elements they are covering. For unity, the plan must indicate the purpose of the text and open with an introductory paragraph and close with a concluding paragraph that links back to all of the individual elements. Unity is that golden (goal-centred) thread that runs through the text…a goalden thread perhaps?

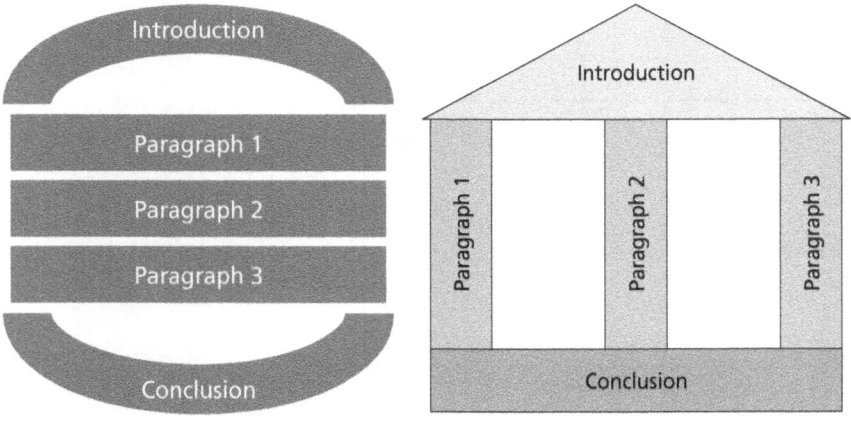

1. Plan the introduction

What is the topic about?

....

....

....

2. Plan the meat of the text

<u>Paragraph 1</u>

Main point _____ Elaborating point 1. _____
Elaborating point 2. _____
Elaborating point 3. _____

<u>Paragraph 2</u>

Main point _____ Elaborating point 1. _____
Elaborating point 2. _____
Elaborating point 3. _____

<u>Paragraph 3</u>

Main point _____ Elaborating point 1. _____
Elaborating point 2. _____
Elaborating point 3. _____

3. Plan the conclusion

Restate the topic

....

Refer to some of the points mentioned

....

Provide closure

....

Drafting – translating the ideas from planning to text

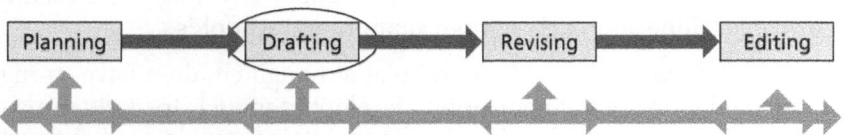

You may well be an excellent artist, but if you are not, you will appreciate the frustration many of us feel being unable to turn our breathtaking mental images into the equivalent magnificent oil painting. We can, similarly, underestimate the challenge of translating ideas for writing into text. One of the reasons is that planning to write is not writing – the map is not the territory! The recipe is not the dish. Something has to be done to achieve the end purpose…and it is usually hard work. There has to be an element of self-trust that the written language we choose to turn our ideas into text will become manifest. Michel Fayol (2016) reminds us that experienced writers understand this and expect and anticipate that it will occur, but that for novice writers, that self-trust will be at best weak and at worst verging on self-doubt. Children will need support, encouragement…and plenty of time translating the ideas in their plans into a draft.

This translating process has two components:

1. **The development of the plan into a mental representation that has the potential to be expanded into a written text.** The text in the plan is not the text. It is not merely a case of transferring the words – many children often do this. There is a cognitive stage here whereby the writer mentally develops the plan into something more purposeful and closer to the goal. For example, before adults write a letter of complaint, they will have a good mental idea of what the complaint aims to achieve and the structure of how it will be developed and the language and tone necessary to achieve the desired outcome.

2. **The transcribing of that mental model into text using words, sentences and paragraphs.** This is where the letter of complaint is actually written. And this is where the words come out…and the trenches are dug!

Adult writers have far richer and more elaborate mental models of text production than children because they have more experience of writing different texts. Lucile Chanquoy and her team (2002) have shown that the more familiar we are with the type of text, the faster the process of translating our plans into that text. We write lots of emails, so we tend to translate our ideas into this type of text pretty quickly. Although even very young children have mental models of some written forms these may not be sufficiently well-developed for them to adopt anything more than a knowledge telling approach without support and scaffolds.

Michel Fayol's research (2016) found that although children have strong mental models for oral composition, developing models for written text types is much more challenging. So, he maintains, pupils need support moving from the translation of ideas orally to the translation of ideas into writing.

Translating ideas into writing poses new and unique constraints for children:

- A reader who is not present and can disengage at any time.
- Less frequently encountered and more precise vocabulary.
- A different syntactic structure.
- Differing tone creation techniques in place of vocal changes and non-verbal cues.
- A variety of structure expectations from the reader.

Fayol (2016) recommends that to promote the effective translation of children's ideas into written text they will need support in three key areas: knowledge, connectedness and writing strategies.

Knowledge

Translation of ideas into text draws on three types of knowledge for a writer: content knowledge (what they are writing about); language knowledge (what language, grammar and sentence structures are appropriate for the text) and procedural knowledge (handwriting and spelling). The more familiar children are with the content knowledge, domain knowledge, text type knowledge, language knowledge, and the more automatic is their handwriting and spelling prior to translation, the higher will be the text's quality.

The old adage of 'write about what you know' could not be more apt than for a novice writer. Remember that knowledge from long-term memory supports the load placed on working memory when we write. Even if pupils are still adopting a 'knowledge telling' approach, the results will be far more successful if they have some knowledge to tell. And it goes without saying that it is impossible to transform knowledge into something fresh with little or no knowledge to start with. If children are to write successfully, much of this knowledge will need collecting in the initial planning phase. That is as important for content knowledge as for language knowledge – children cannot grasp new and appropriate language and vocabulary from thin air, they either have to encounter it regularly or be given it to learn and use. And remember that the writing process is not linear. Content and language knowledge can be gleaned and added at any stage of the writing process and sharing that knowledge through collaborative opportunities supports all.

Using pupils' knowledge from other curriculum areas enables them to access concrete knowledge, helps them manage the working memory load and supports the memorisation and understanding of that knowledge. What's not to like?

Connectedness

Well-written texts are well connected texts. Bereiter and Scardamalia (1987) believed that the creation of greater connectedness within a text indicated a greater awareness of the needs of the reader and a development of a knowledge transforming approach to writing. Philip Durrant and his team (2021) found that texts that received higher marks in exams had a greater number of cohesive devices. Clearly, shoehorning cohesive devices per se won't improve a text; they are there to help the non-present reader make sense of and stay engaged with what they are reading. Often overlooked, the concept of providing readers with clear markers throughout a text is an essential skill for coherent text production. These textual road signs remind the reader where they have come from, which character is being referred to, what has just happened and what might be coming up. Without this vital information readers can become confused as to what is going on.

Fayol (2016) suggests that we should not underestimate their importance when teaching writing and recommends teaching the use of these markers from when children start to compose (orally initially). Teaching, highlighting, analysing and providing markers at all stages of the writing process, he maintains, helps children manage the complexity of translating and connecting ideas in text and ensuring coherence for that non-present reader.

At the macro level, chronology lines, paragraph intentions, narrative lines and character maps all provide markers for children in the planning phase and ensure greater cohesion when they start drafting. At the local level, explicitly identifying opportunities for adding clarity through connectedness in the revising phase will greatly enhance the coherence of a written text, and help keep the reader in mind and a young writer's focus on their writing goals.

Coherence and cohesion

Scott Crossley and Danielle McNamara's (2011) research reveals that one of the strongest indicators of whether writing is considered higher quality is its level of coherence. Coherence is the consistency, continuity and co-ordination within a text. The more coherent a reader finds a text, the more successful that written discourse has been.

Becoming aware of coherence within their written work is therefore essential as young writers develop their composition skills. However, whether a piece of writing is coherent or not is a decision made by the reader not the writer. It is the reader's subjective experience of whether the text is sufficiently well-connected and how that links with their own knowledge as to whether the text delivers them meaning. So, coherence depends on the background knowledge, motivation and purposes that readers bring to the text – readers we don't know, so we have to make decisions in their absence. *You* will decide whether this book is coherent, *not* us.

Again, we find a tension between the micro and a macro structure: how well do individual sentences link together at a local level (local coherence) and how does each sentence contribute to the overall unity of the piece (topic coherence)?

To produce coherent texts, writers must have their purpose and readership in mind – the importance of acknowledging that non-present reader. The writer has to keep in mind not only the readership's potential knowledge and motivation for reading the text but must also provide a sense of connectedness between different elements of a text. This connectedness unifies the text and prevents it from appearing to the reader to be a random collection of incoherent ideas.

Although readers decide whether a text is coherent, writers can create connectedness and cohesion through the use of cohesive devices.

The use of cohesive devices in a text does not automatically infuse the writing with coherence, but their use does correlate with higher quality writing and greater coherence, especially in children's writing according to Linda Struthers (2017). Furthermore, Bereiter and Scardamalia (1987) believed that a growing use of cohesive devices indicates a move towards knowledge transforming writing with a maturing understanding that the writer's message requires markers to guide the reader.

So, we need to teach these. As Virginia Berninger (1999) warned: if school-aged children have not learned these structures and are unable to retrieve them when writing, then they will be unable to manipulate these devices intentionally when composing.

Cohesive devices

Michael Halliday and Ruqaiya Hasan (1976) developed a model for cohesion which suggested that there are a number of cohesive devices that children need to develop to establish cohesion in their spoken and written English and that can be explicitly taught. These should be developed initially within the sentence level aspect of the curriculum in order that they can then be used for authentic communicative purposes in more extended texts. These include:

1. **Reference** uses pronouns and determiners to refer the reader back to information previously mentioned and enhance local connectedness:

   - Mary sniffed the air. *She* could smell perfume.

   - Let's see *that* film again.

2. **Conjunctions** link ideas across phrases, clauses and sentences and also enhance local connectedness:

   - Mary sniffed the air, *but* she could smell nothing.

   - We watched the film again *because* we loved it.

3. **Adverbial phrases** indicate to the reader where, why, how or when the action in the sentence is occurring and enhance local and topic connectedness. They are vital for creating mental models of a text for readers and are significant aids to coherence:

   - *Shortly after midnight*, the army attacked.

   - *On the banks of the river*, the army attacked.

   - *With great stealth*, the army attacked.

   - *To avenge the earlier defeat*, the army attacked.

4. **Connecting adverbs** provide a way of transitioning between two ideas and enhance local connectedness across sentences and topic coherence across paragraphs – moreover, meanwhile, next, then, instead, finally, nonetheless:

   - I was waiting at the clock for my aunt. *Meanwhile*, my aunt was waiting at the library.

   - I was very nervous before the exam. *Nonetheless*, I passed.

5. **Lexical cohesion** uses related words throughout a text to help both local and topic cohesion and includes:

   a. Repetition of the same word

      - The *Thames* is a river in *London*. The *Thames* is the vein of *London*.

  b. Use of synonyms

  - The Thames is a *river* in *London*. It is the main *waterway* through *the capital*.

  c. Use of antonyms, complementary terms, converses throughout the text:

  - hot–cold, sand–beach, ask–answered.

6. **Substitution** uses a generic term to avoid repetition:

- He really wanted an *ice cream*. He got *one*.

7. **Ellipsis** eliminates elements with no loss of meaning as the meaning is implied and clear:

- He was going to go but [*he*] didn't [*go*].

8. **Consistent use of verb tense:** is particularly important across cohesive markers where inconsistency of tenses dramatically undermines coherence for readers.

Lynda Struthers (2017) found that pupils developing the use of cohesive devices in their writing tend to start by using reference and conjunctions before then integrating lexical cohesion. Children find the use of substitution and ellipsis more demanding as this requires greater vocabulary and confidence with sentence structure. Sentence combining activities therefore greatly enhance cohesion at a local level. Furthermore, and importantly for teaching writing, children are far more confident identifying the need for the inclusion of cohesive devices at the reviewing stage of the writing process rather than in the drafting stage. Cohering and connecting text in the moment of writing places a significant load on a young writer's working memory. This doesn't mean they can't manage cohesion; it just means that it is often easier to manage after a bit of drafting. But we must remember to remind them to do it; reminding them to apply what they have previously learned when working on deliberately crafting sentences.

Pupils with learning disabilities and particularly those with language learning disabilities as well as poor readers exhibit far fewer cohesive devices in their writing, which is one of the reasons their writing is often *assessed* as lower quality. These pupils will need extensive explicit instruction and practice in the use of cohesive devices to enhance their writing. They are unlikely to adopt their use through statistical learning alone. Again, adding these connections after drafting is far more likely to be effective rather than expecting them to be included at the moment of writing – working memory again!

We have omitted one cohesive device from the list. We feel that it is so important that it warrants a section all of its own.

Paragraphs

If sentences are the building blocks of writing, paragraphs are the individual elements that the blocks construct. Together they form the whole edifice.

Sticking with our building analogy, take a look at this railway viaduct. It has a clear purpose – to get the train across the gorge – and the whole, rather beautiful but quite intricate, structure enables that purpose to be achieved in a balanced and coherent way. It is built using tiny, innumerable, individual bricks. But it has smaller structural units of differing sizes that bind together to form the whole structure – the arches. They form a link between the numerous bricks and the overall structure.

Like paragraphs in texts, they are instrumental in bridging the gap between whole structure and the micro structures. These linking structures – paragraphs – are particularly important for novice writers who will not have the stamina or cognitive muscle to write at length (they probably won't be writing chapter books) so will be more dependent on paragraphs to structure their whole text.

Judith Hochman and Natalie Wexler (2017) in *The Writing Revolution* spend as many pages developing the teaching of paragraphs as they do on sentence structure. They maintain that effective paragraphing is essential for composing complex, coherent texts. Furthermore, they assert that children gain a sense of pride and confidence from crafting logically sequenced paragraphs that communicate their ideas coherently.

Sentence structure and paragraphing are clearly interlinked (bricks make arches), and Hochman and Wexler (2017) warn that effective paragraphs require secure sentence structure if mechanical errors are not to overwhelm writing – great bricklaying creates secure arches. They go on to emphasise that for children to gain a sense of pride and confidence in creating paragraphs with secure sentence structure, both will need to be taught and there will need to be plenty of practice. Joan Sedita (2023) is similarly exercised by the importance of explicitly teaching pupils how to organise their writing into paragraphs.

But what exactly is a paragraph? We often feel that we inherently know what one is. We can certainly get a sense of them from all of our reading and often assume that we naturally absorb an understanding of their structure in this way. If we need to teach the construct directly, then it would be useful to have a definition. Enter linguist Robert Longacre (1979) with the clearest of definitions. He maintained that a paragraph in non-fiction writing was a grammatical unit characterised by four main characteristics:

1. **Closure:** A sentence introduces the paragraph and a sentence that relates to the idea introduced in the opening sentence ends it.
2. **Thematic unity:** The paragraph is constructed around *one main topic*.
3. **Hierarchical organisation:** The *one main topic* sits at the top of the hierarchy, with all other statements and elaborations occupying subordinate positions.
4. **Recursivity:** It follows the model of how a paragraph is expected to work and appear.

For children this equates to:

- Paragraphs are about one element of the whole text *and only one.*
- Paragraphs always start with a clear introductory sentence to that one element.
- The following sentences elaborate upon that element until it is fully explained.
- A final sentence concludes the paragraph by wrapping up the idea and relating back to the introductory sentence creating a sense of unity.
- Paragraphs have to look like paragraphs.

Sedita (2023) simplifies this into:

- A topic sentence.
- Supporting sentences.
- A concluding sentence.

She also gives a couple of useful visual representations for a paragraph:

- **A burger**, where the top bun is the topic sentence and the bottom bun the concluding sentence, with the different layers in the middle being the elaborating sentences.

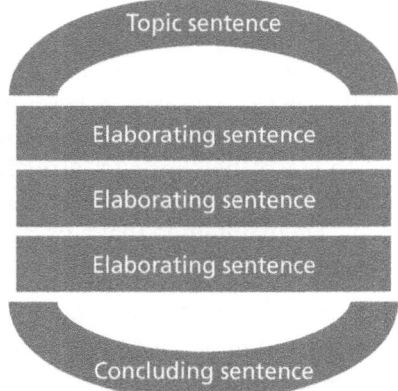

- **A temple**, where the roof is the topic sentence, the foundations the concluding sentence and the pillars the elaborating sentences.

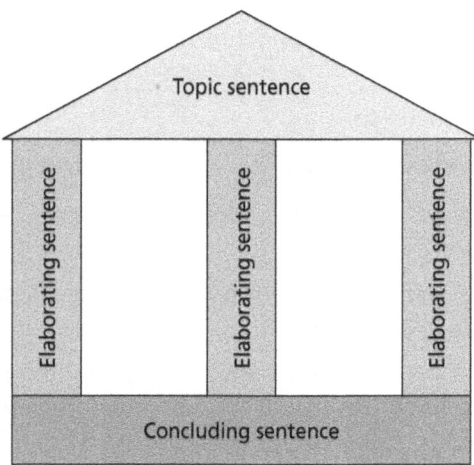

This dovetails nicely with Hochman and Wexler's (2017) paragraph plan (the dotted lines signify notes, rather than complete sentences):

Paragraph plan

Opening sentence: Introduce the main idea of the paragraph

....

....

....

Additional information, in sequence

1. ....

2. ....

3. ....

4. ....

Concluding sentence

....

....

These, of course, relate to non-narrative writing. What about paragraphs in narrative writing?

The narrative writer clearly has much more flexibility (and fewer rules) in the use and effect of paragraphs but that can overwhelm a novice writer. Here are the accepted (but not universal) reasons for starting a new paragraph in narrative writing:

- When the story moves on in time.

- When a new character is introduced to the scene.

- When the location changes.

- When another character speaks.

- For dramatic effect – single word or single sentence paragraphs.

So, when we teach written composition, it will be helpful for us to hold the importance of the paragraph front and centre. Much of children's success understanding composition and actually writing texts will relate to planning, constructing and writing paragraphs.

Paragraphs are the key link between the micro and the macro structures of writing for two vital reasons:

1. Sentences usually don't form a whole text. Sentences make paragraphs and paragraphs make up a whole text. While short picture books buck this trend, typically paragraphs are the link between the local and the whole.

2. The structure of a non-narrative paragraph is the same as a whole non-narrative text. Both require an introduction. Both require a conclusion. The individual elements (points and elaboration) are separate and distinct but integral. A paragraph is a model of a whole text. Nice!

Writing strategy development

Barry Zimmerman and Rafael Risemberg (1997) argued that writing was affected by a writer's self-regulatory skills: how we, personally, approach and manage the writing task. They maintained that there were always personalised social, emotional, and motivational forces at play. After all, if writing is so demanding, then how we manage ourselves during the process is going to be pretty important. Zimmerman and Riesemberg's (1997) self-regulatory model has been highly influential and has been analysed by a considerable body of research. It is extremely useful for us as teachers because it highlights specific areas of pedagogy that can influence the quality of children's writing and their development as individual writers. In other words, we can help children learn strategies and approaches that writers use and, here's the important bit, then apply them to themselves as writers.

Children can be taught:

- Writing can be slowed down, paused, or even halted, while reflection occurs (this is seldom the case in talk).

- Writing is a social activity and collaboration improves writing. Assistance can be sought during writing from multiple sources. In class this may be the teacher or peers. Elements can be read out loud to peers and collaborators for feedback.

- Writing can be temporarily interrupted and returned to (seldom possible when talking). Returning to the problem after time away and viewing it afresh, often helps solve the problem.

- Collecting new information can occur at any time during the writing process.

- During writing the text can be easily reviewed and changed in order to improve it – unlike talk, which is almost always irreversible. Children can find the erasability of writing, or the freedom of drafting liberating and motivating – nothing written during the process needs to be permanent.

- Sentences can be altered and adjusted.

- Paragraphs can be left blank and returned to if the writer is unsure how to approach them.

- Endings can be written before openings.

- Characters can be deleted.

Strategy instruction

Steve Graham and his colleagues (2019) analysed much of the data around Zimmerman and Risemberg's (1997) models, synthetising them into the most effective strategies for teaching writing. They concluded that the explicit teaching of many of these writing strategies has been shown to be effective to help pupils manage, create and improve writing and the explicit instruction of them is associated with highly effective teaching.

They recommend that strategy instruction occurs across the whole writing process. One of the most important elements of strategy instruction is helping children to understand but manage the 'messiness' of the writing process. For strategy instruction to be effective and to embed into long-term memory (and thereby support working memory), instruction must:

- Clearly explain the purpose and rationale of the strategy.

- Clearly explain when and where to use the strategy in relation to the writing process.

- Clearly model the thinking behind the strategy and how to use the strategy multiple times.

- Provide pupils with explicit assistance in applying the strategy until they can use it independently.

- Show pupils how to adapt the strategy in different writing experiences through explicit instruction.

- Highlight and praise when pupils use the strategy and improve their writing as a result and make those gains highly visible.

- Explain that the point of a strategy is that it is ultimately used independently.

- Enable pupils to adapt the strategy and personalise it into their own strategy schema.

They suggest that the research indicates that most effective strategies to teach:

- **Goal setting and monitoring of goals.** This, of course, is at the very heart of developing a knowledge transforming approach to writing. Writing is not just about putting words on paper but about setting goals and then planning, problem solving and evaluating one's writing in light of this.

- **Treating writing as a process.** Being explicit about which phase of the writing process children are working in, and what is required in each phase, can help children to manage their anxieties around writing.

- **Gathering information.** We have discussed the importance of having sufficient content knowledge to attempt to write. Children will also need sufficient vocabulary and language specific to the task.

- **Visualising.** Creating both internalised and actual images of characters, events and settings enhances written descriptions and explanations. Even simple line drawings can support paragraph construction as well as whole text construction. Displaying these visual prompts can remain as secure scaffolds for children who may have less developed working memory capacity.

- **Taking notes.** Writers often make notes at the planning stage. Sometimes a characteristic or a phrase comes to us early in the writing process. We often think we'll remember it when we come to use it. We have almost always forgotten it. This is why writers note them down.

- **Evaluating plans.** The plan is crucial for emergent writers to produce higher quality, well-structured work. They need checking though – by teachers, by collaborators, but also by the writer.

- **Evaluating drafts.** We'll take a closer look at the importance of the revising stage where most evaluation will take place. However, children often find evaluating their own writing difficult, so providing explicit criteria against which they can evaluate will greatly enhance motivation and outcomes.

- **Oral rehearsal** to reduce cognitive load during transcription is not something that comes naturally. We need to teach and model it.

- **Creating the right writing environment.** Quiet surroundings and routines prior to writing will be important in a classroom to create a productive writing environment.

- **Planning and managing time.** Children, like adults, write at different paces. One of the great gifts of written communication is that it is not instant and one of the strongest messages from Steve Graham (2018) to improve children's writing is to give them more time. But we all plan and manage our time before and during the writing process. We have a deadline for the submission of the draft of this book...that we have, as we write, missed!

- **Collaborating with other writers.** We benefit from giving and receiving feedback. Both improve our writing. Securing a supportive but critical writing environment in our classrooms will improve the writing of all children and teaching strategies for feeding back and responding to feedback is beneficial for all.

- **Critically rereading text.** Developing a critical self-evaluation process needs to be modelled for young writers. The sheer effort of producing text may exhaust children to such an extent that the prospect of reading it back and changing it is repellent. It may be important to give them space and time before critically rereading their writing.

It will be important to give them clear criteria against which they are evaluating, and it will be crucial to model how you (the expert writer) approach rereading and evaluating your writing. Steve Graham and Karen Harris (2019) suggest pupils need to have the whole process modelled for them and see 'the struggle, the thinking, the pondering, the messiness of it all – because most struggling writers believe good writers are born, not honed through practice. They need to see that writing is hard and laborious, even for their charismatic and talented teacher.'

Graham and Perin (2007) recommend that to develop their understanding of different text structures children need to study model texts, which provide them 'opportunities to read, analyse, and emulate models of good writing'. The four principles they recommend when introducing pupils to text structures:

1. Reading and analysing similar texts will support the writing of these texts.

2. Children need to study model texts that clearly highlight the features of that specific text type and include those features to be taught and used in writing.

3. The analysis of the structural and language features of the text is heavily scaffolded by the teacher (the expert) – pupils will be unable to 'discover' many of the nuanced features for themselves.

4. Teacher-created texts may be the most effective way of including all the elements of structure and language that any specific class is to be exposed to, to be taught and to be applied.

What Graham and Perin (2007) emphasise, is that pupils should never be required to write a text in a structure that they have little or limited experience of, and they must have sufficient scaffolding to ensure they feel confident to be successful. Without this, the chance of failure increases significantly with all the associated damage to motivation.

Selecting a model to exemplify a particular text being taught will require a nuanced approach. It will depend on the purpose of the text and what is being analysed and taught:

- Where the text is exemplifying the structure and language devices a teacher wants to include in the learning, a teacher-written text is the most effective. This has some significant advantages:

  - The teacher can produce a text with full knowledge of their class.

  - As the writer, the teacher can talk from a position of creative authorial authority – this can be very useful when modelling strategies.

  - The teacher controls all of the content of the text at both the macro and micro level and can include revisiting recently taught content.

  - The teacher is able to refer to their own choices and strategies when discussing and analysing the text with the class and may even discuss changes.

  - The teacher can adapt and adjust the text for all children to ensure access.

- Where the teacher wants to explicitly draw pupils' attention to the choices writers make to develop metalinguistic awareness and strengthen the link between reading and writing, a teacher is more likely to select a text written by a recognised and published writer/author. Often known as 'mentor texts', these enable the teacher to:

  - Focus on those devices and language structures selected and applied by a recognised author and analyse their effects on the reader.

- Encourage deeper thinking about the relationship between linguistic choices and the meanings they create.

- Draw on the authority of a recognised author.

- Enable the pupils to, as Ruth Culham (2014) suggests, 'sit beside the author and study how the text is constructed and how it communicates'.

- Highlight how the author develops clarity, coherence and unity for a non- present reader.

- Highlight the social aspect of writing – what is it achieving, why did the author write it?

- Where a text is demonstrating the quality of writing to which pupils are to aspire by the end of the learning sequence, a text written at that level by a proficient writer can be used. Teacher-written texts offer us numerous opportunities to reveal how writing strategies work for us as writers. Writing lessons provide the chance to make explicit to pupils, in the moment of writing, how a skilled writer uses oral rehearsal, constructs sentences, revises sentences, selects appropriate vocabulary and considers clarity and cohesion with the reader in mind.

Pearson and Gallagher's (1983) slow release model of instruction allows a transfer of responsibility from teacher to pupil. The teacher initially models the skill or strategy being taught. They then incorporate pupil interaction, giving increased responsibility to pupils but monitoring understanding and holding back or returning to modelling where this appears unclear. As with all teaching, pupils must (eventually) be able to use and apply their learning independently.

- **Modelled writing:** The teacher takes the lead, while pupils observe the expert writer. This provides the opportunity for the teacher to demonstrate to the children how to apply new knowledge in small steps and emphasises writing strategies explicitly and can be used at all stages of the writing process. Modelling writing allows the teacher to think aloud, teach and revise writing strategies, enabling the pupils to 'sit beside the author' as they write and study how a text is put together.

- **Shared writing:** Co-constructing a text with an expert (you, the teacher) offers pupils the opportunity to move beyond imitation and helps develop metalinguistic awareness of the possibilities of language choices. They can be supported to reflect on language through questioning, both by the teacher and by the pupils. Further targeted questioning can be directed at specific goals and pupils.

- **Guided writing:** The teacher works with a small group of similar confidence and competence and supports them through knowledge, language and strategy instruction.

- **Independent writing:** Pupils have complete agency, with teacher input and feedback either during the drafting stage or at the reviewing phase. Pupils can be given the opportunity to write independently after modelled or shared writing has taken place to practise what they have observed.

The application of modelled, shared and guided writing supports pupils to not only improve written work, but also to gain confidence when approaching independent writing. These strategies appear particularly effective when adjusting and adapting teaching for specific pupils.

Revising

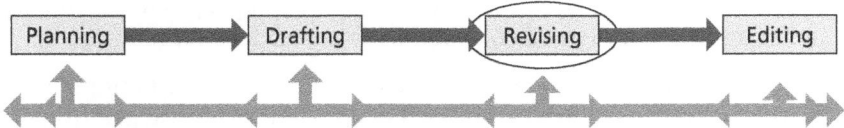

Revising is a crucial part of the writing process and of the teaching of writing composition for two reasons, according to Charles MacArthur (2016).

First, engaging in the revising of drafted writing indicates that a young writer is maturing through the novice stage. Proficient writers will spend a significant amount of time revising their writing to ensure that they achieve their rhetorical goals. Ronald Kellogg's (1994) research indicated that it is at this stage of the writing process that intellectual demands are at their greatest.

This is why novice writers find revising their drafts much more challenging and so tend to make superficial changes at the local level. Attending to the non-present reader and the purpose associated with the macro structure is often ignored in favour of word choices and grammar.

This highlights the second reason for focusing on the revising stage of composition. *This is where the teaching happens.* This is where we can spend significant time developing their understanding of what effective writing looks like to improve the text they are working on, and to build skills, strategies and mental representations that will enable them to take this learning forward to their future writing.

Revising requires the ability to critically reread one's own writing. This criticality applies not only to reading comprehension of the sentences but to a sensitivity to the global organisation of the writing, content knowledge and connections to prior knowledge. As novice writers have a limited task schema, support must focus on both the macro and local level of the writing. For these reasons, Zimmerman and Risemberg's (1997) work indicates that substantial teacher input and scaffolding is necessary at this stage. In primary school, when children are developing their writing as relative novices, the revising stage of composition will require substantial feedback if we are to initiate improvements both to the work in question and to children's future writing.

Teacher feedback at the revision stage, the research suggests, is most effective when it is as close to the point of writing as possible. This suggests that oral feedback, which is more easily actioned in the lesson, is more effective than written feedback. The effect of feedback therefore dissipates where there is a significant delay in reading the written feedback. Richard Beach's research (2006) indicates that feedback on writing needs to be specific to the task and not generalised, with grammar and spelling picked up at the editing stage. He recommends that teacher feedback, which should always be encouraging (but not hyperbolic), clearly identifies and explains the problem as objectively as possible and provides an actionable solution. More dialogic, as opposed to directive, feedback appears to be more motivating but should still clearly identify the problem.

So, 'Well done, this is a very clear description of your character. As the reader, however, I feel I want to know how old they are. Could you add a relative clause indicating this with a reference to their face ...' is more effective than, 'Great description! Can you add their hair colour.'

Peer-to-peer feedback can be effective when reviewing composition even with younger children. However, instruction to pupils – particularly younger pupils – on *how* to feedback and on *what* to feedback seems to be critical according to Charles MacArthur (2016). What this means is that just getting children to 'talk to your partner about their writing ...' is less effective than, 'I want you to read your partner's work and circle all of the explanatory connections from our list ...'. One of the values of children knowing that their work will be read by a peer is that it helps bridge to the non-present reader. Having a reader (or readers) present, who is able to articulate any problems with comprehension and clarity (consider an instruction text), gives the novice writer an opportunity to address any clarity issues. Writers (even novice writers) revise their work more after feedback from a reader.

Computer-generated feedback

Increasingly, Automated Writing Evaluation (AWE) programmes that use AI are able to provide formative and summative feedback on children's writing at the revising phase. There is growing evidence that AWE programmes can have a positive effect on pupils' writing through their high levels of feedback consistency allied to their ability to respond almost instantly and very close to the point of review. When these programmes assess against clear and specified criteria, they are able to deliver specific and actionable feedback along with indications of where extended practice would be beneficial. These programmes are able to support the reviewing phase at both individual and whole class level. Furthermore, it appears that pupils find the use of these programmes motivating for revising their writing.

Use of AWE programmes appears to be more effective at the earlier developmental stages of writing and particularly for grammar, sentence structure, punctuation, spelling and cohesive devices, so tends to improve writing rather than the writer.

Using evaluation criteria in the revising phase

Developing evaluation criteria against which pupils assess their writing and then make revisions has been shown to improve writing outcomes in a meta-study by Steve Graham (2006) and his colleagues. Giving children specific evaluation criteria relevant to the text type being studied is more likely to ensure a higher quality writing outcome. More generalised evaluation criteria that can be applied across a number of text types will develop pupils' mental models of evaluation when revising their writing.

Editing

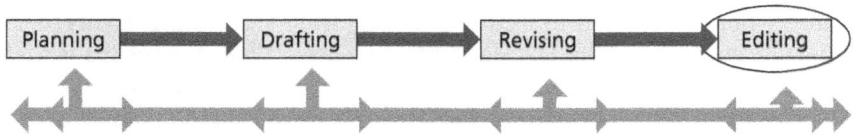

Editing involves identifying and correcting errors in grammar, punctuation, sentence structure and spelling. Pupils will need support proofreading their own and others' writing, and teacher modelling and systematising of the process along with feedback and peer feedback will be essential. An editing checklist can be helpful for pupils who are proofreading their own or others' writing as can proofreading symbols that are standardised across the school. Proofreading other pupils' writing can be an effective way of developing an awareness of writing with a reader in mind and supports proofreading their own work. Again, as with peer-to-peer editing feedback, it is more effective if it focuses on specific details rather than holistic editing.

Practising editing texts that contain intentional errors can be a useful activity when teaching specific punctuation, sentence structure and spelling. This also improves proofreading of pupils' own work.

Editing offers the opportunity for further teaching of grammar, punctuation and spelling in the context of pupils' own writing as well as assessment of what elements may need revision, further practice or more teaching. Editing will need to be modelled and scaffolded. The slow release framework of modelled, shared and guided editing will support the transition to independent editing.

Sharing pupils' written work.

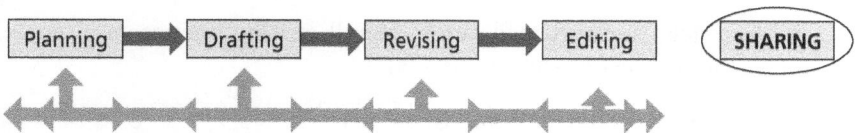

Charles Bazerman (2016) stresses that, particularly in school, understanding that their writing is going to be read develops pupils' belief that writing has a purpose. The non-present reader is made present! This builds not only intrinsic motivation but also affords a further opportunity to receive feedback.

Sharing writing can be as simple as writing a final version knowing that their teacher is looking forward to reading it, that they will read it and offer helpful and encouraging feedback. Reading aloud written work, or specific extracts to the class or sharing the finished piece with peers and relatives also generates motivation and pride. And see also the process of teacher-led peer-to-peer feedback outlined in chapter 9.

It can be more formal, as in publishing blogs, creating and publishing books and sending letters and emails to headteachers, dignitaries or celebrities, where a response may be expected. Formal publication, although motivating for many pupils, should enhance the school's writing environment but not be at the expense of time spent teaching and developing writing.

The identified target audience for any writing may not always be the final readership, but where this is possible – such as a Year 4 class writing for a Year 2 class – then the opportunity for sharing can build motivation during the writing process, identify a specific and known readership and highlight the purpose and clarify the goals of the writing.

Developing a whole school approach to sharing pupils' work with reasonable expectations regarding publication and performance will develop a writing community where writing is seen as supported and valued.

Key messages

- Children will struggle to construct whole texts and the paragraphs that make them up without secure knowledge and application of sentence structure.

- Composition is more than just translating ideas and knowledge into words and sentences.

- Children need support to develop overall writing purpose and goals and a sense of the non-present reader.

- Children need support bridging the gap between writing sentences and constructing quality texts.

- The text structure informs writing decisions made at a local level – the macro defines and influences the micro.

- Helping children build flexible mental models of texts supports them with the macro demands of composition.

- The writing process of planning, drafting, revising and editing is not a linear process. Many sub-processes operate throughout composition. All phases are subservient to the purpose.

- Planning is particularly vital for children if they are to produce quality texts.

- Although not the finished text, planning enables children to see the whole map and therefore build a mental model of their text.

- Single, flexible, narrative and non-narrative planning models support children's mental models of macro structures.

- Translating a plan into text is demanding for children. Having paragraph plans as well as overall plans will support children with the translation process.

- Having strong content and language knowledge relevant to the composition supports translation of ideas from a plan into a draft.

- Teaching and encouraging the use of cohesive devices improves composition.

- Planning, drafting and reviewing individual paragraphs greatly improves their final quality.

- Modelling writing strategies improves writing quality.

- Children should not be expected to compose a text type they have not encountered.

- Model texts that highlight the macro structure and language features of a text should be analysed by children with significant scaffolding from the teacher.

- These texts can be composed by the teacher to give authorial authority and to include contextual nuances relevant to a class.

- Systematically revising drafts is essential for quality composition.

- Revising drafts is cognitively demanding so will require a systematic approach.

- For novice writers, most cohesive devices are added at the revising phase.

- Teacher and peer feedback needs to be clear, encouraging and actionable.

- Editing is different to revising and is a more secretarial review of a composition to ensure correctness of grammar, spelling and punctuation.

- Children should be aware for whom they are writing and that their composition will be read – even if only by their peers and their teacher.

Chapter 8
Motivation for writing

Tim writes: *I hated learning the clarinet...really loathed it. I hated the sounds I made with it, I hated the teacher, I hated the music, I resented the time I spent in lessons and hated practising. I just couldn't get anything right. My fingers felt like bananas, my mouth hurt, the harder I blew the more the thing squealed and squawked, and I hated the faces of my parents as they tried not to wince when I tried to perform to them. I felt a queasiness in my stomach as I awoke on the dreaded day of the lesson. I started bunking off clarinet lessons to avoid the torture and was happy to take the punishments. It took a long and brutal campaign to finally win over my parents to the understanding that the clarinet and I were incompatible, irreconcilable enemies. I still cannot play the clarinet and never attempted another instrument. I cannot read music, cannot play music and my life may be somewhat diminished as a result. Whenever I hear a clarinet being played, however beautifully, I still feel a frisson of spiteful distaste and indifference rise in me. I can honestly say that I am glad to see the back of that small black coffin-case and its loathsome contents. I can live my life without it. But what if I'd felt the same way about writing?*

Writing is more difficult than learning an instrument but more important for navigating life. Even great writers struggle with motivation. Despite the fact most of us will do pretty much anything to put off facing the blank page, we underestimate the importance of motivation for all writers, but particularly novice writers, at our peril. Steve Graham (*cit* Alves, R. 2024) suggests that the development of writing stands on a four-legged chair: knowledge, skills, self-regulation and motivation. Any weakness in any of the legs risks arresting the development. Rui Alves (2024) suggests that the most vulnerable leg is motivation.

Because writing is such hard work, motivating children to do the work necessary to learn how to do it well is a challenge. The profession tends to come up with one of two solutions to the motivation problem; either make sure children have all the tools they need to be successful before expecting much by the way of cognitive trench digging or try to make trench digging seem irresistibly glamorous – 'imagine all those crops you will irrigate!' – so that the effort seems purposeful while skating over learning any tedious mechanics of how to wield your spade effectively.

But in the same way that no one who struggles to decipher a word will ever love reading, not being able to physically write a word will stifle any love of composing.[5] Laboured handwriting will always be a barrier to incentive, especially when your readers are unable to decode your written thoughts. Compared to reading, the teaching of writing has a real disadvantage when it comes to mastering this procedural knowledge: progress is glacially slow and physically and mentally effortful with very small and almost imperceptible improvements. It's a perfect recipe for discouragement and although 'drill and kill' practising will certainly produce greater fluency, it may do so at the cost of enthusiasm as was observed of Quintilian's rigid approach, dismissively compared to 'a fatigue march that would have bored the Gods' (in Bennet, 1991).

But here's the rub: if we focus too much on the allure of the final product without teaching children how to develop technical proficiency, then we risk demotivating them because the whole process becomes impossibly hard. No amount of enthusiastic cheerleading or captivating stimulus, no promise of an eager audience can compensate for the inability to encode one's thoughts into legible, decipherable words. But if we focus on developing one technical process at a time, we remove the motivational effects of producing an authentic piece of writing that someone else might find interesting. When teachers disagree about how best to teach writing, this is mainly because they have tied their colours firmly to one or another mast, perceiving the giving of ground to the alternative perspective as treachery of the highest order. Teaching writing, then, needs to devote sufficient time to enabling children to become successful in the technical enablers of writing (see the previous chapters) while also putting these hard-won skills to use in genuinely communicating with others. As a profession we seem to have an aversion to 'both', preferring the false dichotomies of the either/or.

Self-determination theory (Ryan and Deci, 2000) argues we unconsciously make calculations about whether or not it is worth investing effort in

---

5   There are obvious exceptions where children have a disability that makes them physically unable to write and use non-physical means of transcription.

something based on how much we value the activity; how successful we think we are likely to be and how supported we feel. Our beliefs about our competence are key. When we believe we are going to be successful, we do the work that brings about that success. When we believe we are going to fail no matter how hard we try, it's incredibly challenging to force ourself to put the effort in, even if the atmosphere is supportive and you can see the value of the work. Imagine trying to dig a trench when your spade is made out of paper, when everybody else has one made of steel! At some point, the game isn't worth the candle, and we withdraw our labour and invest our energies in avoiding writing (sometimes excelling in our avoidance strategies). This is why it is so important to have a writing curriculum that enables children to be successful. When children can see that they are being successful, they become more interested and invested in the process and want to try harder. Persistent, visible failure, however, is kryptonite to being a motivated writer.

Self-belief

Developmental psychologist Alfred Bandura (1997) maintained that the greatest influence on motivation was the likelihood of a successful outcome. Let's face it, it's not much fun turning up to school every day knowing that you're only going to succeed at half of what you attempt. Benjamin Bloom (1981) suggested we need to succeed at about 95% to want to come back again. Building that belief and self-confidence as well as the resilience to come back when success is elusive is going to be crucial for children to continue on their path to becoming a competent writer.

Bandura identified a number of factors that can influence children's self-belief:

- The most powerful driver of self-confidence is successful performance. A child's perception that they are writing successfully is the most basic route to developing their self-confidence in writing. Differences in self-belief account for the largest variances in writing competence.

- Assessing their own performance alongside the performance of other children is a potent influence on self-confidence. Children who feel they share similar levels of competence with their classmates, with whom they identify, build self-belief. This comparison is not solely related to success but can also be related to comparative displays of resilience and persistence. Teacher modelling of writing instruction and writing strategies and behaviours (particularly resilience in the face of difficulties) are therefore effective at building self-confidence through establishing social norms.

- Social approval is also important for children's development of self-belief. The expressed belief by others that they can perform successfully builds self-confidence. Encouragement, suggestions and positive feedback are all vital in building self-belief in young writers. This is more than just gratuitous praise and pep talks but requires feedback on *current* performance, rather than *distant* goals. When our long-term communication patterns repeatedly communicate our belief in our pupils their personal agency improves. Children's self-efficacy builds when teachers make specific feedback suggestions and explain their reactions – 'I liked that sentence because the relative clause helped me picture the age of the woman …' rather than, 'great sentence!'

- Labelling emotional reactions can help children understand their apprehensions regarding writing and manage their self-confidence. Many children feel anxious when faced with a challenging writing task and they often interpret this anxiety as an indication that they will perform poorly, thereby lowering self-belief. Writer anxiety leads to weaker writing skills and so to significant consequences for writing development. However, very few adult writers, even professional writers, do not feel a sense of anxiety when faced with the blank page and a complex writing task *(Clare and Tim both have their hands up).* We can label this anxiety as normal to the writing process, explain why the feelings have become apparent, model how to mediate it and express the strategies we use to overcome it and reassure children that they will be scaffolded and supported throughout the process.

Building pupils' self-confidence and self-belief as writers

Charles MacArthur and Steve Graham (2016) maintain that encouraging children to believe they can be successful and helping them to manage negative emotions should be part of writing instruction. Clearly encouragement alone can only go so far. *(Clare shudders as she remembers enthusiastically encouraging Stevie of chapter 3 without actually, you know, teaching him anything.)* Clare's demons notwithstanding, learning that self-doubt comes with the territory and need not be fatal is sensible advice and should be incorporated into any writing curriculum. The reflections of published authors are helpful here. For example, S.F Said, author of primary school classic *Varjak Paw*, describes his writing process in order to encourage children not to give up when it doesn't go right first time.

'I do many drafts. There's a lot of trial and error in my process, and I get it wrong a lot before I get it right. Varjak Paw took me 17 drafts, and those drafts took about five years of my life.' (Said, 2020)

Tanya Santangelo and her colleagues (2016) identified a number of strategies that appear to be effective in building children's success and thereby their self-confidence as writers:

- Analysis of model texts written by the teacher enables the exploration of specific and general features and characteristics of that text. By intentionally including specific features the teacher is able to articulate how these choices have been deliberately made in order to have a specific effect on the reader. This kind of analysis followed by pupils emulating the text appears to improve children's self-belief prior to a writing task. If we think about this in terms of memory demands, by explaining and rehearsing specific features, the learner can draw on what they already know rather than being expected to create *ex nihilo*. This is often deeply reassuring.

- Setting very specific goals for pupils – 'Include three elaborating sentences after your topic sentence one of which is a compound sentence.' David Didau (2014) writes about this way of scaffolding writing – he calls it slow writing – and how liberating many children find it. He describes how novice writers are 'so busy thinking about what to write that there's little space in working memory to consider how it might be written. Giving pupils sentence prompts frees up working memory so they can shape what they know in a more sophisticated way. These constraints provide pupils with the metacognitive prompts for thinking about what they know and allow them to be creative.'

- The use of self-evaluation standards, guides, checklists, and rubrics in the revising phase.

- Developing cognitive strategies prior to writing – generating content before writing in a structured manner – graphic organisers, drama techniques, reading, discussion – produces higher quality writing for pupils compared to unstructured content generation or no prior generation.

- Teaching pupils to use mental images to enhance descriptions during the writing process appears to have positive effects on writing.

- Providing children with authentic purposes and readerships for their writing develops greater writing quality and perception of success.

(This is not surprising if we go back to self-determination theory, which describes motivation as grounded in both social connection and in feeling successful.)

- More interaction with the class teacher during writing results in more positive outcomes for children, reduces anxiety and builds self-efficacy.

- Writing collaboratively improves writing outcomes and enables comparative performance. Well-structured collaboration with peers during writing improves the writing outcome.

- Well-managed group-based activities prior to writing suggest models of decision-making and exposure to different perspectives on the writing task.

- Giving children extra writing time almost always improves the quality of the writing.

Motivation and the social aspect of writing

Robert Beck (2004) maintains that when we write we are not only concerned with the ideas we generate cognitively and how we can best express these ideas in text, but there is also a social dimension; writing is a form of communicating with others. These others may be non-present, but their existence gives writing its purpose. So, when we teach writing, being aware of this social aspect and encouraging children to be aware of it can add a further dimension to children's writing processes and their motivation to write.

This has several implications for writing instruction in primary schools:

- We may need to frame the social situation that the children are participating in as a result of their writing. This is usually the classroom or the school, and the teacher may be the ultimate reader of the writing. Understanding for whom they are writing is vital for writing development and widening the possible readership beyond the classroom (parents, other classes, local politicians, school websites) builds an understanding that writing has a social function. This social side to writing can be very motivating for children. For example, Anne Dyson (2002) found that children often base characters in their writing and drama on friendship networks for greater social impact. Supporting children to consider and appreciate the reader from a social perspective helps them adapt their writing voice.

- Readers understand that writers use a voice. Writers can intentionally develop their voice for greater social impact. Enabling children to share their writing as a social practice develops an understanding of the importance of voice. Identifying and analysing a writer's voice during reading develops understanding of the social imperatives of writing and the importance of voice, according to Timothy Shanahan (2016).

- Understanding that writing has the power to effect material change will motivate children to write. Building opportunities for children's writing to have a material effect will promote writing motivation and develop an understanding of the social consequences of writing. Outcomes of children's writing that effects change (even small changes) in a school develops a belief and trust in the importance of writing and builds motivation to write.

- Ensuring that almost all writing in school is shared, even if just within the classroom as the default, satisfies the social aspect of writing, motivates writing and ensures it is not solely a cognitive and textual activity.

- Collaborative writing is a social activity and exposes children to alternative thinking processes and perspectives which can encourage children to modify their own writing processes. It may require teacher input to assign roles and ensure all are engaged as well as mediate any conflicts. Children appear to revise their texts more when collaborating and talking about their writing with peers, and they develop increased awareness of the dialogic nature of texts – an indicator of writing development.

- Creating a supportive writing environment (the school and the classroom) is one of the most effective motivating practices for improving children's writing and one of the elements of this is creating social structures where children can expect to work together, particularly prior to writing and when revising and sharing.

A competent writer is able to plan, initiate and sustain their efforts throughout a writing task and self-sufficiently undertake the process of writing without the need for external scaffolds. They may seek advice and feedback, but they have the knowledge, skills, and mental models to believe they can complete the task successfully and ignore any advice they feel is inappropriate. But on the way to developing competence, scaffolds are very necessary. The internalised knowledge, skills and mental models start life externalised in word banks, sentence starters, slow writing formats, graphic organisers, planning grids and so on. So, the very foundation of motivating children to write is effective teaching. It is worth repeating that the research is emphatic – writing is very susceptible to teaching. This is not merely teaching the procedural knowledge required to place ideas into sentences and text structures that readers are able to make sense of. It is also vital to assist the development of self-regulation strategies that will help novice writers to cultivate greater independence and self-confidence as well as face and overcome the complex hurdles of communicating ideas in writing.

Ronald Kellogg (1994) argued that the greatest determiner of becoming a productive writer was the amount of time actually spent writing. However, he acknowledged that time alone was not enough. Full engagement in the task is crucial for a higher quality outcome (we all know this as teachers – higher quality outcomes, especially with more novice writers, are far more evident when engagement with the task is complete – think Csikszentmihalyi's flow (1988)). The investment of this time and the level of engagement is also dependent on motivation, and this is itself dependent on the likelihood of success. But even that is not enough, as Elizabeth French and Francis Thomas's (1958) research highlighted all the way back in the 1950s: there has to be a *need* for success for us to persist with complex tasks like writing.

Does anyone really *need* to write. Do children *need* to write? Kellogg (1994) is adamant that we need to write because it is a meaning-making activity that enables us to make that meaning in a specific and unique way in our day-to-day lives. It is different from other forms of meaning-making. In its simplest form, we write a shopping list because it is portable and recordable and memorable – furthermore, our control over its structure supports the efficiency of the shopping task. Once we learn that writing helps our thinking, we are more inclined to write our initial thoughts to support our meaning-making and reflective power – it is as much an act of personal discovery as it is an act of communication. When we write, as David Green and Peter Watson (1982) asserted, what we create is not only something that is part of the world of ideas but also part of ourself. This may seem rather esoteric but it's an important point to communicate to children: when they write they not only think better and understand better, but they also become better. Try it. Write a summary of this paragraph. You'll understand it better, and you'll remember it better, but you'll also create something for yourself and of yourself. Don't believe us? Read your summary out loud to someone. That is why we need to write. We want children to understand their own need to write.

As teachers, we often want to inspire our pupils to develop a passion for a subject and it is no different with writing. We know that what we are trying to do is nurture that need from within. But we also understand that we operate within a school and that in a school, effort is expected whether the children are inspired or not...we want them to get on and do some work. Children's life chances are greatly enriched by being able to communicate in writing for instrumentalist reasons – passing exams, securing employment, navigating bureaucracy and participating in democratic society – but also because writing enhances thinking. Whether or not a child passionately desires to express themselves through creative writing it is our moral imperative to ensure that children learn how to write. Not every child is going to grow up into an adult who writes for pleasure in the same way that not all children grow into adults who read or run or cook or do maths for pleasure. Being able to write easily on demand is a vital skill in a modern, democratic society. As we argued in chapter 1, writing is a social activity that gifts social voice and power, a powerful tool for thinking and it develops language. We can strive to create an ethos where, at the very least, children enjoy having written, in the sense of feeling a sense of satisfaction and achievement at what they have produced and want to share their writing with others.

There's nothing more that we teachers like than inspiring our charges – it's on every advert for teachers and in every job application response. But we all know that inspiring children every minute of every lesson, every day, so that they are intrinsically motivated is a mythical ideal propagated by those who don't have to do the actual teaching...or have forgotten what it's like with thirty Year 4 children all day, every day. There are always situational dynamics that play a part in our motivation to do something. There will be very few teachers who do not, at some point, resort to B.F. Skinner's (1953) behaviourist paradigm of reward and punishment operant conditioning. In other words, we use extrinsic motivation. We use it because we are in control of it...and it works or *can* work and when we are trying to encourage children to do something as complex as writing, any form of motivation is useful.

Very few of us write purely for the love of it and it will be the same for children. Extrinsic motivators exist and can be important. Truman Capote (1957) quipped that he could not imagine writing anything for which he wasn't going to be paid. Nothing was more encouraging to him than money, he added. Teachers write reports at the end of the year because they are contractually obliged to. Headteachers write policies because they are statutory. Most people write social media posts for numbers of 'likes', which in turn can lead to monetary reward. Academics write for citations. These are all powerful extrinsic motivators as acknowledged by Rhona Ochse's (1990) work which indicated that people are indeed motivated to write for a number of extrinsic reasons: fame, admiration, self-esteem, jealousy, egoism and as an act of aggression (take a look at X/Twitter).

Children can be motivated by extrinsic factors: getting good scores, pleasing their teacher and particularly time deadlines – many of us will be aware of just how motivating leaving the writing of an essay until the night before it is due can be for actually getting it completed. They can also be driven by punitive motivators like losing breaktime and completing work at another time – although even Skinner (1953) balked at these being very motivating.

What Kellogg's (1994) work did suggest, and this is important for us as teachers, was that extrinsic motivators were fine for advanced writers but were almost useless for less competent writers where there was no intrinsic motivation. Although extrinsic drivers may be a useful lever to get children underway with a writing task, without intrinsic motivation, once underway, pupils are unable to generate and apply the intensity and focus on the task required to become sufficiently immersed in it to achieve flow.

Motivating intrinsic interest in writing

Extrinsic motivation is far easier to manufacture because we as teachers have control over it, but this tends to be task specific. If we tell you that we will pay you £1000 to write an essay, you probably will, but you are probably not going to write another one without similar reward motivation.

But how do we build our pupils' intrinsic motivation to write? The motivation that, in the long run, is going to turn them into competent writers rather than merely being able to churn out the odd acceptable essay.

Suzanne Hidi and Pietro Boscolo's (2006) work suggested that being interested in something is hugely motivating, particularly for writing. That's probably not a surprise. How many times do pupils, if left to write freely, end up writing about their sport or pastimes. But Hidi and Boscolo were, usefully, more specific, identifying two different types of interest both associated with different levels and sustainability of leverage: situational interest and individual interest.

Situational interest is a response to an event in the environment that focuses attention – a flurry of snow outside a classroom window or a teacher dressed as a Roman soldier, a video clip used as a stimulus, for example. This interest, however, may not have a lasting impact – the snow melts, the teacher changes out of the costume, the clip ends. In writing instruction, it is relatively easy to generate situational interest in a topic, but the interest may wane without *individual interest*. This is more enduring but develops over time and is associated with increased knowledge and value. (How does snow form, what are its structures, how does it affect the environment, why is the gladius so effective, what were the fighting tactics of the Roman army?)

Knowledge and interest affect the quality of writing, but knowledge has more influence, so, to motivate children to write with greater quality it seems important to develop from *situational* interest to the more knowledge-driven *individual* interest. In other words, it is not unreasonable to motivate children to write through grabbing their attention (extrinsic), but it is more important to develop motivation through interest in the content area and a desire to build knowledge of the topic (intrinsic). This is perhaps why using a book that children have enjoyed reading in class can sometimes generate genuine individual interest because children have become emotionally invested in the characters. Some schools manage to carve out time for personal writing projects as well as class writing projects. Having equally high expectations for personal writing projects as for whole class tasks is vital if this time is to be well used, as described by The Writing for Pleasure Centre (2023). (*Clare shudders at memories of pages and pages of incoherent and uninteresting material churned out during Big Writes.*) Investing personal writing projects with the same value and status as class projects, the same expectations with regards to planning, editing, revision and of course sharing makes all the difference.

It is worth repeating MacArthur and Graham's (2016) assertion that developing positive motivation towards writing should be a focus of instruction. We can help children develop a sense of competence and self-belief by designing writing tasks that ensure high levels of success but also that engender the belief in pupils that the success was a result of their *own effort* and learning. By providing writing tasks that are interesting, challenging, and meaningful and that have a social element, we can motivate children to view written communication as useful, important, enjoyable and fulfilling. And being encouraging and supportive, modelling the 'messiness of writing' but also how that mess can be cleared up, and being specific about how to improve writing will all build an intrinsic motivation to view writing tasks as resulting in possible success rather than probable failure.

Key messages

- Because writing is so challenging, a child's motivation is fragile. Once lost it is difficult to rebuild.

- Success and seeing oneself as a success is the greatest motivator. Activities that undermine this and end in failure for the child can be catastrophic for motivation.

- We can model the challenges of writing, and the resilience required to engage with it.

- It is far more motivating for a child to write about something that interests them.

- It is far more interesting to write about subjects that children know a lot about.

- Extrinsic motivators can help to get writing underway, but intrinsic engagement is the only way of achieving 'flow' and higher quality writing.

- Children who are motivated to write, enjoy writing, write more and write higher quality texts.

- Children's self-confidence and belief in their ability to achieve writing success is one of the strongest indicators of future writing quality.

- A focus on developing children's self-confidence as writers is a crucial element of writing instruction.

- Success must be intentionally planned into writing instruction, but that success must be seen by children as a result of their own efforts and learning.

- Encouragement that gives a reason for the success is more valuable than gratuitous (and unwarranted) praise.

- Children who seek to avoid writing tasks will require greater attention to motivation and self-belief if they are not to fall behind in their writing development.

- Writing is a form of social communication. Ensuring children develop their writing in a social environment and write for a social purpose will help motivate them to write.

- Choosing to write is an indication of highly motivated writers. Opportunities to write freely will support this choice.

Chapter 9
Assessing writing

Tim writes: '*I have just read the worst simile ever.' It was after school, and we were sharing our pupils' character descriptions from a morning of writing. 'Her teeth were as far apart as gas molecules.' We laughed, marked the books (probably with a note on improving the simile) and went home. But what was wrong with the simile? It was actually a simile – it compared something with something else – and it was valid – gas molecules are spread out...so were the woman's teeth. So, what was wrong with it? Did the child understand similes? Clearly. Was the child able to use a simile correctly? Absolutely. The fact that we didn't like it seemed to be the issue. In our opinion it was not very high quality...in our opinion. Was it really that important that we didn't like it? Arguably not. Perhaps this is at the heart of the dilemma of assessing writing: do we assess what is correct, or do we assess quality...in our opinion?*

Alfred Hitchcock, when clearly displeased with an actor's performance was asked by the actor how to improve it. 'Act better,' came the terse reply. Not really very helpful. The technical side of an actor's performance can be improved by standing in the right place, speaking at the right volume, hitting the mark and finding the light. But how to improve the quality? Much more difficult...and actors are notoriously dismissive of directors who tell them *how* to say lines. To improve quality, we first have to be able to judge quality and then be able to feed back in a coherent way that is not only understandable to the recipient, but also actionable.

Writing can be technically right or wrong, but it can also be good, indifferent or bad. It can be technically correct, of high quality but utterly forgettable. (*Tim writes: Very much my relationship with Virgina Woolf novels...I know, I know...It's me.*) So, when we assess writing, what are we actually assessing – its technical correctness, its quality or its memorability? Or all three? And if we are doing all three, how are we feeding that assessment back to pupils so that they can improve or at least learn from it and not be overwhelmed by the multiple messages? Or are we really just saying, 'write better'?

This tension between technical correctness, quality and memorability in assessing writing is one of the reasons that writing research is so difficult. How do researchers evaluate the outcomes and possible effects of interventions? How do they evaluate quality? The dilemma goes all the way back to Plato and even he wasn't sure, so, how do we as teachers evaluate quality...and should we even bother?

The writing psychologists are very helpful here. They divide writing assessment into three clear and distinct measures: objective measures, subjective/holistic measures and behavioural measures.

Objective measures

It is relatively straightforward and very useful to assess the technical correctness of a piece of writing. As we write this book, we are using word-processing software, so much of this feedback on our technical writing happens almost automatically (we tend to ignore the suggestions regarding quality – arrogance perhaps but we are meant to be writing this book, and our names are on the front). It checks not only spelling but punctuation and grammar and sentence structure. We have seen that teaching children to become fluent in these areas of writing is crucial to supporting the management of cognitive load when composing. In primary school, much of the focus of our assessment and feedback will be, and should be, concentrated here. Confidence with sentence structure, especially the use of subordination, enables numerous pieces of additional information to be included economically within a sentence. So, technical proficiency here is going to be vital to the development of competence in novice writers (no mention of quality here – complex sentences do not equate to quality, but that's not what we're assessing).

In primary school much of this assessment and feedback of technical accuracy will come during and after new learning and practice associated with a particular new skill. In other words, if the lesson is about sentences, then we will assess correct use of sentence structure being taught in that lesson. When children learn how to construct compound sentences from simple sentences, the assessment and feedback will be related to that learning and those specific lessons. When we are assessing longer writing pieces, we will still need to assess the accuracy of the sentence structure as this indicates fluency in this skill, but we will have to balance this with the cognitive load associated with multiple levels of feedback.

Walter Kintsch (1974) argued that these objective measures can go beyond mere technical accuracy of the writing. His approach systematised the assessment of not only the micro but also the macro structure of a text objectively (leaving aside quality) – for example, in an overall plan, a paragraph plan and the written text. Have all of the structural elements been included? Is there an introduction and conclusion? Have the rules of paragraphing been followed? Is there a topic sentence? Are there elaborating sentences? Is there a concluding sentence? Again, no mention of quality, just objective criteria. We know that their inclusion likely increases the chances of quality writing...but we're not assessing the quality.

Essentially that is what success criteria are: a rubric for objective assessment. We (and pupils and their peers) are assessing the inclusion of the elements of the criteria and not the qualitative effect. The principle is that the inclusion of the elements in the criteria increases the likelihood of quality, otherwise what was the point of teaching them and including them. This can include sentence types, language devices (alliteration perhaps), elements of rhetoric (pathetic fallacy, for example), as well as specific vocabulary and cohesive devices (such as connecting adverbs). There is clear, actionable feedback: if a criterion is not included, then include it. The chances are that the inclusion improves the quality, but we're not assessing the quality...yet.

But when too much emphasis is placed on the inclusion of specific criteria, as is likely when a rubric is used in a high stakes assessment system that judges teachers and schools, quality can take a big hit. This is what has happened with the teacher assessment framework used in England to hold primary schools to account to standards in writing. The problem is not so much with a rubric based system in itself, but with its use in a high stakes system where the inclusion of elements becomes far too make or break. Instead of reflecting on whether or not a specific element makes things clearer or more interesting for the reader, decisions are based on pleasing the mark-scheme. As we saw in chapter 6, teaching writing involves both teaching substantive knowledge (the technical stuff) and disciplinary knowledge (how to use the technical selectively to make writing clear and interesting for the non-present reader). Rubrics are great at assessing the former and are at best a punt for the latter. With rubrics, there is no space for decisions about whether or not to select an element. With rubric based systems, everything goes in, regardless. The development of a reader's ear that reflects on whether this element is really adding anything is completely absent. This isn't a problem where teachers are aware of the issue and alert to the need to undo the over-enthusiastic deployment of the whole *table d'hôte* of potential language features some time later. After all, we've taught certain things and included them in our rubric because we think their inclusion is likely to contribute to, but not guarantee, improving quality. It is like saying adding salt or chilli or cream is likely to improve a recipe. Yes, to a degree, it probably will. And having neither salt, nor chilli nor cream certainly lowers the odds of impending deliciousness. But it depends on both quantity and interaction with other ingredients. We have to be aware of the needs of the non-present eater and add salt, chilli and cream judiciously and maybe not all three at once!

The problem with high stakes assessment systems is that they have an insidious way of becoming the *de facto* curriculum. Teachers can become hoodwinked into believing that the rubric *is* definitive of quality and that the mark-scheme knows better than our non-present reader about what makes writing clear and interesting. More subordinating clauses! The whole panoply of punctuation! Never mind the quality, feel the width! Instead of being a useful diagnostic tool to help teachers identify what we need to help pupils use more fluently, they incentivise unthinking feature bombing. Ofsted – the schools' inspectorate for England – has written about this problem in *Telling the story: the English education subject report*:

'Schools expect pupils to repeatedly attempt complex tasks that replicate national curriculum tests and exams. This is at the expense of first making sure that pupils are taught, and securely know, the underlying knowledge they need.' (Ofsted, 2024)

Similarly, the DfE, in 'The Writing Framework' note:

'While preparing pupils for the assessments is valuable, it can take time away from developing a wider range of skills and knowledge, potentially stifling creativity and critical thinking. The Standards and Testing Agency (STA) says, 'The frameworks [for teacher assessment] are not ... intended to guide individual programmes of study, classroom practice or methodology.' Leaders need to consider what they want their pupils to learn; this – rather than statutory assessments – should inform their writing curriculum and teaching.' (DfE, 2025)

What is more, when rubric-based assessments are taken too seriously as reliable summative assessment, we get into all kinds of nonsense. Having a rubric might make it *feel* objective – there's a list and everything – but there is abundant research that reveals otherwise (Harlen, 2004). Using the same rubric is not a guarantee that different markers will agree. It doesn't even guarantee that a marker will agree with themselves if they mark a piece of work twice. This is because humans are not very good at making absolute judgements and much better at making judgements that compare one thing with another: the system of comparative judgement we discuss below.

Perhaps one of the most useful objective assessment tools is one of the least known. It comes from corpus studies. These studies contain large amounts of writing whose quality has already and separately (no rubrics here) been accepted, having been marked by experts. The writing is then analysed and elements correlated with the higher quality (higher marks) texts are grouped. As the quality has already been decided, the results give us some objective markers. Philip Durrant (2021) and his team's work indicated that for children writing with greater competence and maturity we would expect to see:

- Additional words beyond a single subject and a single verb – 'the dog barked.' = 'The fierce dog barked at the lazy cat.'

- Greater use of low frequency words – richer and wider vocabulary.

- Greater use of abstract nouns and verbs.

- The main verb appearing deeper in the sentence.

- A higher ratio of subordinate clauses to main clauses.

- An increase in noun phrase length and greater use of noun phrases.

- Increased use of noun clauses.

- Increased use of relative clauses.

- Premodification of adjectives (additional words before the adjective = a *very* cold day.

- Post modification of adjectives by prepositional phrases = a very cold day *in December.*

- Use of passive voice.

- Increased use of adverbial clauses.

- Increased use of adverbial clauses at the end of the sentence (as opposed to the beginning).

- Greater use of cohesive devices – the greatest indicator of higher quality writing.

- Texts structured in a hierarchical manner.

- Paragraphs clearly defined with ideas ordered.

- Ideas separated into distinct paragraphs and not tangled across paragraphs.

Ronald Kellogg (1994) noted that the above were indications of a move away from a 'knowledge telling' approach to writing towards a 'knowledge transforming approach'.

Again, the use of these does not guarantee quality but their use is associated with higher quality writing, and we should certainly be teaching them in primary school. Noticing their use in our reading and then reminding novice writers to apply them, then monitoring and practising their use will likely improve writing quality. It is interesting how heavily associated vocabulary is to quality writing; not because that's surprising, but because most of the research is into how vocabulary affects reading comprehension.

So, objective measures of writing are specific in what they are assessing and often have a list of criteria. Assessments include:

- Handwriting speeds.

- Handwriting legibility.

- Spelling accuracy.

- Sentence structure accuracy.

- Punctuation accuracy.

- Use of cohesive devices.

- Use of rhetorical devices.

These can be particularly useful for identifying skills gaps and as a screening for when children join a school. They are also very informative for assessing what support children might benefit from and avoid that catchall 'they struggle with writing' by enabling focus on which particular element of writing they are struggling with. Such systems are useful tools to help the development of writing quality. They are less useful, as we have rehearsed at some length above, at enabling the valid or reliable assessment of writing quality.

Subjective and holistic measures

So, the quality of a piece of writing is to some extent a subjective assessment by the reader of the text. Having said that, there is, according to Ronald Kellogg (1994), often little variation between experts on the assessment of a text's quality. This is why academic essays are double, and triple marked and why the system persists and is considered robust, though we don't think such a system is likely to be adopted with any enthusiasm in schools! It's why the writing moderation assessment process is in place at KS2, though here the existence of the teacher assessment framework interferes with the subjective reflection on whether or not this piece feels any good to me – in my role as ambassador to future non-present readers – and instead imposes an objective definition of quality based on feature bombing.

Holistic measures of writing tend to assess the whole writing piece for its overall effect on the reader. This is an assessment of the impression of the overall quality of a piece of writing. This might even include a scoring rubric to quantify that impression and is often comparative. Daniel Kahneman (2011) found that those pieces assessed early in the marking often received lower marks as the assessor started to set their assessment markers and anchors, even when the assessors were experts – he would often re-mark his first ten essays. Not a workload friendly practice we would suggest for teachers!

Perhaps the most robust way of mitigating any bias is through the use of comparative judgements with large sample sizes and extensive numbers of assessors. Numerous texts on the same subject are read by assessors. Each time two texts are compared and the one of higher quality is identified. This creates a strata of texts across the whole sample. San Verhavert and his colleagues (2019) found that this form of quality assessment was highly reliable and, perhaps more importantly, there was little difference between assessment by experts or novices. The greater the number of comparisons, the more reliable were the results. Ofqual, the regulatory body in the United Kingdom that oversees qualifications, examinations and assessments, came to similar conclusions (Ofqual, 2017). And now that AI can be used in comparative assessments, with or without including at least some humans in the loop (we would very much advocate *with*), the process is now incredibly speedy and also, highly reliable (Christodoulou, 2025).

Assessing self-regulation

As discussed in chapter 8, developing self-sufficiency as writers is important for children's development, particularly in secondary school. As pupils develop their mental models for different writing tasks they can write with greater self-regulation. However, allowing pupils to write with fewer scaffolds and models enables teachers to assess how these mental representations are embedding and whether the scaffolds need to remain in place. This can provide valuable feedback for both teachers and pupils. Hence the usefulness of the 'cold write' which pupils attempt without any prior teaching and no access to scaffolding. Teachers sometimes decry the (often disappointing) results as not representative of what a child can really do. But if a child can only do a thing with a lot of cognitive handholding, then it just isn't true that they can 'really do' a thing – except with a lot of help. This is not to deride help as a supportive short- or medium-term strategy. In the long term though, we need pupils to be able to do the things our curriculum intends them to do, all by themselves.

Reading assessments

Children who struggle with reading almost always struggle with writing, so it is worth keeping a close eye on all reading assessments and correlating them with progress in writing. As with most assessments, making general assumptions from them is often unhelpful, but they may indicate specific difficulties in writing progress.

- **Phonics assessments** are particularly useful. As we have seen, development of grapheme/phoneme understanding is a crucial Rubicon to be crossed both for reading and writing. It is particularly important for spelling and more fluent handwriting. Children will struggle to learn to write without considerable knowledge of this so where there are gaps in knowledge, support in this area will support writing as well as reading. The Phonics Screening Check can be particularly useful as an indicator of spelling and writing progress.

- **Reading fluency assessments.** Poorer reading fluency may indicate issues with spelling and sentence structure both of which support reading rate and accuracy.

- **Reading comprehension assessments.** Ironically, these may be more useful for writing evaluation than reading, where many issues may be conflated. Poor comprehenders seldom compose well, and a child with excellent reading comprehension but poor composition is more likely to be struggling at the micro level of writing. Perhaps more important, poor comprehension is often an indication of modest vocabulary and the non-recognition of writing markers (cohesive devices in particular). The more that young writers notice cohesive devices as they read, the more likely they are to use them effectively in their writing.

Self-evaluation

Steve Graham's (2006) work has shown that teaching children how to evaluate their own writing using strategy instruction and rubrics as well as specific monitoring of specific aspects of their writing improves writing outcomes. This is often an element that we ignore, but modelling by teachers how to critically reread one's own writing develops children's criticality both of their own and others' texts.

Feedback

There is little point assessing a child's writing if the child cannot benefit from it and improve and learn or know what to practise. Assessment is therefore integrally linked to feedback. Most feedback that children receive from their teacher will likely be at the revising stage of the writing process.

The research suggests that the most effective teacher feedback:

- Tends to be more oral than written and is close to the point of learning and writing rather than afterwards.

- Is specific to the writing task, is not generalised and does not focus on surface features like spelling and grammar – unless this is the focus of the task.

- Explains clearly what the problem is and what the solution is and includes actionable improvements.

- Is more dialogic than directive – discussion is more effective than instruction particularly regarding language.

- Needs to be supportive and encouraging but not exaggerated.

- References the reader and what the reader might need to know or have clarified.

- Is systematic and not entangled – sentence structure, then language, then cohesive devices, then rhetoric.

For EAL learners and struggling writers:

- Clear and specific feedback on writing is essential and can be transformational.
- Feedback on errors should be selective and driven by error patterns.

Peer-to-peer feedback can be effective when reviewing composition even with younger children. However, instruction to pupils – particularly younger pupils – on *how* to feedback and on *what* to feedback seems to be critical according to Charles MacArthur (2016). Martin Nystrand's (1986) work indicates that peer feedback encourages children to read critically and apply recommended solutions to their own writing.

Clare writes: A group of talented teachers in the primary school where I last worked developed a powerful peer-to-peer revision and editing process as a replacement for the previous ineffective and time intensive practice of the teacher individually marking children's work. This was driven by tightly structured whole class feedback and paired work. The first section of the feedback lesson – after a first draft had been completed – focused initially only on editing. The teacher would share with the class three or four sentences or short groups of sentences written by different members of the class that correctly showcased the use of commas in a list, or consistent past tense, for example. To get around differences in handwriting clarity that might detract from the thing they wanted the class to note as praiseworthy, they would often type up these sentences, crediting each pupil with their mastery. As well as reminding everyone about punctuation or tense use or whatever, this also showcased excerpts from a range of children and exposed the rest of the class to their ideas and vocabulary at the same time.

The teacher would then remind the class that they had been working on speech punctuation, for example. They would then share an anonymous (or possibly teacher invented) wrongly punctuated sentence and model how to correct it. A second example was then shared for children to correct, working together in pairs on mini white boards. After two or three different examples, children would then move to edit their own work, with the help of a partner. For the first five minutes, both children read the work of the first child, checking for anywhere that might need changing. The non-author child was not allowed to write in the author's book, only make suggestions that the author might or might not decide to pay attention to.

The second part of the lesson focused on revising, and we only did this with KS2. During this part, the teacher again shared longer extracts from a range of children, explaining what it was that each child had done to make the sentence, paragraph or (occasionally) couple of paragraphs particularly clear, interesting, dramatic or useful. Again, not only did this reinforce key learning, it also ensured that the whole class heard great sentence structure, or vocabulary or clever use of cohesive devices or showing not telling or whatever from their peers.

The teacher would once again share a couple of less successful anonymous or fictitious examples that the children would discuss together how these might be improved. Often the points under discussion related to success criteria for the lesson. Having finished this section, children then returned to their own work and worked independently revising it. Their partner was, however, available for advice should they need it and when they had finished.

Not only did this approach work amazingly well at scaffolding how to edit and revise one's work, but the children also absolutely loved it. It became their favourite lesson of the week. We hadn't anticipated this. We had thought it would be good for them – but not that they would really like it! But of course, we had made writing into a social activity, provided a genuine readership for their work by making the non-present reader highly, and volubly, present!

Computer-generated feedback

Computer-based writing assessments have been around for some time but there are now an increasing number of automated writing assessment programmes available to schools. Not only can these convert pupils' handwriting into digital text, but they can also evaluate writing against a widening assessment criteria. Meta-studies indicate that automated feedback can significantly enhance the quality of pupils' writing. There is a growing consensus that, appropriately applied, feedback from Automated Writing Evaluation (AWE) can have a positive effect on pupils' writing and can offer some significant advantages. It can:

- Assess large amounts of text almost instantly.

- Provide high levels of consistency of corrective feedback.

- Offer pupils almost instant formative feedback, ensuring practice is focused and deliberate and thus more effective (this immediacy can improve pupils' writing and offer the opportunity for the necessary extended practice that promotes the development of writing skills).

- Specify where deliberate practice is beneficial and provide practice exercises.

- Assess against clear, specified goals and deliver actionable feedback against those goals with no other distracting feedback.

- Track revisions and keep records of the revising process.

- Offer fast, accurate, holistic and qualitative feedback at both individual pupil and whole class level.

- Promote motivation in pupils.

- By supporting self-assessment, allow pupils to develop more accurate evaluations of their writing progress.

- When monitored by teachers, reduce workload and improve subject knowledge.

- Provide reliable summative assessment quickly and efficiently.

There are, nonetheless, some potential shortcomings with AWE, which:

- Tends to be more effective at the earlier stages of writing development (good for primary schools).

- Is more effective for feedback on grammatical accuracy and lexical appropriateness rather than in content or structure.

- Tends to improve the *writing* rather than the *writer.*

- Tends to be less effective in improving argumentation, discourse and organisation.

- Is built on statistical analysis of large data sets so tends not to value originality, creativity, succinctness and clarity.

- May give pupils the impression that writing is an academic exercise rather than a lifelong skill.

However, the technology is improving exponentially and Laura Allen and Scott Crossley (2025) recently concluded that it holds significant promise as an educational technology not only to support assessment but also for writing instruction. The research, they maintain, demonstrates that the technology is effective for feedback and writing development and they suggest that it can play a valuable role in enhancing pupils' writing abilities if integrated thoughtfully within schools. We need to start embracing the technology.

Conclusion

There seems to be a growing enlightenment on the thorny problem of assessing writing and providing appropriate feedback to pupils. The quality versus subjective/objective equation is starting to look simpler. As we move forward, the technical aspects of writing require assessing separately from the qualitative and this is increasingly more effective when delivered by technology which can also design appropriate and bespoke deliberate practice. The qualitative elements of writing are then left to the teacher. However, the more teachers that are involved in that evaluation of quality, and where possible, large samples delivering comparative judgements, the more robust will be the assessment.

Key messages

- Assessing children's writing is a combination of objective evaluations and subjective/holistic as well as behavioural judgements.

- The technical aspects of writing are right or wrong and require acknowledgement.

- Other objective aspects relate to criteria that, although they do not guarantee quality, would usually be expected in a quality piece.

- Many of these objective aspects have been indicated by corpus studies and should all be taught.

- Holistic measures of assessment relate to an overall impression of the quality of the writing and often require a level of expertise to assess accurately.

- Comparative judgements with large samples of assessors and texts mitigate the need for large numbers of experts with reliable evaluations and have strong reliability.

- Assessment should deliver feedback for pupils or possible intervention or specific instruction or practice or curriculum or teaching improvement. Otherwise, it is pointless.

- Assessment should generate opportunities for deliberate practice.

- The reviewing phase will require teachers to engage with significant feedback for children to be able to revise and edit their work.

- Specific, actionable feedback is essential.

- Oral feedback appears to be more effective than written feedback.
- Feedback should be encouraging but fair and accurate and actionable.
- Children should be taught self-evaluation strategies.
- Peer-to-peer feedback can be effective where the teacher has defined feedback criteria.
- Automated Writing Evaluation (AWE) technology is increasingly accurate and effective and offers encouraging promise for assessing, feeding back on and improving children's writing.

Chapter 10
Vocabulary

Tim writes: *One week I used the term 'draconian' to my Year 4 class several times. I explained what it meant and used it a few more times. In The Big Write that Friday (Remember them? Pages of writing that defined the law of diminishing returns and that all needed marking by Monday morning – and this being Year 4 always ended with a deus ex machina moment because everyone had lost the will to live.) I was horrified. The word 'draconian' appeared in every script at least half a dozen times. They were littered with the word. Strewn everywhere. Draconian looks and glances. Draconian replies. Draconian shouts. Draconian walks. Draconian eyes. Draconian noses. What vocabulary monster had I created? I was appalled and banned the word from use ever again. But looking back, I think I should have been delighted. I had introduced vocabulary that they found interesting, useful and unusual and they enjoyed using it. Had we persisted with using the word, they probably would have started to use it more sparingly and correctly. I could have introduced more words like this. But I didn't. I banned it. Banning draconian was…well, draconian…and profoundly stupid.*

We saw in the previous chapter from the corpus studies that higher quality writing contains more advanced and less frequently used vocabulary. That is hardly a great surprise. It really seems very obvious. Having a wider vocabulary not only allows us to express ourselves more clearly and coherently to our readers, but it has the added advantage of helping us manage our cognitive load when writing. Vocabulary that sits in long-term memory and is easily accessible enables us to write with greater fluency.

What is perhaps surprising then, is that virtually all of the research into vocabulary acquisition and application relates to reading and its effect on comprehension. Now this is, of course, important. Vocabulary has a significant influence on reading comprehension. Ray Reutzel and Robert Cooter (2013) suggested that up to 80% of the variances in comprehension test scores were as a result of vocabulary knowledge. But being able to apply vocabulary in our writing is a far greater indicator that we have embedded both the meaning and the accessibility of the word.

Our reading vocabulary is **receptive**: we already have the word in front of us, and if we don't know it, we can use the context in the text, our knowledge of morphology and etymology to hazard an educated guess at the meaning. Our writing vocabulary is **productive**: we have to know what we want to express, find the right word in our brain's lexicon and then transcribe it into the text. It is sometimes far harder to find the right word to write (or speak) compared to recognising a word and understanding it in a text.

Building vocabulary

At first, we build our oral vocabulary through exposure to words in context when we hear others speak those words. Most common, day-to-day words are learned in this way. We expand our vocabulary further when we are able to read and encounter more expressive language. We also increase our vocabulary purposely when we encounter subject-specific words we need to learn to engage in a discipline. A child may have heard of a volcano and have a reasonable representation of the meaning of the word but may have to learn what the words lava and magma mean in order to understand how volcanoes erupt. In the same way, when watching a new sport, there is an essential vocabulary needed to access the sport (bowler, batter, fielder, wicket, runs in cricket).

Building a language-rich environment

According to psychologist Keith Rayner (2012), creating schools and classrooms where rich and expressive language is used and shared is essential for children's vocabulary development. Much of this will be through talk and spoken interactions, particularly the language used regularly by teachers and support staff. However, children will be exposed to far richer and more expansive vocabulary through reading. This takes two forms: the books that children read themselves and the books that teachers and others read to them, which can be above instructional level with richer language. Jeff McQuillan's (2019) research suggests that there is no better way of extending children's vocabulary than by reading to them regularly and for extended periods. Reading to children gives the teacher the opportunity to scaffold meaning, explain new vocabulary and give added and exaggerated expression along with body language and movement to indicate the meaning of words and new vocabulary. Children's books contain far richer language and vocabulary than they encounter in speech and, according to the study by Maria Korochkina (2024) and her team, they will encounter up to 28% of words in books that they will never encounter orally (including radio and television). Most of our vocabulary appears to develop in this way.

However, Steve Graham and Michael Harris's (2018) research also indicates that an effective strategy for building vocabulary is through direct instruction.

Specific vocabulary instruction

Isabel Beck and her colleagues in their seminal book on vocabulary instruction *Bringing Words to Life* (2013), categorise words into three tiers. Basic vocabulary sits in Tier 1 and pupils will acquire these easily through speech (cat, walk, run, happy). Tier 3 words are subject-specific words that are encountered only when studying the specific subject and are taught within the subject domain (respiration). Tier 2 words are those that are encountered less regularly than Tier 1 words but are found across a wide range of genres and texts (ponder, influence, notion). Tier 2 words enable us to add complexity and precision to our writing, both of which help make our writing clearer and more interesting to our non-present reader.

Although Tier 2 words will be encountered through wide reading and exposure to texts, it is these words that Beck and her colleagues consider good targets for teachers to select for direct instruction.

They suggest that a Tier 2 word considered for direct instruction should be:

- Unknown to most pupils.
- Encountered in class texts that week.
- Used in their writing that week.
- From an age-appropriate word list.

They suggest that between seven and ten words each week can be introduced and taught. So the word has a high chance of becoming embedded in long-term memory we should ensure that pupils:

- Explore the meaning of the word using pupil-friendly explanations rather than dictionary definitions.

- Encounter the words in different ways:
  - In a sentence attached to pupils' experiences.
  - With a multiple-choice quiz with distractor definitions.
  - With two close examples, only one of which is correct e.g. berate – 'the coach yelled at the player who missed the open goal.' OR 'the coach shouted at the player to swap positions.'
  - Experience the word in different contexts.
  - Use the word in talk.
  - Use the word in writing.
  - Analyse literal and more abstract meanings of the word.
  - Analyse the morphology and etymology of the word.
- Focus their attention directly on the word at least ten times.
- Revise the word in future and experience the word in speech, reading and writing.

Morphology and etymology

As discussed in chapter 3, the study of a word's **morphology** can support spelling, but it can also support vocabulary, according to Peter Bowers and his colleagues (2010). This may help in the understanding of a word when reading it but also in the use of words when writing. For example, when a teacher teaches the meaning of the adjective 'robust', it is useful for children to know that they can apply the word as an adverb – robustly – and a noun – robustness – delivering three occasions to use the word rather than one.

Words in English are not random strings of letters. Their patterns have a logic and represent meaning, much of which comes from (usually) Latin and Greek roots – particularly words of more than one syllable. By teaching these roots and applying them to words, children have a better attack strategy for unknown words in their reading, but they also make words more memorable and hence more likely to be used in writing. It is suggested by Tim Rasinski (2008) that **etymology** instruction and analysis should form part of direct vocabulary instruction.

For example, a teacher might introduce children to the word 'robust' with their own definition: 'strong, healthy, tough and not likely to knocked over or off course and likely to last a long time.' They discuss its etymology from the Latin *robur* meaning 'of oak' and how that links to the meaning. The teacher gives examples: 'The oak tree was very robust and survived many storms.' 'The ship proved to be very robust and was not blown off course by the strong wind.' 'The prince did not have a very robust character and was always changing his mind.' During the week the pupils encounter the word in their reading and their talk, they engage with a multiple choice of definitions of the word, decide between two close examples and use the word when writing about the Roman army. They discuss the morphology of the word and the meaning of 'robustly' and 'robustness'. Never assume that children will easily be able to transport a word across word classes naturally – some will of course but other children will not unless we explicitly point this out.

Teaching vocabulary for writing

Effective evidence-based practice studied by Steve Graham and his colleagues (2007) suggests that highly effective teachers improve the quality of their pupils' writing through the specific teaching of vocabulary for specific types of writing. What appears to be important is the identification of words that will improve the quality of the written activity. These words should be connected to the writing but also potentially useful and relevant for children's use orally. Many will be Tier 2 words that are more frequently encountered and may be applied across domains. Once identified by the teacher as potentially useful vocabulary, Isabel Beck's (2013) principles of teaching and embedding that vocabulary apply.

Writing and vocabulary processing in the brain

So, what is going on in our brains when we select vocabulary to use when we write and speak as opposed to when we read? And can this help us when we teach?

Emilia Kerr and her team (2023) suggest that the process begins with our desire to represent a particular thought or proposition in written or oral form (it's the same process for either) so a variety of meanings will come to mind, which we will associate with a variety of possible different word forms that could be used to build words to articulate the idea or concept we are communicating. We then select the word form. This is usually the word form most closely related to the desired meaning and is usually the most common – it's why we tend to speak with less complex vocab. There may be competition from other words, but we tend to select the one most frequently activated. Whichever word form wins that competition is selected. We then select and encode the word using our phonological and orthographic knowledge. This knowledge often influences the word form we select – if we can spell it quickly it often wins the competition – subconsciously. In other words, the stronger the link between the word, its letter patterns and the meaning, the more likely we select that word.

This process, Gill Fitzgerald (2025) suggests, gives us some rich instructional direction and insight when it comes to written vocabulary development.

First, she proposes, the assumption that poor vocabulary use is solely due to lack of word meaning knowledge is probably not always accurate. Pupils may be aware of certain meanings and vocabulary, but because the word's orthographic pattern (spelling) is weak, the word is not strongly associated with the meaning so loses the selection competition – this is not conscious, it is just that the word doesn't 'occur' to us with any great strength so an alternative word that flashes more brightly is selected.

Second, word meanings are not static. They are not dictionary definitions. So, words and meanings are located in different brain regions and associated with semantic subsystems. Selecting the right word is not merely about finding the word in a mental store but about the association of that word with experiences of meaning. Thus, the more opportunities we have to experience the word in different and nuanced contexts, the higher the likelihood of the word appearing in the vocabulary beauty parade. It is not just about learning the meaning, it is about building networks of meaning in a variety of contexts.

Perhaps even more important, Fitzgerald (2025) suggests, is making pupils explicitly aware of this beauty parade of words that materialises in the brain. The selected word will usually be the one that wins the competition, and this is the most frequently occurring word. But, she suggests, what if we make pupils aware of the competition and which words usually win it? If we encourage children to consider 'the right word' rather than the one that appears the most swiftly, we build the strategy of vocabulary consideration. Not for every word, but for important words. We encourage them to interfere in the competition and consider some of the other competitors. They may be more appropriate.

And finally, because this word competition has a built-in bias towards words we can spell, Fitzgerald (2025) once again emphasises the importance of spelling proficiency and sound orthographic knowledge linked with morphological study for vocabulary selection during composition.

Interestingly, Fitzgerald (2025) also warns against the instructional trope of encouraging pupils to use 'fancy' (or 'wow') words. She suggests that the choice of words will be dependent on the text type that will define the appropriateness of word selection. Just because sophisticated words are often associated with quality texts, their use as a metric for quality endangers the adoption of Goodhart's law – where a measure becomes a target.

The selection of vocabulary in writing is a different process to the comprehension of vocabulary in reading. When children compose, they are not merely selecting a word from a mental word store, but are engaged in a more nuanced process, with interaction between the lexical system (words) and the various discourse systems. There is a complex mix of factors that influence word selection: task, reader, language, disciplinary rhetoric, social consideration, cohesion and text type.

Key messages

- More sophisticated and appropriate vocabulary is associated with higher quality writing.
- Creating a language-rich environment in all classrooms will support and promote vocabulary development.
- Vocabulary development supports the cognitive load associated with writing and promotes fluency.
- Much vocabulary development is associated with reading and being read to.
- Books contain a far higher percentage of more complex vocabulary than will ever be experienced orally.
- Vocabulary instruction is vital in promoting written vocabulary and should occur weekly.
- Tier 2 and Tier 3 words should be identified and taught.
- The study of words' etymologies can improve written vocabulary.
- Children should be taught to consider 'the right word' and not merely 'the first word'.
- Spelling and morphology both improve vocabulary choices.
- Selecting vocabulary when composing is a more complex mental process than merely choosing words from the brain's word bank.

Chapter 11
Pupils who need more support

Tim writes: *I taught many children who struggled to read and to write. I tried hard. I was always supportive and encouraging. I gave them simpler books and writing activities and highlighted them to the Special Needs lead. If I am brutally honest, however, I failed every one of them. The reason for this is that I had no knowledge and no expertise of how the processes of learning to read and write developed. I floundered in a sea of good intentions, and they drowned in the briny ocean of my ignorance. Not being able to teach struggling writers meant I didn't really know how to teach writing.*

Clare writes: *One salutary thing I learned over the years was that what might look like a special education need getting in the way of a pupil making progress in writing can often – not always, but often – be unwittingly created by the pedagogical and curriculum choices we make. Once we actually taught handwriting really explicitly for example, it turned out that several children didn't have special education needs after all. The same was true of phonics and of focusing on sentence structure and giving sufficient time to oral composition. Getting children to read each other's work in a structured, supportive way was a game changer for motivation. Instead of believing it was sad but regrettable that certain children found writing so hard, we (eventually) did something to make it much less hard. Sometimes our ideological commitments are a form of luxury belief – a belief that makes us look inclusive or caring or committed to creativity when in reality, these beliefs can inflict significant negative consequences on children who, for whatever reason, find writing more challenging than others. We feel sorry for these children but don't do the things that would make life easier for them.*

If you have gotten this far in the book, you will be very clear just how challenging learning to write is: cognitively, emotionally, socially, personally and technically. We make no apologies for hammering this nail home. But if writing is difficult for a child developing in line with the majority of their classmates, consider how difficult it may be for a child with a social, environmental, cognitive or developmental frailty or issue that directly undermines elements of their writing progress.

Many children have difficulties when learning to write. There are three conditions, according to Virginia Berninger (Berninger and May, 2011), that appear to be specifically associated with increased difficulty in writing development: **dyslexia, developmental language disorder** and **dyspraxia.** Many of the difficulties experienced with all three may overlap so it is important to heed the words of Julie Dockrell and Barbara Arfé (2014):

'When children have developmental difficulties or academic problems, their needs can be assessed and understood in a number of different ways. One approach is to search for a diagnostic label ... These labels may provide indicative information about the difficulties pupils have with producing written text. However, such approaches fail to address the considerable overlap in difficulties with text production pupils might have.' (Dockrell and Arfé, 2014)

In other words, address the difficulties, not the diagnosis – the barrier, not the label.

Dyslexia

Kate Nation (2011) describes dyslexia as a developmental learning debility categorised by a difficulty in learning to read and spell. The majority of children with dyslexia have difficulty with the phonological aspects of reading and spelling, she explains, resulting in deficits at the word level. Julie Dockrell and Barbara Afré (2014) suggest that these word-level deficits affect writing, with strong evidence that pupils with dyslexia do not progress as well as their peers in writing.

The difficulties that pupils with dyslexia experience learning to *read* will affect their *writing* development.

- Reading is a key resource in learning to write. Learning to read contributes to reading comprehension and improves vocabulary and grammatical knowledge. Dyslexic pupils will have greater difficulty in acquiring these elements of writing development from reading alone. Furthermore, fluent reading enables quick and effective reviewing of text, particularly a text a pupil is writing. Dyslexic pupils will find this key strategy, associated with higher quality writing, more demanding.

- The poor spelling associated with dyslexia is a double disadvantage. First, poorer representation of words slows down the writing and second, this is exacerbated by the additional demand of selecting an alternative word from memory that they can spell. Much of the problem is associated with the act of writing rather than speech as dyslexic pupils are able to produce narratives of equal lexical diversity as their peers when the narrative is spoken. Poor spelling will also impact writing tasks that do not require composition, such as dictation and copying affecting the efficiency of transcription even when working memory demands are fewer. Dyslexic pupils struggle to develop multiple spelling strategies, with morphology a particular weakness. Spelling continues to be a demanding task for most individuals with dyslexia into adulthood.

- Although children with dyslexia can form letters when handwriting as quickly as their peers, the greater number of pauses when writing reduces their handwriting speed. Research suggests that this appears to be associated with poor and hesitant spelling.

Language learning disorder

Vince Connelly and Julie Dockrell (2016) have found that pupils who have difficulties with the acquisition and processing of oral language experience a protracted rate of language development. This, they suggest, places them at significant risk of literacy difficulties, which has a direct impact on their writing development with written texts shorter and more error prone than their peers.

The development of increased oral language proficiency is associated with increased written language facility so any difficulties acquiring oral language will affect pupils' writing development in a number of ways:

- Pupils will struggle with decoding and reading comprehension, which will constrain their written texts, and problems with decoding are associated with poorer spelling.

- Many pupils who develop oral language more slowly have smaller vocabularies and may struggle to retrieve words and word forms, placing them at a disadvantage when composing texts. These children are far more likely to select the first and most frequent word.

- Pupils with language learning disorder experience difficulties with the grammatical elements of speech. Thus, the move to the more complex syntax of writing is even more difficult.

- As with dyslexic pupils, spelling is a key constraint for pupils with language learning disorder and this constraint slows their handwriting as greater hesitations occur.

Dyspraxia/developmental coordination disorder

Pupils with dyspraxia have difficulty performing and learning everyday movement tasks and this often includes difficulties with handwriting. Connelly and Dockrell (2016) assert that this may impact the whole writing process as the transcription process will place greater demands on working memory to the detriment of other elements of the writing process.

Support for pupils with writing difficulties

The reason this section comes near the end of this book is important. It is **NOT** because we consider it to be less crucial and merely an add-on given the current focus on SEND provision. We hope that the knowledge and expertise you have acquired from the earlier chapters can now be applied. As you read through the difficulties children experience in writing who have these conditions, we hope that you are able to start to apply that knowledge and consider what might be a supportive instructional action. As Julie Dockrell and Barbara Afré (2014) implied at the beginning of the chapter, children who struggle with learning to write will still proceed through the same developmental process. They still need to learn to transcribe.[6] They still need to develop the syntax of writing. They still need to write sentences and develop mental models of text structures. They may need significantly more support, instruction, practice, time and patience. And where a debility creates an insurmountable barrier to an element of the progress and process, there may well be a digital solution. Typing can be an alternative for a small minority of pupils – though in almost all cases it is still worth developing their handwriting in tandem since research indicates writing by hand has cognitive benefits that typing does not – and speech typing is liberating for a very small minority. Such decisions to offer alternative solutions have profound long-term consequences and schools need robust systems to ensure they

---

6   There will be exceptions here for children with physical difficulties.

are not undertaken inappropriately. For some pupils however, they are truly emancipating.

Given the integrated nature of writing, when teachers examine the final writing product of pupils with writing difficulties, these pupils may well appear to be weak across all areas of assessment. The diagnostic labels may be useful, but evidence suggests that writing difficulties experienced are similar across pupils *with* and *without* conditions. Back to Dockrell and Arfé (2014):

'When specific instructional choices have to be made, teachers will need to move beyond diagnostic labels and identify the areas in the writing process that are challenging the pupil ... Accurate targeting of interventions requires that the pupil's difficulties can be reliably ascertained, and that these differ from what would be expected by children developing typically in that educational and social context. It is also implicit that children have been exposed to appropriate instruction...' (Dockrell and Arfé, 2014)

We think that is worth repeating – ' ... *identify the areas in the writing process that are challenging the pupil* ... ' And we can only do that if we have deep expertise in that process.

Support and additional instruction and intervention for pupils with writing difficulties

- Consistent across all categories is that all pupils who have writing problems appear slow to write, *even when they are improving*. Extra time to complete writing activities, beyond that afforded to their peers, is essential for pupils who have difficulty writing.

- Explicit spelling instruction leads to gains for pupils that are sustained over time and formal spelling instruction is beneficial for ALL learners in ALL year groups and ALL levels of literacy.

- Interventions that improve handwriting improve the quality of composition for struggling writers – struggling writers may well have reduced working memory capacity so automatisation is going to be crucial.

- Pupils with language learning disorder often struggle to apply knowledge from one context to another situation so benefit from additional scaffolding particularly when writing in other curriculum areas.

- Using digital devices can support pupils with writing particularly where transcription is a barrier to composition. Digital support can also help with sentence structure and punctuation and AI software now even supports text and paragraph structuring.

Having a sound knowledge of the process that underpins writing enables us to respond flexibly to the challenges faced by pupils experiencing difficulties writing. An awareness and understanding of the barriers created by poor spelling and handwriting for struggling writers empowers us to address and mitigate the obstacles for children. We saw how fragile motivation to write is. For children who are struggling with this complex task this fragility will be even more brittle and delicate. Our perceptions of handwriting, spelling and vocabulary can negatively affect assessment of the quality of written work – keep the assessment objective. This appears particularly important in KS3 when children with writing difficulties are taught by subject specialists who are using writing for learning.

Pupils who need support with writing

After Year 1, writing starts to become more integrated across the curriculum. Pupils who struggle to write will not be able to engage fully with the curriculum and are in danger of developing a lack of self-belief as writers and of becoming demotivated. They may well develop avoidance strategies, talk less in class, and be excluded from the social aspects of writing.

Identifying pupils who need support

Although the evaluation of writing is often subjective (see chapter 9), when identifying struggling older writers we should use an objective assessment framework.

- Pupils who read little out of school are likely to write less and have restricted vocabulary. Ensuring that these pupils have a rich language experience within school with opportunities to read and be read to can support their language development.

- Pupils' decoding skills should be assessed. Pupils who will struggle to decode will also struggle to encode and will require phonics support to help them develop the spelling element of their transcription skills.

- Pupils should be regularly assessed as to the rate and legibility of their handwriting. Pupils who struggle with handwriting will find it difficult to compose as their working memory will be heavily loaded with the transcription element of writing. These pupils require additional instruction and opportunity to practise their handwriting. This should be promoted as a matter of urgency and monitored. Older pupils who struggle with transcription should not be excluded from the composing element of writing. Scribing, dictation software and word-processors can support them. They will still need handwriting instruction and practice. For children to improve their writing they need more practice and more time.

- Pupils should have systematic spelling lessons and be regularly assessed. Pupils who struggle with spelling will again struggle with transcription and find it difficult to attend to composition. These pupils will require additional spelling instruction.

- Pupils should be assessed as to their competence in forming and extending sentences. All pupils will need to have regular and systematic instruction in sentence structure and grammar and have opportunities in that instruction to practise what they have learned. Pupils who do not develop the ability to create coherent and cohesive sentences will struggle to make their writing understood. They may require additional instruction and practice to mediate this and regular reminders from teachers how to form sentences. Regular sentence combining activities will support sentence construction.

- Holistic assessments of composition will help identify pupils who struggle with composing texts. When approaching written composition, these pupils will require additional support and scaffolds, models and structures with more atomised steps to support the cognitive load associated with composition. Teachers can support all pupils with models, worked examples and scaffolds. Pupils who find composition more challenging require more detailed structures, more explicit modelling and regular feedback. They may require additional relevant vocabulary to support their language use.

- Monitoring pupils' motivation to write is essential. Pupils who struggle with writing are in danger of losing self-belief and becoming demotivated. Ensuring that they have regular successful writing experiences is vital for them not to lose faith in themselves. Praise should, however, not be gratuitous, but encouraging and linked to improvements and goals.

- Children who talk less in class often find writing more difficult. Modelling strategies that support thinking aloud, oral rehearsal and peer-to-peer collaboration can help encourage greater amounts of talk. Creating a supportive social writing environment in classrooms will support more talk as will teacher and peer collaboration and dialogic practices.

The key to supporting children who are struggling with writing development, whether diagnosed with a specific condition or not, is to focus on the barriers that are making progress difficult. Objective assessments can give us useful data on what these specific barriers might be and how to mediate them. Our knowledge of the writing process and the developmental hurdles that require traversing, will give us a greater likelihood that we can successfully support these pupils with targeted and effective action.

Key messages

- Teaching handwriting, phonics (including encoding) and sentence structure, as well as prioritising oracy, especially early, are all protective factors that will prevent some children being deemed to have special educational needs in the first place.

- Many children struggle with writing, whether diagnosed with a specific condition or not.

- Dyslexia, dyspraxia (developmental coordination disorder) and developmental language disorder are diagnosable conditions associated with difficulties writing.

- For all struggling writers, whether diagnosed with a condition or not, it is the *difficulties* that should inform teaching and support rather than the condition.

- Using forensic, objective assessments will offer us a greater likelihood of analysing the difficulty and applying the most appropriate support.

- Children who struggle with decoding, handwriting, spelling and sentence structure will all find writing difficult. These areas can be assessed and mitigating support put in place and monitored.

- Children who find elements of writing difficult are at far greater risk of becoming demotivated and will seek to avoid writing. The fragility of their motivation needs robust attention, and they will need to experience successes regularly.

Chapter 12
Leading writing

Tim and Clare write: If writing is difficult and teaching writing is extremely difficult, then to develop an effective writing curriculum across a whole school or group of schools may be one of the most demanding challenges facing school leaders. But the more expert you are, the more credibility you will have, and the clearer what is right and wrong will become. There is probably not a school in the world that does all of the following list perfectly, but you will definitely be doing some of it. You can work on the rest a bit at a time. Think of this as a five-year project, rather than something you can tick off your development plan in a term or a year. It's a summary of what the research and evidence in this book suggests we should be doing.

- The school's approach to writing and its curriculum acknowledges the cognitive load and working memory demands associated with writing and learning to write and explicitly and intentionally is planned to manage this load to ultimately ensure pupils can focus on composition.

- The school's approach to writing and its curriculum acknowledges that writing exists to communicate.

- The school creates a rich writing community that all children can be part of and where writing is respected for its cognitive, social, language and creative gifts. Plentiful opportunities exist for sharing writing at a variety of scales (often with peers and the teacher, sometimes further afield).

- The school explicitly directs young pupils' attention to print and helps them build the muscle strength required for writing.

- Children's attention, from the very start of their school experience, is drawn to the macro elements of written text structures – both narrative and non-narrative. Initially this is through being read to and through the collective oral retelling of stories.

- Teachers and pupils are cognisant of the writing process.

- Teachers and pupils are cognisant of the non-present reader and how when we write we need to be both clear and interesting. Grammatical structures are taught with these aims in mind, not as an end in themselves.

- A schoolwide approach to handwriting is taught and practised in all year groups to build fluency. It is assessed and monitored.

- Handwriting is taught separately from phonics instruction.

- A school-wide approach to spelling that acknowledges and includes phonology, orthography and morphology is taught in all year groups. It is assessed and monitored.

- The move from oral syntax to written syntax is explicitly bridged for younger writers.

- Oral rehearsal prior to writing is taught and expected with the expectation that over time this will become interiorised and silent.

- Progressive sentence structure, grammar and punctuation is timetabled and explicitly taught across all year groups with a view to developing secure and strong mental representations for young writers. It is assessed and monitored.

- Vocabulary is explicitly taught but is also developed through language-rich environments and regular and timetabled reading, both by and to pupils.

- Macro structures of writing are explicitly highlighted and mental models built.

- Paragraphing is explicitly taught when children are secure enough with sentences to develop and elaborate on separate but interrelated themes within a text. Consistency is monitored.

- Across the school, consistent structures for narrative and non-narrative texts build mental models of writing structures for pupils. This consistency is monitored.

- Pupils are never expected to write a text type they have not encountered and have significant experience of.

- Teachers provide model and exemplar texts that indicate the structure and language requirements of a text type.

- Teachers build and use model texts to scaffold writers' structure, language and meaning.

- Consistency is not a straitjacket. Teachers have sufficient knowledge to be able to be flexible when this is appropriate.

- The school's approach to the teaching of writing affords pupils sufficient time for planning, writing and reviewing their work and emphasises quality over quantity.

- Teachers model writing strategies, explain them, recommend them and monitor them, highlighting their successful application.

- Oral feedback is privileged over written feedback.

- All feedback, whether teacher or peer, oral or written, is specific and actionable by the recipient.

- Pupils are explicitly taught how to deliver peer-to-peer feedback.

- Teaching and support staff receive regular training on the school's approach to the teaching of writing, with regular revisiting and revision.

- Reading and writing are linked with references to writers when reading and readers when writing.

- Teachers develop pupils' writing strategies through modelled, shared and guided writing.

- Pupils are explicitly and progressively taught cohesive devices that connect their written ideas to develop coherence for readers.

- Pupils always have sufficient content knowledge of a subject before writing about it.

- The school uses a range of assessment and screening protocols to evaluate writing and writing progress and identify pupils who may need more support in a specific area. Most of these will be objective (e.g. handwriting rate and legibility, spelling accuracy, sentence accuracy, text structure accuracy and consistency). Some will be holistic and subjective and relate to perceived quality of writing (e.g. comparative judgement).

- The school has robust assessment and screening protocols for the identification of pupils who require more support along with evaluated interventions to provide that support.

- Pupils who struggle to make progress in writing are quickly identified with their difficulties addressed through expert teaching founded on research and evidence.

- A high value is placed on pupils' motivation to write. It is monitored, developed and recognised.

- Pupils experience high degrees of success in writing lessons.

Bibliography

Ahmed, Y., Wagner, R.K. and Lopez, D. (2014). 'Developmental relations between reading and writing at the word, sentence and text levels: A latent change score analysis'. *Journal of Educational Psychology*, 106, 419–434.

Alexander, P.A., Graham, S. and Harris, K.R. (1998). 'A perspective on strategy research: Progress and prospects'. *Educational Psychology Review*, 10(2), 129–154.

Allen, L and Crossley, S. (2025). 'Advances in automated writing evaluation', in C. MacArthur, S. Graham and J. Fitzgerald (eds.) *Handbook of writing research* (3rd ed.). Guilford Press.

Allende, I. (2025). Interview with John Wilson, 2 January 2025. *This Cultural Life*, BBC Radio 4.

Almond, N. (2025). 'Handwriting: More than just fluency and more important than ever', in T. Bennet and S. Lockyer (eds.) *The ResearchEd guide to primary literacy*. John Catt Educational.

Alves, R. (2024). 'The early steps in becoming a writer: Enabling participation in a literate world', in J. Horst and J. von Koss Torkildsen (eds.) *International handbook of language acquisition*. Routledge.

Andrews, R., Torgerson, C., Beverton, S., Freeman, A., Locke, T., Low, G., Robinson, A. and Zhu, D. (2004). 'The effect of grammar teaching (syntax) in English on 5 to 16 year olds' accuracy and quality in written composition'. *Research Evidence in Education Library*. EPPI Centre, Social Science Research Unit, Institute of Education.

Applebee, A.N. (1978). *The child's concept of story: Age two to seventeen*. University of Chicago Press.

Armbruster, B., Lehr, F. and Osborn, J. (2001). *Put reading first: The research building blocks for teaching children to read.* Education Publishing Centre.

Bandura, A. (1997). *Self-efficacy: The exercise of control.* Freeman.

Bara, F. and Bonneton-Botté, N. (2017). 'Learning letters with the whole body: Visuomotor versus visual teaching in kindergarten.' *Perceptual and Motor Skills,* 125(1), 190–207.

Barnett, A.L., Prunty, M. and Rosenblum, S. (2018). 'Development of the handwriting legibility scale (HLS): A preliminary examination of reliability and validity.' *Research in Developmental Disabilities,* 72, 240–247.

Barton, C. (2018). *How I wish I'd taught maths.* John Catt Educational.

Barton, G. (2005). *Grammar survival: A teacher's toolkit.* David Fulton Publishers.

Bazerman, C. (2016). 'What do sociocultural studies of writing tell us about learning to write?', in C. MacArthur, S. Graham and J. Fitzgerald (eds.) *Handbook of writing research* (2nd ed.). Guilford Press.

Beach, R. and Friedrich, T. (2006). 'Response to writing', in C. MacArthur, S. Graham and J. Fitzgerald (eds.) *Handbook of writing research* (1st ed.). Guilford Press.

Beck, I.L., McKeown, M.G., Sandora, C., Kucan, L. and Worthy, J. (1996). 'Questioning the author: A yearlong classroom implementation to engage students with text'. *The Elementary School Journal,* 96(4), 385–414.

Beck, I.L., McKeown, M.G. and Kucan, L. (2013). *Bringing words to life: Robust vocabulary instruction.* Guilford Press.

Beck, R.C. (2004). *Motivation: Theories and principles* (5th ed.). Pearson/Prentice Hall.

Bennet, B.S. (1991). 'The rhetoric of Martianus Capella and Anselm de Besate in the tradition of Menippean satire'. *Philosophy & Rhetoric,* 24(2), 128–142.

Bereiter, C. and Scardamalia, M. (1987). *The psychology of written composition.* Lawrence Erlbaum Associates.

Berman, R.A. and Nir-Sagiv, B. (2007). 'Comparing narrative and expository text construction across adolescence: A developmental paradox'. *Discourse Processes,* 43(2), 79–120.

Berninger, V.W. (1999). 'Coordinating transcription and text generation in working memory during composing: Automatic and constructive processes', *Learning Disability Quarterly*, 22(2), 99–112.

Berninger, V.W. (2000). 'Development of language by hand and its connections with language by ear, mouth, and eye'. *Topics in Language Disorders*, 20(4), 65–84.

Berninger, V.W., Abbot, R.D., Abbot, S.P., Graham, S., Richards, T. (2002). 'Writing and reading: Connections between language by hand and language by eye'. *Journal of Learning Disabilities*, 35(1), 38–56.

Berninger, V.W. and May, M.O. (2011). 'Evidence-based diagnosis and treatment for specific learning disabilities involving impairments in written and/or oral language'. *Journal of Learning Disabilities*, 44(2), 167–183.

Berninger, V.W., Vaughan, K., Abbott, R.D., Begay, K., Coleman, K.B., Curtin, G., Hawkins, J. M. and Graham, S. (2002). 'Teaching spelling and composition alone and together: Implications for the simple view of writing'. *Journal of Educational Psychology*, 94(2), 291–304.

Bernstein, B. (1964). 'Elaborated and restricted codes: Their social origins and some consequences'. *American Anthropologist*, 66(6), Part 2: The Ethnography of Communication (December, 1964), 55–69.

Bloom, B.S. (1981). *All our children learning: A primer for parents, teachers and other educators*. McGraw-Hill.

Bourdieu, P. (1974). 'The School as a conservative force: Scholastic and cultural inequalities', in L. Eggleston (ed.) *Contemporary research in the sociology of education*, pp. 32–46. Methuen.

Bowers, P.N., Kirby, J.R. and Deacon, S.H. (2010). 'The effects of morphological instruction on literacy skills: A systematic review of the literature'. *Review of Educational Research*, 80, 144–179.

Capote, T. (1957). Interview with Hill, P. 'The Art of Fiction No. 17'. *The Paris Review*, 16.

Castles, A., Rastle, K. and Nation, K. (2018). 'Ending the reading wars: Reading acquisition from novice to expert'. *Psychological Science in the Public Interest*, 19(1), 5–51.'

Chanquoy, L. and Alamargot, D. (2002). 'Mémoire de travail et rédaction de textes: Evolution des modèles et bilan des premiers travaux'. *L'Année Psychologique*, 102(2), 363–398.

Chatta app. (2020). Available at https://chattalearning.com/

Chipere, N. (2003). *Understanding complex sentences: Native speaker variation in syntactic compete*nce. Palgrave Macmillan.

Chomsky, N. (1965a). *Persistent topics in linguistic theory.* International Council for Philosophy and Humanistic Studies.

Chomsky, N. (1965b). *Aspects of the theory of syntax.* MIT Press.

Christodoulou, D. (2025). 'What is Comparative Judgement and why does it work?'. Available at https://substack.com/home/post/p-172967037?selection=6905e76a-a6ba-41a8-8d23-40e8902515bb

Cikszentmihalyi, M. and Csikszentmihalyi, I.S. (eds.). (1988). *Optimal experience: Psychological studies of flow in consciousness.* Cambridge University Press.

Clay, M. (1991). *Becoming literate.* Heinemann.

Connelly, V. and Dockrell, J. (2016). 'Writing development and instruction for students with learning disabilities: Using diagnostic categories to study writing difficulties', in C. MacArthur, S. Graham and J. Fitzgerald (eds.) *Handbook of writing research* (2nd ed.). Guilford Press.

Crossley, S.A. and McNamara, D.S. (2011). 'Text coherence and judgments of essay quality: Models of quality and coherence', in L. Carlson, C. Hoelscher and T.F. Shipley (eds.) *Proceedings of the 29th annual conference of the cognitive science society*, pp. 1236–1241. Cognitive Science Society.

Culham, R. (2014). *The writing thief: Using mentor texts to teach the craft of writing.* International Literacy Association.

Cummins, J. (1979). 'Cognitive/academic language proficiency, linguistic interdependence, the optimum age question and some other matters', *Working Papers on Bilingualism*, 19, 121–129.

DfE. (2025). 'The writing framework'. Available at https://assets.publishing.service.gov.uk/media/68bec95444fd43581bda1c86/The_writing_framework_092025.pdf

Didau, D. (2014). 'Revisiting slow writing – How slowing writing might speed up thinking'. *Learning Spy.* Available at https://learningspy.co.uk/literacy/revisiting-slow-writing-improving-writing-improves-thinking/

Didau, D. and Cole, R. (2026). *Writing fitness: From beginner to 5K.* Routledge.

Dixon, R.C. (1993). *The surefire way to better spelling: A revolutionary new approach to turn poor spellers into pros.* St. Martin's Press.

Dockrell, J. and Arfé, J. (2014). 'The role of oral language in developing written language skills: Questions for European pedagogy?', in B. Arfe, J. Dockrell, and V. Berninger (eds.) *Writing development in children with hearing loss, dyslexia or oral language problems: Implications for assessment and instruction,* pp. 3–15. Oxford University Press.

Donica, D., 2010. 'A historical journey through the development of handwriting instruction (part 2): The occupational therapists' role'. *Journal of Occupational Therapy, Schools, and Early Intervention,* 3(1), 32–53.

Durrant, P. Brenchley, M. and McCallum, L. (2021). *Understanding development and proficiency in writing – Quantitative corpus linguistic approaches.* Cambridge University Press.

Dyson, A.H. (2002). 'The drinking god factor'. *Written Communication,* 19(4), 545–577.

Elimelech, A., Aram, D. and Levin, I (2020). 'Mothers teaching their children the Hebrew writing system', in R. Alves, T. Limpo and R. Joshi (eds.) *Reading and writing connections: Towards integrative literary science.* Springer.

Fayol, M. (2016). 'From Language to text: The development and learning of translation', in C. MacArthur, S. Graham and J. Fitzgerald (eds.) *Handbook of writing research* (2nd ed.). Guilford Press.

Fisher, R., Jones, S., Larkin, S. and Myhill, D. (2010). *Using talk to support writing.* Sage.

Fitzgerald, G. (2025). 'Vocabulary in writing', in C. MacArthur, S. Graham and J. Fitzgerald (eds.) *Handbook of writing research* (3rd ed.). Guilford Press.

French, E.G. and Thomas, F.H. (1958). 'The relation of achievement motivation to problem-solving effectiveness'. *The Journal of Abnormal and Social Psychology,* 56(1), 45–48.

Frith, U. (1985). 'Beneath the surface of developmental dyslexia', in, K. Patterson, J.C. Marshall and M. Coltheart (eds.) *Surface dyslexia: neuropsychological and cognitive studies of phonological reading.* Erlbaum.

Galbraith, D. (1996). 'Self-monitoring, discovery through writing and individual differences in drafting strategy', in G. Rijlaarsdam, H. van den

Bergh and M. Couzijn (eds.) *Theories, models and methodology in writing research*, pp. 121–141. Amsterdam University Press.

Gathercole, S. and Alloway, T. (2004). 'Working memory and classroom learning'. *The Psychologist*, 15(5).

Geary, D. (2002). 'Principles of evolutionary educational psychology'. *Learning and Individual Differences*, 12(4), 317–345.

Geary, D. (2007). 'Educating the evolved mind', in J. Carlson and J. Levin (eds.) *Educating the evolved mind: Conceptual foundations for an evolutionary educational psychology*. Information Age Publishing.

Goodman, K. (1970). 'Reading: A psycholinguistic guessing game'. *Journal of the Reading Specialist*, 6(4), 126–135.

Gough, P. and Tunmer, W. (1986). 'Decoding, reading and reading disability'. *Remedial and Special Education*, 7(1), 6–10.

Graham, S. (2006). 'Strategy instruction and the teaching of writing: a meta-analysis', in C. MacArthur, S. Graham and J. Fitzgerald (eds.) *Handbook of writing research* (1st ed.). Guilford Press.

Graham, S. (2018). 'A revised writer(s)-within-community model of writing'. *Educational Psychologist*, 53(4), 258–279.

Graham, S. (2020). 'Reading and writing connections: A commentary', in R. Alves, T. Limpo and R. Joshi (eds.) *Reading and writing connections: Towards integrative literary science*. Springer.

Graham, S and Harris, K. (2018). 'Evidence-based writing practices: A meta-analysis of existing meta-analyses'. *Design Principles for Teaching Effective Writing: Theoretical and Empirical Grounded Principles*, 34, 13–37.

Graham, S. and Harris, K. (2019). 'Evidence-based practices in writing', in S. Graham, C. MacArthur and M. Hebert (eds.) *Best practices in writing instruction*. Guilford Press.

Graham, S. and Hebert, M. (2010). *Writing to read: Evidence for how writing can improve reading*. Carnegie Corporation.

Graham, S. and Santangelo, T. (2014). 'Does spelling instruction make students better spellers, readers and writers? A meta-analytic review'. *Reading and Writing*, 27(9), 1703–1743.

Graham, S., MacArthur, C. and Hebert, M. (2019). *Best practices in writing instruction*. Guilford Press.

Graham, S. and Perin, D. (2007). *Writing next: Effective strategies to improve writing of adolescents in middle and high schools. A report to Carnegie Corporation of New York.* Alliance for Excellent Education.

Graham, S., Berninger, V., Weintraub, N. and Schafer, W. (1998). 'Development of handwriting speed and legibility in grades 1–9'. *The Journal of Educational Research*, 92(1), 42–52.

Graham, S., Harris, K.R. and Chambers, A.B. (2016). 'Evidence-based practice and writing instruction: A review of reviews', in C. MacArthur, S. Graham and J. Fitzgerald (eds.) *Handbook of writing research* (2nd ed.). Guilford Press.

Graham, S., McKeown, D., Kiuhara, S.A. and Harris, K.R. (2012). 'A meta-analysis of writing instruction for students in the elementary grades'. *Journal of Educational Psychology*, 104(4), 879–896.

Graves, D. 1983. *Writing: Teachers and children at work.* Pearson.

Green, D.W. and Wason, P.C. (1982). 'Notes on the psychology of writing'. *Human Relations*, 35(1), 47–56.

Halliday, M.A.K. and Hasan, R. (1976). *Cohesion in English.* Longman Group.

Harlen, W. (2004). 'A systematic review of the evidence of the impact on students, teachers and the curriculum of the process of using assessment by teachers for summative purposes'. *Research Evidence in Education Library.* EPPI Centre, Social Science Research Unit, Institute of Education, University of London.

Harris, K.R., Graham, S. and Mason, L. (2006). 'Self-regulated strategy development for 2nd-grade students who struggle with writing'. *American Educational Research Journal*, 43, 295–340.

Havelock, E. (1976). *Origins of Western literacy* (1st ed.). Harvard University Press.

Hayes, J.R. and Flower, L.S. (1980). 'Identifying the organization of writing processes', in L.W. Gregg and E.R. Steinberg (eds.) *Cognitive processes in writing*, pp. 3–30. Erlbaum.

Hidi, S. and Boscolo, P. (2006). 'Motivation and writing', in C. MacArthur, S. Graham and J. Fitzgerald (eds.) *Handbook of writing research* (1st ed.). Guilford Press.

Hochman, J. and Wexler, N. (2017). *The writing revolution.* Jossey-Bass.

Horton, S. (1990). *Thinking through writing*. Johns Hopkins University Press.

Hudson, R. (2016). 'Grammar instruction', in C. MacArthur, S. Graham and J. Fitzgerald (eds.) *Handbook of writing research* (2nd ed.). Guilford Press.

Hyland, K. (2021). *Teaching and researching writing* (4th ed.). Routledge.

Jacob, L., Lachner, A. and Scheiter, K. (2020). 'Learning by explaining orally or in written form: Text complexity matters'. *Learning and Instruction*, 68.

James, K.H., Jao, R.J. and Berninger, V. (2016). 'The development of multileveled writing systems of the brain', in C. MacArthur, S. Graham and J. Fitzgerald (eds.) *Handbook of writing research* (2nd ed.). Guilford Press.

Johnson-Laird, P.N. (1983). *Mental models: Towards a cognitive science of language, inference and consciousness*. Cambridge University Press; Harvard University Press.

Johnston, R. and Watson, J. (2004). 'Accelerating the development of reading, spelling and phonemic awareness skills in initial readers'. *Reading and Writing*, 17(4), 327–357.

Juel, C., Griffith, P. and Gough, P. (1986). 'Acquisition of literacy: A longitudinal study of children in first and second grade'. *Journal of Educational Psychology*, 78, 243–255.

Kahneman, D. (2011). *Thinking, fast and slow*. Penguin Books.

Kellogg, R., (1994). *The psychology of writing*. Oxford University Press.

Kerr, E., Ivanova, B. and Strijkers, K. (2023). 'Lexical access in speech production: Psycho- and neurolinguistic perspectives on the spatiotemporal dynamics', in R. Hartsuiker and K. Strikers (eds.) *Language production*, pp. 32–65. Routledge.

Kim, Y.G. (2020). 'Toward integrative reading science: The direct and indirect effects model of reading'. *Journal of Learning Disabilities*, 53(6), 469–491.

Kim, Y.G. and Schatschneider, C. (2017). 'Expanding the developmental models of writing: A direct and indirect effects model of developmental writing (DIEW)'. *Journal of Educational Psychology*, 109(1), 35–50.

Kim, Y.G. and Park, S.H. (2019). 'Unpacking pathways using the direct and indirect effects model of writing (DIEW) and the contributions of higher order cognitive skills to writing'. *Reading and Writing*, 32, 1319–1343.

Kim, Y.G. and Graham, S. (2022). 'Expanding the direct and indirect effects model of writing (DIEW): Reading–writing relations and dynamic relations as a function of measurement/dimensions of written composition'. *Journal of Educational Psychology*, 114(2), 215–238.

King, S. (2020). *On writing*. Hodder and Stoughton.

Kintsch, W. (1974). *The representation of meaning in text*. Lawrence Erlbaum Associates.

Klein, P., Bildfell, A., Dombroski, J.D., Giese, C., Sha, K.W.Y. and Thompson, S.C. (2022). 'Self-regulation in early writing strategy instruction'. *Reading & Writing Quarterly*, 38(2), 101–125.

Korochkina M., Marelli, M., Brysbaert, M. and Rastle, K. (2024). 'The children and young people's books lexicon (CYP-LEX): A large-scale lexical database of books read by children and young people in the United Kingdom'. *Quarterly Journal of Experimental Psychology*, 77(12), 2418–2438

Korzybski, A. (1933). *Science and sanity. An introduction to non-Aristotelian systems and general semantics*. The International Non-Aristotelian Library Pub. Co.

Kress, G. (1994). *Learning to write*. Routledge.

Leith, S. (2024). *The haunted wood: A history of childhood reading*. Oneworld Publications.

Lewis, C. (1959). Letter to Thomasine, 14 December.

Lobina, D.J., García-Albea, J.E. and Demestre, J. (2020). 'Parsing for position'. *Experimental Psychology*, 67(1), 40–47.

Longacre, R.E. (1979). 'The paragraph as a grammatical unit', in T. Givón (ed.) *Syntax and semantics 12: Discourse and syntax*, pp. 115–134. Academic Press.

Luria, A.R. (1929/1983). 'The development of writing in the child', in M. Martlew (ed.) *The psychology of written language*, pp. 237–277. John Wiley and Sons.

Adler, M. and Van Doren, C. (1972). *How to read a book*. Touchstone.

MacArthur, C. (2016). 'Instruction in evaluation and revision', in C. MacArthur, S. Graham and J. Fitzgerald (eds.) *Handbook of writing research* (2nd ed.). Guilford Press.

MacArthur, C. and Graham, S. (2016). 'Writing research from a cognitive perspective', in C. MacArthur, S. Graham and J. Fitzgerald (eds.) *Handbook of writing research* (2nd ed.). Guilford Press.

McArthur, G. and Castles, A. (2017). 'Helping children with reading difficulties: Some things we have learned so far'. *Science of Learning*, 2, 10.

McCutchen, D. (1995). 'Cognitive processes in children's writing: Developmental and individual differences'. *Issues in Education: Contributions from Educational Psychology*, 1, 123–160.

McQuillan, J. (2019). 'Where do we get our academic vocabulary? Comparing the efficiency of direct instruction and free voluntary reading'. *The Reading Matrix: An International Online Journal*, 19(1), 129–138.

Mercer, N. and Hodgkinson, S. (2008). *Exploring talk in school: Inspired by the work of Douglas Barnes*. Sage.

Myhill, D. and Jones, S. (2015). 'Conceptualizing metalinguistic understanding in writing'. *L1-Educational Studies in Language and Literature*, 27(4), 839–867.

Myhill, D., Jones, S., Watson, J. and Lines, H. (2016). *Essential primary grammar*. OUP.

Myhill, D., Jones, S., Lines, H. and Watson, A. (2012). 'Re-thinking grammar: The impact of embedded grammar teaching on students' writing and students' metalinguistic under-standing'. *Research Papers in Education*, 27, 139–166.

Myhill, D., Lines, H., Jones, S. (2020). 'Writing Like a reader: Developing metalinguistic understanding to support reading-writing connections', in R. Alves, T. Limpo and R. Joshi (eds.) *Reading and writing connections: Towards integrative literary science*. Springer.

Nation, K. (2011). 'Disorders of reading and writing', in P.C. Hogan (ed.) *The Cambridge encyclopaedia of the language sciences*, pp. 267–269. Cambridge University Press.

National Literacy Trust. (2018a). 'Mental wellbeing, reading and writing'. Available at https://literacytrust.org.uk/research-services/research-reports/mental-wellbeing-reading-and-writing/

National Literacy Trust. (2018b). 'Mental wellbeing, reading and writing'. Available at https://nlt.cdn.ngo/media/documents/Mental_wellbeing_reading_and_writing_2017-18_-_FINAL2_qTxyxvg.pdf

Nickerson, R.S., Perkins, D.N. and Smith, E.E. (1985). *The teaching of thinking.* Psychology Press.

Nystrand, M. (1986). *The structure of written communication: Studies in reciprocity between writers and readers.* Academic Press.

Ochse, R. (1990). *Before the gates of excellence: The determinants of creative genius.* Cambridge University Press.

Ofqual. (2017). Marking reliability studies 2017: Rank ordering versus marking – which is more reliable? Available at https://assets.publishing.service.gov.uk/media/5e25c44940f0b62c4ccf5ac9/Marking_reliability_-_FINAL64494.pdf

Ofsted. (2024). 'Telling the story: The English education subject report'. Available at https://www.gov.uk/government/publications/subject-report-series-english/telling-the-story-the-english-education-subject-report

Olive, T. and Kellogg, R.T. (2002). 'Concurrent activation of high- and low-level production processes in written composition'. *Memory and Cognition,* 30, 594–600.

Ose Askvik, E., van der Weel, F.R. and van der Meer, A.L. (2020). 'The importance of cursive handwriting over typewriting for learning in the classroom: A high-density EEG study of 12-year-old children and young adults'. *Frontiers in Psychology,* 11, 1810.

Ouellette, G., Martin-Chang, S. and Rossi, M. (2017). 'Learning from our mistakes: Improvements in spelling lead to gains in reading speed'. *Scientific Studies of Reading,* 21(4), 350–357.

Palmer, S. (2006). *The complete set of skeleton books for non-fiction writing.* TTS Skeleton.

Paratore, J.R., Cassano, C.M. and Schickedanz, J.A. (2011). 'Supporting early (and later) literacy development at home and at school: The long view', in M.L. Kamil, P.D. Pearson, E.B. Moje and P.P. Afferbach (eds.) *Handbook of reading research,* vol. IV, pp. 107–135. Routledge.

Payne, J. and Whitney, P. (2002). 'Developing L2 oral proficiency through synchronous CMC: Output, working memory and interlanguage development'. *CALICO Journal,* 20, 7–32.

Pearson, P.D. and Gallagher, M.C. (1983). 'The instruction of reading comprehension'. *Contemporary Educational Psychology*, 8(3), 317–344.

Perfetti, C. (1997). 'The psycholinguistics of spelling', in C.A. Perfetti, L. Rieben and M. Fayol (eds.) *Learning to spell: Research, theory and practice across languages*. Lawrence Erlbaum Associates, 21–38.

Rasinski, T.V., Padak, N., Newton, R. and Newton, E. (2008). *Greek and Latin roots: Keys to building vocabulary*. Shell Educational Publishing.

Rastle, K. (2019). 'The place of morphology in learning to read in English'. *Cortex: A Journal Devoted to the Study of the Nervous System and Behavior*, 116, 45–54.

Rayner, K., Pollatsek, A., Ashby, J. and Clifton, C. (2012). *Psychology of reading*. Psychology Press.

Reutzel, D.R. and Cooter, R.B. (2013). *Teaching children to read: The teacher makes the difference*. Pearson.

Ryan, R.M. and Deci, E.L. (2000). 'Self-determination theory and the facilitation of intrinsic motivation, social development and well-being'. *American Psychologist*, 55(1), 68–78.

Saddler, B. (2012). *Teacher's guide to effective sentence writing*. Guilford Press.

Said, S. F. (2020). 'Talk for writing'. Available at https://www.talk4writing. com/wp-content/uploads/2020/05/SF-Said.pdf

Santangelo, T., Harris, K.R. and Graham, S. (2016). 'Self-regulation of writing: meta-analysis of the self-regulation processes in Zimmerman and Risemberg's model', in C. MacArthur, S. Graham and J. Fitzgerald (eds.) *Handbook of writing research* (2nd ed.). Guilford Press.

Scarborough, H. S. (2001). 'Connecting early language and literacy to later reading (dis)abilities: Evidence, theory and practice', in S. Neuman and D. Dickinson (eds.) *Handbook for research in early literacy*, pp. 97–110. Guilford Press.

Schmandt-Besserat, D. (1992). *How writing came about*. University of Texas Press.

Sealy, C. (2025). 'What are we teaching when we teach writing?'. Available at https://primarytimery.com/2025/05/20/what-are-we-teaching-when-we-teach-writing/

Sedita, J. (2023). *The writing rope. A framework for explicit writing instruction in all subjects*. Paul H. Brookes Publishing.

Shanahan, T. (2016). 'Relationships between reading and writing development', in C. MacArthur, S. Graham and J. Fitzgerald (eds.) *Handbook of writing research* (2nd ed.). Guilford Press.

Skinner, B.F. (1953). *Science and human behavior*. Macmillan.

Sternberg, R.J., (1988). *The nature of creativity: Contemporary psychological perspectives*. Cambridge University Press.

Stone, L. (2021). *Spelling for life*. Routledge.

Struthers, L., Lapadat, J. and MacMillan, P. (2017). 'Assessing cohesion in children's writing: Development of a checklist'. Assessing Writing, 18(3), 187–201.

Suggate, S. (2016). 'A meta-analysis of the long-term effects of phonemic awareness, phonics, fluency and reading comprehension interventions'. *Journal of Learning Disabilities*, 49, 77–96.

Tan, C.-Y., Chuah, C.-Q., Lee, S.-T. and Tan, C.-S. (2021). 'Being creative makes you happier: The positive effect of creativity on subjective well-being'. *International Journal of Environmental Research and Public Health*, 18(14), 7244.

The Adult Literacy Trust. (2026). *The impact of poor literacy*. Available at https://alt.org.uk/impact-of-illiteracy/ (Accessed: 14 March 2026).

The National Literacy Strategy. (2000). *Grammar for writing*. DfEE.

The Writing for Pleasure Centre. (2023). *Pursue personal writing projects*. Available at https://writing4pleasure.com/personal-writing-projects/ (Accessed: 14 March 2026).

Toczek, M.C, Fayol, M. and Dutrévis, M. (2012). 'Marked dictation or not? Analysis of the spelling mistakes of schooled pupils'. *Revue Francaise de Pedagogie*, 178, 85–96.

Tolchinsky, L. (2016). 'From text to language and back. The emergence of written language', in C. MacArthur, S. Graham and J. Fitzgerald (eds.) *Handbook of writing research* (2nd ed.). Guilford Press.

Torrence, M. (2016). 'Understanding planning in text production', in C. MacArthur, S. Graham and J. Fitzgerald (eds.) *Handbook of writing research* (2nd ed.). Guilford Press.

Tower Hamlets EMA team. (2009). 'Progression in language structures: Some suggestions for class teachers in planning for children's academic language development'. Available at https://www. solgrid.org.uk/wp-content/uploads/sites/43/2020/02/TowerHamlets-AProgressionInLanguageStructures.docx

Treiman, R. (2018), 'Teaching and learning spelling'. *Child Development Perspectives*, 12, 235–239.

Trivette, C.M., Hamby, D.W., Dunst, C.J. and Gorman, E. (2013). *Emergent writing among young children from twelve to sixty months of age.* Center for Early Literacy Learning.

Van Galen, G. (1991). 'Handwriting: Issues for a psychomotor theory'. *Human Movement Science*, 10, 165–191.

Verhavert, S., Bouwer, R., Donche, V. and De Maeyer, S (2019). 'A meta-analysis on the reliability of comparative judgement'. *Assessment in Education: Principles, Policy and Practice*, 26(5), 541–562.

Vinter, A. and Chartrel, E. (2010). 'Effects of different types of learning on handwriting movements in young children'. *Learning and Instruction*, 20(6), 476–486.

Vygotsky, L.S. (1935/1978). *Mind in society: The development of higher psychological processes.* Harvard University Press.

Whitehead, A.N. (1929). *The aims of education and other essays.* Free Press.

Wyse, D., Aarts, B., Anders, J., Gennaro, A., Dockrell, J., Manyukhina, Y., Sing, S. and Torgerson, C. (2022). *Grammar and writing in England's national curriculum: A randomised controlled trial and implementation and process evaluation of Englicious.* UCL.

Zimmerman, B.J. and Risemberg, R. (1997). 'Becoming a self-regulated writer: A social cognitive perspective'. *Contemporary Educational Psychology*, 22, 73–101.

Personalised professional development from Hachette Learning Academy

A simple way to boost career progression, staff motivation and educational excellence.

Our online courses are:

 Aligned with **teaching competency frameworks**

 Written by experts in education, including Hachette Learning authors (formerly John Catt)

 Created to enable educators to **develop competencies** linked to their professional development aspirations

 **Powered by adaptive learning,** to accommodate a diverse range of skills, knowledge and understanding

 Designed to support **effective learning and high-impact teaching**

www.hachettelearning.com/academy